The Grammar Handbook 2

A handbook for teaching Grammar and Spelling

Sara Wernham and Sue Lloyd
Illustrated by Lib Stephen

Edited by Rachel Stadlen

Jolly Learning Ltd

Published June 2001
Reprinted 2005, 2007

Jolly Learning Ltd
Tailours House
High Road
Chigwell
Essex
IG7 6DL
United Kingdom

Tel: (+44 or 0) 20 8501 0405
Fax: (+44 or 0) 20 8500 1696

Printed and bound in England.

The Photocopy Sections in this book use 'Sassoon Infant', a typeface designed for children learning to read and write. Sassoon is a registered trade mark of Sassoon and Williams. For more information see the following website: www.clubtype.co.uk

The front cover shows two children doing the action for conjunctions.

The page numbers in this book have been kept within the binding, at the base of each page, so that the numbers do not appear on copies of the photocopiable pages.

ISBN: 978-1-870946-96-4

Acknowledgements

Our sincere thanks go first to Professor Alice Coleman, whose work has been an inspiration to us and a profound influence on this project.

We are grateful also to Trudy Wainwright and the staff of St. Michael's Primary School, Stoke Gifford, as of course to our colleagues at Woods Loke Primary School. Their hard work and support in testing our material has greatly benefited this book.

Finally we would like to thank Jennifer Chew O.B.E., whose expertise has been invaluable.

Contents

PART 1

PART 2 Photocopiable material

Extra Activities

Introduction

The Grammar Handbook 2 is designed to follow *The Phonics Handbook* and *The Grammar Handbook 1.* It is intended to:

- introduce new elements of grammar,
- teach new spelling patterns systematically,
- develop dictionary and thesaurus skills,
- improve vocabulary and comprehension, and
- reinforce the teaching in *The Grammar Handbook 1.*

The teaching is multisensory and active. It places emphasis on consolidating the children's learning and helping them to apply their skills. Each part of speech is taught with its own action and colour. The actions enliven the teaching, and make the learning easier. The colours, which are useful for identifying parts of speech in sentences, match those used by Montessori Schools. *The Grammar Handbooks 1* and *2* provide all the essential teaching ideas, and can be used alone, or with the valuable support of the *Jolly Grammar Big Books 1* and *2.*

Children's achievement

The most dramatic improvements to result from using *Jolly Grammar* will be found in the children's writing. The children will spell and punctuate more accurately, use a wider vocabulary, and have a clearer understanding of how language works.

In their first year at school, *Jolly Phonics* teaches children to write independently, by listening for the sounds in words and choosing letters to represent the sounds. This enables the children to write pages of news and stories. It is a joy to read their work and to see the great pride and confidence they derive from their newly-acquired skill. However, it is important to build on this foundation in the following years. *Jolly Grammar* provides teaching ideas for developing writing skills. The children become more aware that they are writing for a purpose: that their words are intended to be read and understood. They learn that writing is easier to understand if it is grammatically correct, accurately spelt, well punctuated and neatly written – and that if the words used are interesting too, their writing can give real pleasure. Even in the early stages, it is valuable for children to have a simple understanding of this long-term goal.

The format of *The Grammar Handbook 2*

The programme consists primarily of photocopiable activity sheets for two lessons a week. Each lesson is designed to be about one hour in duration, and material is provided for 36 weeks. Teaching ideas are offered alongside each activity sheet.

There are two elements to the programme, namely spelling and grammar. Each week the first lesson is devoted to spelling and the second to grammar. These terms are loosely used and there is some overlapping: punctuation, vocabulary development and dictionary work are among the areas covered in both spelling and grammar lessons. This is deliberate: when mixed together, the two elements complement each other.

The teaching is intended to be envisaged as part of a broader literacy programme. If two days' literacy sessions are devoted to *Jolly Grammar* each week, this leaves three for other areas, such as comprehension, group and individual reading, formal and creative writing, and handwriting practice. The children should be shown how spelling and grammar relate to their other literacy work. For instance, if they have recently covered contractions, and there is an example of one in the text they are studying, the children should be encouraged to look at it and identify which letter(s) the apostrophe is replacing.

The teaching ideas alongside each activity sheet give useful suggestions and reminders. More detailed explanations and advice are provided in the following two chapters: 'Teaching Ideas for Grammar' and 'Teaching Ideas for Spelling'. Relevant material from *The Grammar Handbook 1* has been included for easy reference.

To avoid confusion, *Jolly Grammar* follows the convention of using different symbols to distinguish between letter names and letter sounds. Letter names are indicated by the symbols ‹ ›, e.g. 'Ship' begins with the letter ‹s›. By contrast, letter sounds are indicated by the symbols / /, e.g. 'Ship' begins with the /sh/ sound.

Teaching Ideas for Grammar

The benefits of learning grammar are cumulative. In the first instance, a knowledge of grammar will give the children more conscious control over the clarity and quality of their writing. Later it will also help them to understand more complicated texts, learn foreign languages with greater ease, and use Standard English in their speech.

Spoken language is living and varies from region to region. The grammar we first learn, through our speech, varies accordingly. However, sometimes there is a need for uniformity. This uniformity improves communications, and is one of the main ways of uniting people in the English-speaking world. An awareness of this helps children who do not speak Standard English to understand that the way they speak is not wrong, but that it has not been chosen as the standard for the whole country. The children need to learn the standard form of English, as well as appreciating their own dialect.

In the first year of *Jolly Grammar*, *The Grammar Handbook 1* introduced the concepts of sentences, punctuation and parts of speech. The children learnt about proper and common nouns, pronouns, verbs, adjectives and adverbs, and they learnt to use verbs to indicate whether something happened in the past, present or future.

The Grammar Handbook 2 aims both to extend the children's knowledge, and to deepen their understanding. Their knowledge of sentences is refined, and they learn to punctuate with greater variety and precision. They are introduced to new concepts, such as irregular verbs, and to new parts of speech, namely possessive adjectives, conjunctions, prepositions, and comparatives and superlatives.

In addition to this new material, *The Grammar Handbook 2* provides a systematic approach to revision. This enables even the slowest learners to keep up, while ensuring that more able ones master their skills thoroughly and develop good grammatical habits. Every lesson should include some revision. Suggestions are provided in the teacher's notes alongside the activity sheets. However, teachers should feel free to use their own judgement as to which areas their children need to revise.

The term 'grammar' is used broadly with children of this age. Definitions of the parts of speech, and of what constitutes a sentence, have necessarily been simplified to age-appropriate 'working definitions'. As the children grow older, the definitions can be expanded and refined.

Proper Nouns

A noun denotes a person, place or thing. There are four kinds: common nouns (e.g. 'table'), proper nouns (e.g. 'Linda'), abstract nouns (e.g. 'warmth') and collective nouns (e.g. 'the group').

The children were introduced to proper nouns in *The Grammar Handbook 1.* A proper noun starts with a capital letter, and is the particular name given to a:

- person, including that person's surname and title;
- place: e.g. river, mountain, park, street, town, country, continent, planet;
- building: e.g. school, house, library, swimming pool, cinema; and
- date: e.g. day of the week, month, religious holiday.

In *The Grammar Handbook 2*, the children revise proper nouns through focus on learning the names of the months, including their correct spelling and sequence. Use the above list to start a class collection of the types of word that are proper nouns, adding to it whenever examples of new categories arise, such as the names of books, films and pop groups.

Action: The action for a proper noun is to touch one's forehead with the index and middle fingers. This is the same action as that used for 'name' in British Sign Language.

Colour: The colour for nouns is black.

Common Nouns

The children were introduced to common nouns in *The Grammar Handbook 1.* Only concrete nouns are taught in these early stages. Abstract nouns (e.g. 'pleasure') are more difficult for young children to grasp.

Everything we can see has a name by which we can refer to it, such as 'table', 'chair' and 'pencil'. As these names are not specific to any one object, but refer to tables, chairs, etc. in general, they are called common nouns and not proper nouns. At this stage the children find it useful to think of nouns as the names for things they can see and touch. To help the children decide if a word is a noun, they can see whether it makes sense to say the word 'a', 'an' or 'the' before it, e.g. 'the table', 'a chair', 'an elephant'. ('A', 'an' and 'the' are the three articles, which are explained later.)

Action: The action for a common noun is to touch one's forehead with all the fingers of one hand.

Colour: The colour for nouns is black.

In general children understand the concept of nouns easily, and have no trouble when asked to think of examples. As they find it harder to identify nouns in sentences, this is the main focus in *The Grammar Handbook 2.* In any spare moments, encourage the children to identify the nouns in sentences on the board, or in big books.

Plurals

Most nouns change in the plural, i.e. when they describe more than one. *The Grammar Handbook 1* introduced two regular ways in which the plural can be formed. The first is by adding an ‹-s› to the noun, as in 'dogs', 'cats' and 'girls'. The second applies to those nouns which end with ‹sh›, ‹ch›, ‹s›, ‹z› or ‹x›. These words usually form the plural by adding ‹-es›, as in 'churches', 'wishes', 'kisses', 'buzzes' and 'foxes'.

Both plural endings are revised in *The Grammar Handbook 2.* In addition, the children learn how to form the plural of nouns which end with the letter ‹y›. There are two possible endings. If the letter immediately before the ‹y› is a vowel, then the plural is simply made by adding ‹-s›, as in 'days', 'boys' and 'monkeys'. However, if the letter immediately before the ‹y› is a consonant, then the plural is formed by replacing the ‹y› with ‹i› before adding ‹-es›, as in 'flies', 'babies' and 'puppies'. The children should already know that 'shy ‹i›' does not like to be alone at the end of a word, and so is often replaced by 'toughy ‹y›'. This helps them understand that while we would be unlikely to find 'shy ‹i›' at the end of a word like 'puppy', 'toughy ‹y›' is no longer needed to replace it when the word is extended in the plural.

Through later spelling lists, *The Grammar Handbook 2* also introduces some common irregular or 'tricky' plurals, such as 'mice' for 'mouse'. Tricky plurals can be formed by modifying the base word, altering its pronunciation, adding an unusual ending, or a combination of the three. Sometimes the pronunciation of the base word alters even when the spelling does not, so the letter ‹i› in 'child' makes a long /ie/ sound, whereas in 'children' it makes a short /i/.

Personal Pronouns

Pronouns are the little words used to replace nouns. The children were introduced to the personal pronouns in *The Grammar Handbook 1.* The relative pronouns (e.g. 'who'), possessive pronouns (e.g. 'mine') and reflexive pronouns (e.g. 'myself') can be taught when they are older.

There are eight personal pronouns (see the list below). Although in modern English the second person pronoun 'you' is used for both singular and plural, this is not the case in many foreign languages. In order to make learning such languages easier later on, *Jolly Grammar* introduces children to the distinction between 'you' for the singular and 'you' for the plural.

The Grammar Handbook 2 revises the personal pronouns when introducing the possessive adjectives, which are explained later. The children also practise using the personal pronouns whenever they conjugate verbs, as in 'I swim, you swim, he swims, she swims, it swims, we swim, you swim, they swim'.

Actions:	I	*(1st person singular)*	– point to self
	you	*(2nd person singular)*	– point to someone else
	he	*(3rd person singular)*	– point to a boy
	she	*(3rd person singular)*	– point to a girl
	it	*(3rd person singular)*	– point to the floor
	we	*(1st person plural)*	– point in a circle to include self and others
	you	*(2nd person plural)*	– point to two other people
	they	*(3rd person plural)*	– point to the next-door class

Colour: The colour for pronouns is pink.

Verbs

A verb denotes what a person or a thing does, and can describe an action, an event, a state or a change. It is easiest for children to think of verbs as 'doing words' at first. The infinitive form, or name, of a verb is made by putting the word 'to' before the verb root, as in 'to run', 'to hop', 'to sing' and 'to play'.

The children were introduced to verbs in *The Grammar Handbook 1*, and learnt to conjugate regular verbs in the present, past and future. Conjugating means choosing a particular verb, and saying the pronouns in order, with the correct form of the verb after each. Conjugating verbs aloud with the pronoun actions is very good for children. It promotes a strong understanding of how verbs work, which helps them make sense of their own language, and is invaluable when they come to learn foreign languages later on. Revise the conjugations regularly, using the pronoun actions:

Past	*Present*	*Future*
I jumped	I jump	I shall/will jump
you jumped	you jump	you will jump
he jumped	he jumps	he will jump
she jumped	she jumps	she will jump
it jumped	it jumps	it will jump
we jumped	we jump	we shall/will jump
you jumped	you jump	you will jump
they jumped	they jump	they will jump

The children need to remember the following points:

- In the present, the verb changes after he, she and it: with regular verbs, an ‹s› is added to the root. This is called the third person singular marker.
- The simple past tense of regular verbs is formed by adding the suffix ‹-ed› to the root. If the root ends with an ‹e›, as in 'bake', this must be removed before the ‹-ed› is added. The ‹-ed› can be pronounced in one of three ways: /t/, as in 'slipped', /d/, as in 'smiled' or /id/, as in 'waited'.
- With simple verbs, when we speak of future time we use the verb root and add the auxiliary 'shall' or 'will'. 'Will' can be used with all the pronouns but 'shall' should only be used with 'I' and 'we', the first person singular and plural.

The Grammar Handbook 2 revises these regular conjugations and introduces some irregularities. The children learn some of the most common irregular or 'tricky' past forms, such as 'sat' for 'to sit' and 'ran' for 'to run'. They also learn to conjugate and identify the irregular verb 'to be' in both the present and past tenses. This is especially useful for those children who are not in the habit of using standard forms in their speech, and who say, for example, 'we was' for 'we were'. Chanting the conjugations regularly will help these children avoid making similar mistakes in their written work. Because it is so irregular, children often find it difficult to identify parts of the verb 'to be' in sentences. It is important to overcome this problem, as 'to be' is used so frequently. When the children learn that every sentence must contain a verb, they need to be able to identify verbs in sentences with confidence. Familiarity with the verb 'to be' will also help the children later, as it is used to form the continuous tenses (see the table overleaf).

Since verbs in English are very complicated, *The Grammar Handbooks 1* and *2* introduce only the simple tenses. Later, when the children learn the continuous and perfect modes of the verb, they can be told that the verbs they first learnt were known as the simple tenses. For reference, the table below shows all three modes in past, present and future:

	Past	*Present*	*Future*
Simple	looked	look	will look
Continuous	was looking	is looking	will be looking
Perfect	had looked	have looked	will have looked

In preparation for the continuous tenses, *The Grammar Handbook 2* introduces the ‹-ing› suffix. At this stage, it is sufficient that the children learn how to use this suffix correctly. Later they will learn that the ‹-ing› suffix is used to make either (i) the gerund, or noun form of a verb, as in 'I like running,' (ii) the present participle for continuous tenses, as in 'I am running,' or (iii) the present participle used as an adjective, as in 'There was no running water.' Like ‹-ed›, the ‹-ing› suffix may be added in one of several different ways, depending on how the verb root is spelt (see the rules for adding suffixes on page 24).

Technically there is no future tense in English since, unlike the past tense, the future is not formed by modifying the verb root itself. At this stage, however, it is helpful for the children to think of verbs as taking place in the past, present and future. The complexities are better left until they are older.

Actions: The action for **verbs** is to clench fists and move arms backwards and forwards at sides, as if running.

The action for the **present tense** is pointing towards the floor with the palm of the hand.

The action for the **past tense** is pointing backwards over the shoulder with a thumb.

The action for verbs which describe the **future** is pointing to the front.

Colour: The colour for verbs is red.

Use the actions for pronouns and verbs in the past, present and future to play 'Guess what I am saying?' with the class. First choose a verb, and mime the action for it, e.g. hop for 'to hop'. Then do the action for a pronoun, e.g. point to the next-door class for 'they'. Next indicate when the action took place, e.g. point backwards over the shoulder with a thumb for the past. After watching the mime and actions the children should be able to respond, 'They hopped'.

Adjectives

An adjective is a word that describes a noun or pronoun. It can be used either directly before the noun or pronoun, as in 'the big dog', or elsewhere in the sentence, as in 'The dog was big'.

The children were introduced to adjectives in *The Grammar Handbook 1*, and learnt how to use them before a noun. *The Grammar Handbook 2* provides revision of adjectives and of identifying them, whether they are placed before the noun or elsewhere in the sentence. The children are encouraged to use adjectives imaginatively in their writing.

Action: The action for an adjective is to touch the side of the temple with a fist.

Colour: The colour for adjectives is blue.

Possessive Adjectives

The Grammar Handbook 2 extends the children's understanding of adjectives to include the eight possessive adjectives, which are 'my', 'your', 'his', 'her', 'its', 'our', 'your' and 'their'. These correspond to the eight personal pronouns, 'I', 'you', 'he', 'she', 'it', 'we', 'you' and 'they'. A possessive adjective replaces one noun and describes another, by saying whose it is. For example, in the sentence 'Lucy fed her cat', the possessive adjective 'her' is used in place of 'Lucy's' and describes 'cat', by saying whose cat it is. (Because the possessive adjectives also function as pronouns, they are sometimes known as the weak set of possessive pronouns. However, to avoid confusion with the strong set of possessive pronouns, 'mine', 'yours', 'his', 'hers', 'its', 'ours', 'yours' and 'theirs', *Jolly Grammar* does not use this terminology.)

Action: The action for an adjective is to touch the side of the temple with a fist.

Colour: The colour for adjectives is blue.

Comparatives and Superlatives

The adjectives the children learnt to use in *The Grammar Handbook 1* are called positives. A positive is an adjective which describes a noun or pronoun without comparing it to anything else, as in 'The girl is young'. *The Grammar Handbook 2* introduces adjectives which describe a noun or pronoun by comparing it with one or more other items. These are called comparatives and superlatives. A comparative is used for comparing a noun with one other item, as in 'The boy is younger than the girl', and a superlative for comparing it with two items or more, as in 'He is the youngest of the four children'.

Short adjectives usually form their comparatives and superlatives with the suffixes ‹-er› and ‹-est›, whereas longer ones often use the words 'more' and 'most', so we say 'harder' and 'hardest', but 'more difficult' and 'most difficult'. The focus in *The Grammar Handbook 2* is on adding the ‹-er› and ‹-est› suffixes correctly (see the rules for adding suffixes on page 24). With the children, practise saying an adjective followed by its comparative and superlative, e.g. 'clean, cleaner, cleanest'. Ask the children which spelling they would use in each case.

Action: The action for an adjective is to touch the side of the temple with a fist.

Colour: The colour for adjectives is blue.

Adverbs

An adverb is similar to an adjective, but describes a verb rather than a noun. Usually adverbs describe how, where, when or how often something happens. They can also be used to modify adjectives or other adverbs, but the children do not need to know this at this stage.

The children were introduced to adverbs in *The Grammar Handbook 1*. At first it helped them to think of an adverb as often ending with the suffix ‹-ly›. *The Grammar Handbook 2* revises adverbs, and encourages the children to identify less obvious ones by looking for the verb and thinking which word is describing it. For example, in the sentence 'We arrived late last night', the adverb 'late' tells us something about the past tense verb 'arrived'. Point out examples in texts whenever possible, to help the children develop this understanding.

Action: The action for an adverb is to bang one fist on top of the other.

Colour: The colour for adverbs is orange.

Prepositions

A preposition is a word that relates one noun or pronoun to another. (Later, when they learn about subject and object, the children will learn that a preposition relates the subject to the object.) In the sentence 'He climbed over the gate', for example, the preposition 'over' relates 'he' to 'gate'. 'Pre' means 'before', 'position' means 'place' and together, 'preposition' means 'placed before', because it is placed before a noun or pronoun (in this case 'gate'). A preposition is also placed before any describing words which may already come before the noun or pronoun, such as adjectives, possessive adjectives or the articles 'a', 'an' or 'the', as in 'under the bridge', 'in my purse', 'after a long pause' and 'by her favourite author'.

Prepositions often describe where something is or where it is moving towards, and this is how they are first presented to the children in *The Grammar Handbook 2*. Practice prepositions by calling out examples and asking for nouns to go with them. For 'in', for example, the children might suggest 'the box' or 'the classroom', and for 'under' they might suggest 'the mat' or 'the table'. Many common prepositions are short words like 'at', 'by', 'for', 'of', 'in', 'on', 'to' and 'up'. Other common examples are 'above', 'after', 'around', 'behind', 'beside', 'between', 'down', 'from', 'into', 'past', 'through', 'towards', 'under' and 'with'. However, many of these words can also function as adverbs if they do not come before a noun or pronoun. For example, in the sentence 'I fell down', 'down' is an adverb describing 'fell', whereas in 'I fell down the stairs', it is a preposition relating 'I' to 'stairs'.

Action: The action for prepositions is to point from one noun to another.

Colour: The colour for prepositions is green.

Conjunctions

A conjunction is a word used to join parts of a sentence which usually, but not always, contain their own verbs. *The Grammar Handbook 2* introduces conjunctions through focus on six of the most useful ones: 'and', 'but', 'because', 'or', 'so', and 'while'. Other common conjunctions are 'although', 'if', 'now', 'once', 'since', 'unless', 'until', 'when' and 'whether'. Conjunctions allow the children to write longer, less repetitive sentences. Instead of writing, for example, 'I eat fish. I eat chips. I like the taste', the children could use the conjunctions 'and' and 'because' to write, 'I eat fish and chips because I like the taste'. Whereas the shorter sentences were stilted and repetitive, the new one is flowing and concise. The ability to vary the length of their sentences will greatly improve the quality of the children's writing. Display a list of common conjunctions in the classroom to encourage the children to use others besides 'and'.

Action: The action for conjunctions is to hold the hands apart with palms facing up. Move both hands so one is on top of the other.

Colour: The colour for conjunctions is purple.

a / an / the

The words 'a', 'an' and 'the' are known as articles. 'A' and 'an' are used before singular nouns and are called the indefinite articles, as in 'a man' and 'an egg'. 'The' is used before singular and plural nouns and is called the definite article, as in 'the dog' and 'the boys'. The articles are a special sort of adjective.

The Grammar Handbook 1 taught the children when to use 'an' instead of 'a'. As a simple rule of thumb, they learnt to look at the word after the article. If it starts with a vowel sound, the article is 'an', as in 'an ant', 'an eagle', 'an igloo', 'an octopus', 'an umpire'. Note that it is the first sound that is important, not the first letter, so if, for example, a word starts with a silent consonant and the first sound is actually a vowel, the article is 'an', as in 'an hour'.

Sentences

The full definition of a sentence is complicated and more than children can cope with at this stage. In *The Grammar Handbook 1*, they learnt that a sentence must start with a capital letter, end with a full stop, and make sense. In *The Grammar Handbook 2*, this definition is refined when the children learn that a sentence must contain a verb. Later they will learn that it must contain a subject too. A sentence can end with a question or exclamation mark instead of a full stop, and the children are encouraged to think about the meaning of each sentence to decide which punctuation mark to use.

Punctuation

The Grammar Handbook 2 emphasises the importance of punctuation. The teaching aims to help the children understand that their writing will be easier to read if it is accurately punctuated. The children revise full stops, question marks and speech marks, and are introduced to exclamation marks, commas and apostrophes.

Exclamation Marks

An exclamation mark (!) is used at the end of a sentence instead of a full stop, to show that the speaker or writer feels strongly about something. To exclaim is to cry out suddenly, especially in anger, surprise or pain.

Commas

Sometimes in the middle of a sentence, where it would be wrong to use a full stop, it is necessary to indicate a short pause. This helps the reader separate one idea from another. For this sort of pause we use a comma (,). The children will be used to being told to pause when they see a comma in their reading. However, learning when to use commas in writing is more difficult. *The Grammar Handbook 2* introduces two of the most straightforward ways commas are used.

- We use commas to separate items in a list of more than two items, such as 'red, white and blue', or 'Grandma, Grandpa, Aunt and Uncle'. Note that before the last item in a list a comma is not used, but is replaced by the word 'and'.
- We also use commas in sentences which include direct speech, to indicate a pause between the words spoken and the rest of the sentence. If the speech comes before the rest of the sentence, the comma belongs after the last word spoken but inside the speech marks, e.g. '"I am hungry," complained Matt.' (If the words spoken are a question or an exclamation, then a question or exclamation mark is used instead of a comma, in the same position.) If the speech comes after the rest of the sentence, the comma belongs after the last word that is not spoken but before the speech marks, e.g. 'Matt complained, "I am hungry."'.

Apostrophes

The Grammar Handbook 2 introduces both of the main ways that apostrophes (') are used. There are clear rules for using apostrophes, and it is important to teach them early, before any children develop bad habits in their writing. Apostrophes are very often incorrectly used.

- An apostrophe with the letter ‹s› is used after a noun to indicate possession, as in 'Ben's new toy' or 'the girl's father'. The apostrophe is needed to show that the ‹s› is not being used to make a plural. Understanding this will help the children use apostrophe ‹s› correctly. Encourage them to think about the meaning of what they write, and whether each ‹s› is being used to make a plural or the possessive case.

  Later they will learn how to use apostrophe ‹s› with plurals that already end with ‹s› (e.g. 'the boys' room') and with names that end with ‹es› (e.g. 'James' cat').

  Although the possessive adjectives (my, your, his, etc.) indicate possession, there is no risk of confusion with the plural, so they do not need an apostrophe. Help the children avoid the common mistake of writing the possessive adjective 'its' as 'it's'.

- An apostrophe is also used to show that a letter or letters are missing. Sometimes we shorten a pair of words by joining them together and leaving out some of their letters. We use an apostrophe to show where the missing letter or letters used to be. This is called a contraction. There are many common contractions, such as 'I'm' for 'I am', 'didn't' for 'did not' and 'you'll' for 'you will'. Encourage the children to listen to each contraction and identify which sound or sounds are missing. This will help them leave out the appropriate letters and put the apostrophe in the right place, thereby avoiding some common mistakes. In 'haven't', for example, the /o/ of 'not' is missing, so the apostrophe goes between ‹n› and ‹t›, to show where ‹o› used to be. It does not go between ‹e› and ‹n›, to make 'have'nt'.

  When 'it is' is contracted to 'it's', as in 'It's late', an apostrophe is needed to show that the second ‹i› is missing. The children need to think about the meaning of what they are writing, to avoid confusion with the possessive adjective 'its'. When it is short for 'it is', 'it's' always needs an apostrophe.

  It is important that the children learn how to spell and punctuate contractions correctly. However, they should only use contractions when writing direct speech or informal notes. Contractions are not traditionally used in formal writing.

Parsing: identifying parts of speech in sentences

Parsing is identifying the function of words in sentences. Each word must be looked at in context to decide which part of speech it is. This skill is worth promoting, as it reinforces the grammar teaching and helps the children develop an analytical understanding of how our language works. Many words can function as more than one part of speech, e.g. 'light' can be the noun 'a light', the verb 'to light', or the adjective in 'a light colour'. It is only by analysing a word's use within a sentence that its function can be identified.

Begin by writing extremely simple sentences on the board, e.g. 'I pat the dog', which can be parsed as: pronoun, verb, (article), noun. Ask the children to identify the parts of speech they know. They enjoy taking turns to underline the parts of speech in the appropriate colours.

Gradually, when most of the children have mastered this, move on to more complicated sentences which use more parts of speech, e.g. 'She cheerfully wrote a long letter to her friend'. This can be parsed as: pronoun, adverb, verb (the infinitive of which is 'to write'), (article), adjective, noun, preposition, possessive adjective, noun. Remind the children that every sentence must contain at least one verb. They should begin parsing a sentence by identifying its verb or verbs, and should supply each verb in the infinitive form. If there is time, the children should then identify as many of the other parts of speech as possible, underlining them in the appropriate colours. Regular practice in odd moments will help the children become quick and competent at parsing.

Alphabetical order, dictionary and thesaurus work

Many reference materials, including dictionaries, thesauruses, encyclopedias, indexes and directories, organise their material alphabetically. The more familiar the children are with the order of the alphabet, the better they will become at using these resources independently.

In *The Grammar Handbook 1*, the children were introduced to the order of the alphabet and to using the dictionary. To help them find words, the children imagined dividing the dictionary into four approximately-equal parts, which would divide the letters into the following groups:

1. Aa Bb Cc Dd Ee
2. Ff Gg Hh Ii Jj Kk Ll Mm
3. Nn Oo Pp Qq Rr Ss
4. Tt Uu Vv Ww Xx Yy Zz

Knowing these groups saves the children time when using the dictionary. Before looking up a word, they decide which group its initial letter falls into, and then narrow their search to that section of the dictionary. For the word 'pony', for example, the first letter is ‹p› which is in the third group, so the children would turn to the third quarter of the dictionary.

The Grammar Handbook 2 improves the children's alphabet skills, by teaching them to look beyond the initial letter of each word. They practise putting into alphabetical order words which share the first two letters, e.g. 'sheep' and 'shoe', and then words which share the first three letters, e.g. 'penny', 'pencil' and 'penguin'.

Most children can become quite proficient at using a dictionary designed for schools. When they finish a piece of writing they should proofread it, identify any words that look incorrectly spelt, and look them up in the dictionary. The children are also encouraged to use the dictionary to look up meanings. Practice is provided through focus on homophones, which are words which sound similar to one another but which have different spellings and meanings, e.g. 'hear' and 'here'. *The Grammar Handbook 2* also introduces thesauruses, which are books that list words with similar meanings to one another. The children practise finding alternatives to commonly-overused words, e.g. 'nice'.

It is helpful to give each child a Word Book, for keeping a note of the weekly spellings and any additional topic or tricky words which arise. The Word Books can then be used to help the children in their independent writing. The following extension ideas are also useful for improving alphabet and dictionary skills in any spare moments, or for children who finish their work ahead of time:

- The children take the words on one page of their Word Book and re-write them in alphabetical order.
- Write up groups of words. For each group, choose a word which uses a sound with alternative spellings, e.g. 'disturb' uses the /er/ sound. Write up several versions of this word, only one of which is correctly spelt, e.g. 'disterb', 'distirb' and 'disturb'. The children use the dictionary to check which spelling is correct.
- In pairs, the children race one another to find a given word in the dictionary.

Teaching Ideas for Spelling

Most children need to be taught to spell correctly. In *Jolly Grammar*, spelling is the main focus for one lesson each week. The aim of the spelling work in *The Grammar Handbook 2* is to introduce groups of words which use new spelling patterns, and to revise the alternative spellings of vowel sounds.

The children first learnt to spell by listening for the sounds in words and writing the letters to represent those sounds, and by systematically learning key irregular, or 'tricky' words by heart. After one year of *Jolly Phonics* and one year of *Jolly Grammar*, most children have a reading age of at least seven years, and are starting to spell with far greater accuracy. As research has shown, children with a reading age of seven years or more are able to use analogy in their reasoning. This is a useful strategy for spelling. Children who want to write 'should', for example, might notice that it sounds like a word they already know, such as 'would'. They could then use the spelling of 'would' to write 'should', by replacing the /w/ sound with /sh/. If the children are unsure of a spelling, they may be able to find it by writing the word in several ways, e.g. 'should' and 'shood', and then trying to choose the correct version. If they have already encountered the word several times in their reading, they will probably be able to choose the right spelling. By introducing groups of words which use each of the new spelling patterns, *The Grammar Handbook 2* encourages the children to think analogically.

Focus on revising the alternative spellings of vowel sounds helps the children consolidate their learning. Now they are ready to learn, not only the main ways of spelling the vowel sounds, but which words take which spelling.

The Grammar Handbook 2 introduces the following spelling features:

- vowel digraphs,
- alternative spellings of vowel sounds,
- new spelling patterns,
- silent letters,
- syllables,
- identifying the short vowels,
- spelling rules, and
- tricky word families.

These eight features are outlined in greater detail in the pages following.

Vowel digraphs

The vowel digraphs were introduced in *The Grammar Handbook 1.* The focus in *The Grammar Handbook 2* is on consolidating this learning. 'Vowel digraph' is the term for two letters which make a single vowel sound, one or both of the letters being a vowel. Often the two letters are next to each other, e.g. ‹ay›, ‹ea›, ‹ou›, ‹oi›, ‹ew›. Two vowel letters are usually needed to make a so-called 'long vowel' sound, i.e. one of the vowel letter names: /ai/, /ee/, /ie/, /oa/ or /ue/. Generally the sound they make is that of the first vowel's name. Hence the well-known rule of thumb, 'When two vowels go walking, the first does the talking'.

Sometimes the long vowel sound is made by two vowels separated by one or more consonants. In one-syllable words, the second vowel is usually an ‹e›, known as a 'magic ‹e›' because it modifies the sound of the first. Digraphs with a magic ‹e› can be thought of as 'hop-over ‹e›' digraphs: ‹a_e›, ‹e_e›, ‹i_e›, ‹o_e› and ‹u_e›. Once again, the sound they make is that of the first vowel's name; the 'magic ‹e›' is silent. Children like to show with a hand how magic from the ‹e› hops over the preceding consonant and changes the short vowel sound to a long one.

This is an alternative way of making the long vowel sounds, as in such words as 'bake', 'these', 'fine', 'hope' and 'cube'. The children need to be shown many examples, which are available in the *Jolly Phonics Word Book*. It helps the children understand if a piece of paper is held over the ‹e›, and the word is read without it. For example, 'pipe' becomes 'pip', 'hate' becomes 'hat', 'hope' becomes 'hop' and 'late' becomes 'lat'. It does not matter if, as in this last example, the children find themselves producing nonsense words; the exercise will still help them to understand the spelling rule. When looking at texts on the board or in big books, it is helpful for the children to look for and identify words with a 'magic ‹e›'.

As there are only a few words with the '‹e› hop-over ‹e›' spelling, e.g. 'these', 'scheme', 'complete', and as they are rather rare and usually found in complicated words, this spelling was not taught as one of the main alternatives for the long vowel sounds. However, it should be introduced to the class.

Alternative spellings of vowel sounds

Children who have learnt to read with *Jolly Phonics* are used to spelling new words by listening for the sounds and writing letters to represent those sounds. This enables them to spell accurately the many regular words that do not use vowel sounds with more than one spelling, e.g. 'hot', 'plan', 'brush', 'drench' and 'stinging'. However, words like 'train', 'play' and 'make' present a problem. All three words feature the same /ai/ sound, but in each case it is spelt differently. The list below shows the first spelling taught for each letter sound and the main alternatives introduced:

First spelling taught for sound:	*Alternative spellings of sound:*	*Examples of all spellings in words:*
ai	ay, a_e	rain, day, came
ee	ea	street, dream
ie	igh, y, i_e	pie, light, by, time
oa	ow, o_e	boat, snow, home
ue	ew, u_e	due, few, cube
er	ir, ur	her, first, turn
oi	oy	boil, toy
ou	ow	out, cow
or	au, aw, al	corn, haunt, saw, talk

The alternative spellings of vowel sounds were taught in *The Grammar Handbook 1*, and should be familiar to the children. Now it is important to consolidate this teaching. The spellings should be regularly revised, both with flash cards, and by asking the children to list the alternative spellings for a particular sound. The children should be able to do so automatically, and be able to apply their knowledge when writing unfamiliar words. For a word like 'frame', for example, they should be able to write 'fraim, fraym, frame' on a scrap of paper, and then try to decide which version looks correct.

New spelling patterns

The Grammar Handbook 2 introduces the new letter sound /air/, and the three main ways it can be spelt, which are ‹air›, ‹are› and ‹ear›, as in 'hair', 'care' and 'bear'. This sound was not included in *The Phonics Handbook* or *The Grammar Handbook 1*, as it is relatively unusual.

The children also learn many new, less usual spellings of familiar sounds. The list below shows the first spelling taught for each letter sound(s) and the new spelling introduced:

First spelling taught for sound(s):	*New spelling of sound(s):*	*Examples of new spelling in words:*
ai	ei, eigh	veil, eight, sleigh
cher*	ture	capture, nature, picture
e	ea	breakfast, deaf, ready
ee	ey	chimney, key, valley
ee	ie	field, piece, thief
ee	y	any, daddy, fairy
f	ph	graph, orphan, photo
j	'soft' g	gem, giant, gymnast
k	ch	chemist, chord, echo
k	ck	block, cricket, duck
or	ore	more, snore, wore
s	'soft' c	cell, city, cycle
shun*	sion	mission, tension, vision
shun*	tion	fiction, lotion, station
u	o	front, love, month
u	ou	couple, touch, young
ool*	le	handle, little, nibble
w	wh	whale, whistle, why
wo	wa	swan, was, watch

The children need to memorise which words use each of these new spelling patterns. It is helpful to make up silly sentences for each spelling, using as many of the words as possible. For the ‹ie› spelling of the /ee/ sound, for example, the children could chant 'I believe my niece was the chief thief who came to grief over the piece of shield she hid in the field.' This would help them remember to write the words 'believe', 'niece', 'chief', 'thief', 'grief', 'piece', 'shield' and 'field' with the ‹ie› spelling.

* As the relevant teacher's lesson notes explain, this is only an approximation of the sound made by the new spelling.

Silent letters

A number of English words contain letters which are not pronounced at all, known as 'silent letters'. Some silent letters, such as the ‹k› in 'knee', show us how the word used to be pronounced. Others, such as the ‹h› in 'rhyme', reflect the word's foreign origins. *The Grammar Handbook 2* introduces the following silent letters:

silent ‹b›, as in 'lamb',
silent ‹c›, as in 'scissors',
silent ‹h›, as in 'rhubarb',
silent ‹k›, as in 'knife' and
silent ‹w›, as in 'wrong'.

Practising with the 'Say it as it sounds' method helps children remember these spellings. For the word 'lamb', for example, say the word to the class, pronouncing it correctly as /lam/. The children respond by saying /lam**b**/, emphasising the /b/ which would normally be silent.

Syllables

An understanding of syllables will help improve the children's spelling. Some spelling rules depend on the children's ability to identify the number of syllables in a given word. Later, when they learn about where the stress is placed in words, their understanding of syllables will be even more important. Although the rules of English often let us down, they are worth acquiring. The more the children know, the more skillful they become, and the better equipped they are to deal with irregularities.

'Chin bumps' is a fun, multisensory way of teaching syllables. The children each use one hand, which should be flattened as if to pat something. They each touch their chin by placing this hand underneath it. Then they slowly say a word, and count the number of times they feel their chin go down. For 'cat', for example, they feel one bump, which means it has one syllable; 'table' has two bumps, so two syllables; 'any' has two bumps and two syllables; 'screeched' has one bump and one syllable; 'idea' has three bumps and three syllables.

Identifying the short vowels

One of the most reliable spelling rules in English is that of consonant doubling. Consonant doubling is governed by the short vowels, so the children need to be able to identify short vowel sounds confidently. For an entertaining way of helping them listen for short vowels, a puppet such as the Inky Mouse puppet and a box can be used.

For /a/, put the puppet **a**t the side of the box.

For /e/, make the puppet wobble on the **e**dge of the box.

For /i/, put the puppet **i**n the box.

For /o/, put the puppet **o**n the box.

For /u/, put the puppet **u**nder the box.

Then the children pretend that their fist is the box and their other hand is the puppet.

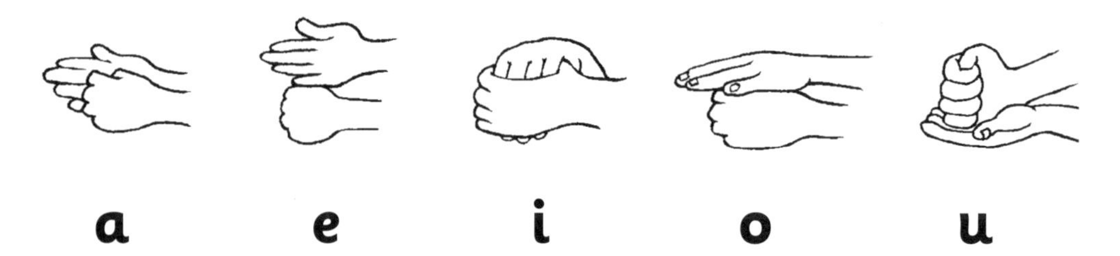

Start by calling out short vowel sounds. For each one, the children do the appropriate action with their hands. Then call out short words which have a short vowel, e.g. 'pot', 'hat', 'bun', 'dig', 'red'. The children should listen for the vowel sound in each word, and do the action. When most of the children have mastered this, progress to calling out short words with a variety of vowel sounds. For those which do not have a short vowel sound, the children must keep their hands still.

Activities like these help to keep the children 'tuned in' to identifying the sounds in words, as well as preparing them for the consonant doubling rules.

Spelling rules

Being able to identify syllables and short vowels will help the children apply the following rules for consonant doubling and adding suffixes.

Rules for consonant doubling:

a. In a one-syllable word with a short vowel sound, if the last consonant is ‹f›, ‹l›, ‹s› or ‹z›, this is doubled: e.g. 'cliff', 'bell', 'miss', 'buzz'. (The exceptions include the tricky two-letter words: 'as', 'if', 'is', 'of' and 'us'.)

b. In a one-syllable word with a short vowel sound, if the last consonant sound is /k/, this is spelt as ‹ck›: e.g. 'back', 'neck', 'lick', 'clock', 'duck'.

c. If there is only one consonant after a short, stressed vowel sound, this consonant is doubled before any suffix starting with a vowel, such as ‹-ed›, ‹-er›, ‹-est›, ‹-ing›, or ‹-y›, as in 'hopped', 'wetter', 'biggest', 'clapping' and 'funny'. Note that when ‹y› is a suffix, it counts as a vowel because it has a vowel sound. (This rule does not apply if the consonant is ‹x›, which is never doubled, even in words like 'faxed', 'boxing' and 'mixer'.)

   It helps the children to think of the two consonants as forming a wall. If there were only one consonant, the wall would not be thick enough to prevent 'magic' hopping over from the vowel in the suffix and changing the short vowel sound to a long one. With two consonants the wall becomes so thick that the 'magic' cannot get over. (See adding suffixes, rule 'c'.)

d. When a word ends with the letters ‹le› and the preceding syllable contains a short, stressed vowel sound, there must be two consonants between the short vowel and the ‹le›. This means that the consonant before the ‹le› is doubled in words like 'paddle', 'kettle', 'nibble', 'topple' and 'snuggle'. No doubling is necessary in words like 'handle', 'twinkle' and 'jungle' because they already have two consonants between the short vowel and the ‹le›.

Rules for adding suffixes:

a. If the base word ends with a consonant which is not immediately after a short vowel sound, simply add the suffix. So 'look' + ‹-ing› = 'looking' and 'quick' + ‹-est› = 'quickest'.

b. If the base word ends with the letter ‹e› and the suffix starts with a vowel, remove the ‹e› before adding the suffix. So 'brave' + ‹-er› = 'braver' and 'like' + ‹-ing› = 'liking', whereas 'like' + ‹-ness› = 'likeness'.

c. If the base word ends with a consonant immediately after a short, stressed vowel sound and the suffix starts with a vowel, double the final consonant before adding the suffix. So 'run' + ‹-ing› = 'running' and 'sad' + ‹-er› = 'sadder', whereas 'sad' + ‹-ness› = 'sadness'. Remind the children that this is because two consonants are needed to make a wall, to prevent magic from the vowel in the suffix jumping over to change the short vowel sound. (See consonant doubling, rule 'c'.)

d. If the base word ends with the letter ‹y› immediately after a consonant, replace the ‹y› with ‹i› before adding the suffix. So 'dirty' + ‹-est› = 'dirtiest', 'beauty' + ‹-ful› = 'beautiful' and 'hurry' + ‹-ed› = 'hurried'. However, if the suffix starts with the letter ‹i›, the rule does not apply, so 'worry' + ‹-ing› = 'worrying'.
   The letter ‹y› is unique in being able to function as either a vowel or a consonant. As a vowel, ‹y› replaces ‹i›. With *Jolly Phonics*, the children learnt that 'shy ‹i›' does not like to go at the end of a word, so 'toughy ‹y›' takes its place. As the last syllable of multi-syllabic words, the sound ‹y› makes is somewhere between the short /i/ in 'tin' and the long /ee/ in 'bee'. (This is also true of the rare instances when ‹i› is found as the last syllable of a multi-syllabic word, such as 'taxi'.) Despite this confusing pronunciation, it is important for the children to think of ‹y› as replacing 'shy ‹i›'. This will help them remember that the ‹i› returns when such words are extended.

Tricky word families

Each week, *The Grammar Handbook 2* introduces two words from a 'word family'. The 'word families' are groups of useful words, many of which are 'tricky' words, with irregular spellings that need to be learnt. The first group consists of family words, e.g. 'cousin'. The others are month names, number words, measuring words and tricky plurals. For completeness, a few regular words are included, e.g. 'March' and 'fifteen'. Although these present fewer problems, they are still important and need to be learnt.

Photocopy Section 1

Grammar and Spelling Lesson Sheets

For each lesson there is a photocopiable activity sheet for the children to complete, accompanied by a page of teacher's lesson notes. The recommendations in the notes are intended to be followed systematically. However, if a suggestion seems inappropriate to a particular class situation, it can of course be adapted to suit.

All the lesson notes feature a notepad in the top right-hand corner. This shows a brief checklist of what to prepare for teaching, and is intended for easy reference once the teaching notes have been read. (Items which are useful, but not essential, are shown in brackets.)

The **grammar notes** all follow the same format:

a. Aim
b. Introduction
c. Main point
d. Grammar sheet
e. Extension activity
f. Rounding off

Each grammar lesson has its own particular focus, and the teacher's notes vary accordingly. However, the standard format helps to give the lessons a recognisable shape.

Grammar 3 – Speech Marks

Aim: Develop the children's ability to use speech marks.

Introduction: Show the children a comic or book which uses speech bubbles. Ask what the speech bubbles are for. Choose the words in one of the speech bubbles, and ask the children how they would write the spoken words if they were writing a story. On the board, write the spoken words in a sentence that explains who the speaker is. Use speech marks around the words that are actually spoken. Remind the children how to write speech marks and where to position them above the line.

Example: *Words in speech bubble:* I want to go home. *Sentence on board:* "I want to go home," said Karen.

Main point: Show the children Grammar sheet 3, which can be enlarged, using a photocopier. With the children, read the sentences at the top of the worksheet. Ask where the speech marks should be, to indicate which words were actually spoken. Then look at the picture and ask the children to suggest what each character might say next. Choose one of the suggestions and write it in the appropriate speech bubble.

Grammar sheet 3: The children write inside the outlined speech marks. Then they add speech marks to the sentences. Next they look at the picture, decide what each character says next and write it in the appropriate speech bubble. Finally they write out the words in the speech bubbles, in sentences. Remind the children to explain which character is speaking and to put in the speech marks, in each sentence. The Writing Master on page 176 may be photocopied onto the back of the grammar sheets for the children to write on.

Extension activity: The children could continue the conversation, still using the back of their sheets.

Rounding off: Go over the sheet with the class, checking where the speech marks belong. Ask some of the children to read out what they wrote in the speech bubbles.

The **spelling notes** also follow a standard format:

a. Revision
b. Main point
c. Spelling sheet
d. Dictation
e. Spelling list

Two boxes at the bottom of each page show the words and sentences for dictation, and the weekly spelling list.

Many teaching points are common to all the spelling lessons, so these are explained in further detail below.

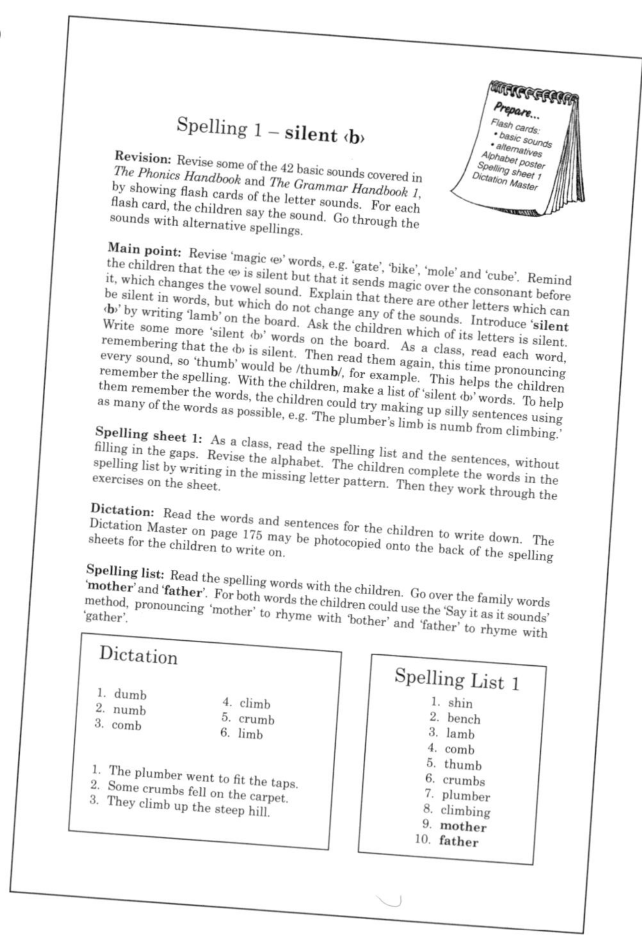

Spelling 1 – **silent ‹b›**

Revision: Revise some of the 42 basic sounds covered in *The Phonics Handbook* and *The Grammar Handbook 1*, by showing flash cards of the letter sounds. For each flash card, the children say the sound. Go through the sounds with alternative spellings.

Main point: Revise 'magic ‹e›' words, e.g. 'gate', 'bike', 'mole' and 'cube'. Remind the children that the ‹e› is silent but that it sends magic over the consonant before it, which changes the vowel sound. Explain that there are other letters which can be silent in words, but which do not change any of the sounds. Introduce '**silent ‹b›**' by writing 'lamb' on the board. Ask the children which of its letters is silent. Write some more 'silent ‹b›' words on the board. As a class, read each word, remembering that the ‹b› is silent. Then read them again, this time pronouncing every sound, so 'thumb' would be /thum**b**/, for example. This helps the children remember the spelling. With the children, make a list of 'silent ‹b›' words. To help them remember the words, the children could try making up silly sentences using as many of the words as possible, e.g. 'The plumber's limb is numb from climbing.'

Spelling sheet 1: As a class, read the spelling list and the sentences, without filling in the gaps. Revise the alphabet. The children complete the words in the spelling list by writing in the missing letter pattern. Then they work through the exercises on the sheet.

Dictation: Read the words and sentences for the children to write down. The Dictation Master on page 175 may be photocopied onto the back of the spelling sheets for the children to write on.

Spelling list: Read the spelling words with the children. Go over the family words '**mother**' and '**father**'. For both words the children could use the 'Say it as it sounds' method, pronouncing 'mother' to rhyme with 'bother' and 'father' to rhyme with 'gather'.

Dictation

1. dumb
2. numb
3. comb
4. climb
5. crumb
6. limb

1. The plumber went to fit the taps.
2. Some crumbs fell on the carpet.
3. They climb up the steep hill.

Spelling List 1

1. shin
2. bench
3. lamb
4. comb
5. thumb
6. crumbs
7. plumber
8. climbing
9. **mother**
10. **father**

a. Revision

Each lesson should start with a short burst of revision. In the early lessons, concentrate on the 42 main letter sounds and the alternative spellings of vowel sounds, using flash cards. Over the course of the year, other areas can be added, such as words and sentences featuring new spelling patterns, and chanting the letter names of tricky words.

b. Main Point

Most of the spelling lessons introduce a new spelling pattern, e.g. ‹ph›. Each of the remaining lessons features one of the vowel sounds with alternative spellings, e.g. /ai/. Where before the children practised the alternative spellings one at a time, now they practise them together and must memorise which words take which one.

c. Spelling sheet

The focus of each spelling sheet reflects the main teaching point, whether it is a new spelling pattern or a vowel sound with alternative spellings. The exercises also provide practice with the week's spelling words, reading, and revision of the previous week's grammar.

d. Dictation

As a weekly exercise, dictation is useful in a number of ways. It gives the children regular practice in listening for sounds in the words they write, and is a good way of monitoring their progress. It helps the children develop in their independent writing, and encourages the slower writers to increase their speed.

Each dictation list consists of six words and three simple sentences. These all revise the spelling introduced that week, and in previous spelling lessons. For example, if the focus for a particular week is the 'soft ‹g›' spelling, then the six dictation words usually feature it.

Begin by calling out the first word for the children to write down. Then ask one of them to sound it out. As the child calls out the sounds, write the letters for them on the board. On reaching the spelling of the week, the child should say the sound, e.g. /j/, and then name the letter(s) used to spell it, in this case ‹g›. The other children check whether they have written the word correctly and, if so, give themselves a tick. If there is time after the sentences have been dictated, check that the regular words in the sentences have been sounded out properly and the tricky words spelt correctly. Where appropriate, have the children say the names of the letters in the tricky words.

When the majority of children have finished a word or sentence, go on to the next. The few children who have not finished should leave the item incomplete, and move on. This encourages them to get up to speed. For extra practice, these children could be given words for dictation homework.

Without regular practice, some children lose the ability to hear the sounds in words. These tend to be the children who were slowest to acquire phonemic awareness in the first place. It is easy to identify problems by looking at the children's independent writing. For example, if a child writes the word 'brown' as 'bowrn', this usually indicates that the child needs to be taught to listen more carefully when writing. Regular listening practice is particularly important for such children.

There are a number of activities introduced in *The Phonics Handbook*, which can be used to improve phonemic awareness with a class, group or individual, such as:

- holding up one finger for each sound in a word, e.g. five fingers for 'thirsty',
- orally 'chopping' sounds off a word, one by one, e.g. 'clap, lap, ap, p',
- splitting a word into onset and rime, e.g. 'scr-eam',
- splitting a word into syllables, e.g. 'ho-li-day', and
- making new words by changing one sound at a time, e.g. 'fun, fin, thin, thick, sick, sing, song, wrong'.

e. Spelling list

Each week the children are given ten spellings to learn for a test. It makes sense to give the spelling homework at the beginning of the week, and to test at the end of the week or on the following Monday.

The words have been carefully selected to enable every child to have some success, with the majority achieving full marks.

Words 1 and 2 in each spelling list are regular and usually feature a consonant blend, e.g. '**cr**ab' and 'le**nd**'. All the children should be able to spell these correctly by listening for the sounds. Words 3, 4, 5, 6, 7 and 8 feature the spelling of the week. Number 8 is often a longer word. The children need encouragement in tackling long words to build their confidence. Words 9 and 10 are from the 'word families' introduced. Many of these are tricky words, with irregular spellings that need to be learnt.

Spelling List 1

1. shin
2. bench
3. lamb
4. comb
5. thumb
6. crumbs
7. plumber
8. climbing
9. **mother**
10. **father**

It is important to go over the words on the list during the spelling lesson, looking carefully to see which words are regular and which are not. For words identified as irregular, the teacher's notes suggest suitable learning strategies. Usually one of the three techniques already familiar from *Jolly Phonics* and *The Grammar Handbook 1* will be suitable; these are: 'Look, Copy, Cover, Write, Check', 'Say it as it sounds', and Mnemonics. It is not enough simply to send home a list of words for the children to learn. At odd moments during the week ask the class, or individual children, to spell or sound out words from the list, or to test each other in pairs.

Each child takes the spellings home in a small vocabulary-size exercise book. In Photocopy Section 3 the spelling words are set out in the groups of ten, ready for photocopying. At the beginning of each week, stick the right section into each child's Spelling Homework Book, or ask the children to write out the spellings themselves. If the children do the writing, check that they have copied the words clearly and accurately before the books go home.

Test and mark the spellings each week. The results should be written in the Spelling Homework Book for the parents to see, shown either as a mark out of ten, or with a coded system if preferred. A coloured star system might be used, for example, with a gold star for 10/10, a silver star for 9/10 and a coloured star for 8/10. A letter of encouragement to parents is provided on page 185. Most parents like to be involved in the homework, and are interested in how many words their child spelt correctly and which words were mis-spelt.

Children need to be aware that accurate spelling is important for their future. There is no magic wand that can be waved to make them good at spelling. In addition to knowing the letter sounds and alternative spellings thoroughly, a certain amount of dedication and practice is needed.

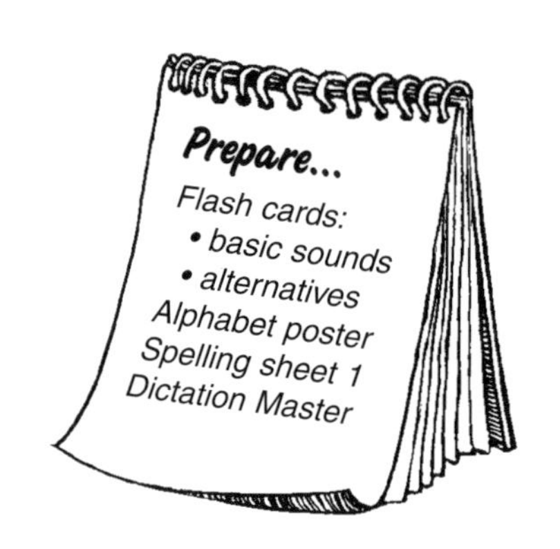

Spelling 1 – **silent ‹b›**

Revision: Revise some of the 42 basic sounds covered in *The Phonics Handbook* and *The Grammar Handbook 1*, by showing flash cards of the letter sounds. For each flash card, the children say the sound. Go through the sounds with alternative spellings.

Main point: Revise 'magic ‹e›' words, e.g. 'gate', 'bike', 'mole' and 'cube'. Remind the children that the ‹e› is silent but that it sends magic over the consonant before it, which changes the vowel sound. Explain that there are other letters which can be silent in words, but which do not change any of the sounds. Introduce '**silent ‹b›**' by writing 'lamb' on the board. Ask the children which of its letters is silent. Write some more 'silent ‹b›' words on the board. As a class, read each word, remembering that the ‹b› is silent. Then read them again, this time pronouncing every sound, so 'thumb' would be /thum**b**/, for example. This helps the children remember the spelling. With the children, make a list of 'silent ‹b›' words. To help them remember the words, the children could try making up silly sentences using as many of the words as possible, e.g. 'The plumber's limb is numb from climbing.'

Spelling sheet 1: As a class, read the spelling list and the sentences, without filling in the gaps. Revise the alphabet. The children complete the words in the spelling list by writing in the missing letter pattern. Then they work through the exercises on the sheet.

Dictation: Read the words and sentences for the children to write down. The Dictation Master on page 175 may be photocopied onto the back of the spelling sheets for the children to write on.

Spelling list: Read the spelling words with the children. Go over the family words '**mother**' and '**father**'. For both words the children could use the 'Say it as it sounds' method, pronouncing 'mother' to rhyme with 'bother' and 'father' to rhyme with 'gather'.

Dictation

1. dumb
2. numb
3. comb
4. climb
5. crumb
6. limb

1. The plumber went to fit the taps.
2. Some crumbs fell on the carpet.
3. They climb up the steep hill.

Spelling List 1

1. shin
2. bench
3. lamb
4. comb
5. thumb
6. crumbs
7. plumber
8. climbing
9. **mother**
10. **father**

Spelling List
1. shin
2. bench
3. lam _
4. com _
5. thum _
6. crum _ s
7. plum _ er
8. clim _ ing
9. mother
10. father
Silent ‹b›
Write some ‘silent ‹b›’ words in the lamb.
Choose a word from the list to fit each sentence.
1. I ______________ my hair every morning.
2. A baby sheep is called a ______________.
3. The girls were ______________ the tree.
4. There are cake ______________ on the table.
mother
_ o _ h _ r
m _ t _ e _
m _ _ h e _
father
_ a _ _ e r
f _ t h _ _
f _ _ h _ _
Write the alphabet in capital and lower-case letters.
A a

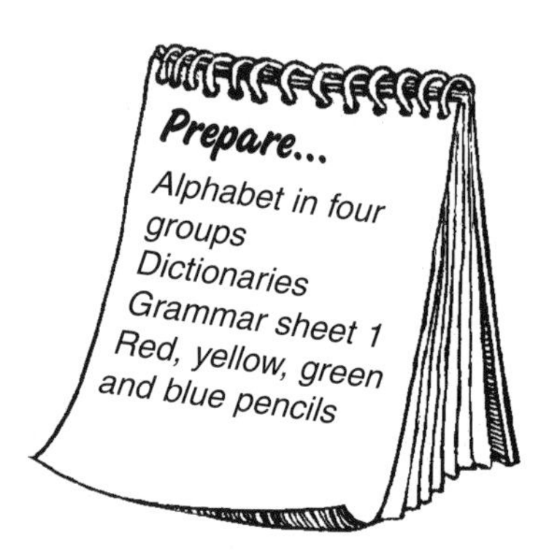

Prepare...
Alphabet in four groups
Dictionaries
Grammar sheet 1
Red, yellow, green and blue pencils

Grammar 1 – Alphabetical Order (1)

Aim: Develop the children's familiarity with the alphabet, and with the four dictionary groups.

Introduction: Revise the alphabet. Call out a letter and ask which letters come before and after it. Repeat with other letters. Then write groups of three or four letters on the board. With the children, sort them into alphabetical order.

Main point: Remind the children that if a dictionary were divided into four approximately-equal parts, the letters would fall into the following groups:

1. Aa Bb Cc Dd Ee
2. Ff Gg Hh Ii Jj Kk Ll Mm
3. Nn Oo Pp Qq Rr Ss
4. Tt Uu Vv Ww Xx Yy Zz

Revise the four dictionary groups. The children say the alphabet, holding up a finger for each group and pausing between groups. Call out a letter and ask the children which group it belongs to. Repeat with other letters. If possible, give out dictionaries to all the children. Call out a letter and ask the children to try opening the dictionary in the right group for that letter.

Grammar sheet 1: The children write inside the outlined lower-case letters. They use a different coloured pencil for each group: red for group 1, yellow for group 2, green for group 3 and blue for group 4. Then they write the capital letters next to the lower-case ones. Next they put the groups of letters into alphabetical order. Remind them to use capital letters. Finally they read through the words at the bottom of the page, and try looking up each one in the dictionary. When they find a word, they write its page number on the line provided. Make sure that all the words are included in the dictionaries being used, and replace any words that are not. If the dictionaries do not have page numbers, ask the children to write the word which comes after the one they looked up. This ensures that the children really have found the words in their dictionaries.

Extension activity: Write more words on the board for the children to find in their dictionaries.

Rounding off: Go over the sheet, with the class checking their answers.

Alphabetical Order

Use a different colour for each section of the alphabet.
Write the capital letters next to the lower-case letters.

___a ___b ___c ___d ___e

___f ___g ___h ___i ___j ___k ___l ___m

___n ___o ___p ___q ___r ___s

___t ___u ___v ___w ___x ___y ___z

Put these sets of letters into alphabetical order.

D A B E	M L K J	U V T W
___ ___ ___ ___	___ ___ ___ ___	___ ___ ___ ___
J H G I	**N A M D**	**P O Z Q**
___ ___ ___ ___	___ ___ ___ ___	___ ___ ___ ___

Look up these words in the dictionary. Beside each word, write its page number.

stable ______ ark ______ chess ______

zebra ______ plate ______ kettle ______

Spelling 2 – **silent ‹w›**

Revision: Revise some basic sounds. Go through the sounds with alternative spellings.

Main point: Some letters in words are silent. Revise some 'silent ‹b›' words. Introduce '**silent ‹w›**' by writing 'wreck' on the board. Read the word to the children and ask what it means. Ask which of its letters is silent. Write some more 'silent ‹w›' words on the board and read them together. Then read them again, this time pronouncing every sound, so 'wrap' would be /**w**-rap/, for example. This helps the children remember the spelling. With the children, make a list of 'silent ‹w›' words. To help them remember the words, the children could try making up silly sentences using as many of the words as possible, e.g. 'The wren writes two wrong answers.'

Spelling sheet 2: As a class, read the spelling list and the sentences, without filling in the gaps. Revise how to put words into alphabetical order. The children complete the words in the spelling list by writing in the missing letter pattern. Then they work through the exercises on the sheet.

Dictation: Read the words and sentences for the children to write down. The Dictation Master on page 175 may be photocopied onto the back of the spelling sheets for the children to write on.

Spelling list: Read the spelling words with the children. Point out that the /ie/ sound in 'write' is spelt ‹i_e›. Go over the family words '**sister**' and '**brother**'. For 'brother' the children could use the 'Say as it sounds' method, pronouncing it to rhyme with 'bother'. They could also remember that 'Brothers are bother!'

Dictation

1. wrap
2. write
3. wren
4. two
5. wring
6. wreck

1. The plumber may be wrong.
2. My wrist is numb.
3. The sheep has two lambs.

Spelling List 2

1. chat
2. cash
3. write
4. wrist
5. wreck
6. wrong
7. answer
8. swordfish
9. **sister**
10. **brother**

Spelling List

1. chat
2. cash
3. _rite
4. _rist
5. _reck
6. _rong
7. ans_er
8. s_ordfish
9. sister
10. brother

Silent ‹w›

Write some 'silent ‹w›' words in the wreck.

Choose a word from the list to fit each sentence.

1. She got the answer ________.
2. Then she got the ________ right.
3. I must ________ to my pen friend.
4. He sprained his ________.

sister

_ _ s t _ _

s i _ t e _

s _ s t e _

brother

b _ _ t h _ r

_ r _ t _ e r

b r _ _ h _ _

Put these words into alphabetical order.

1. clown acrobat tent juggler

________ ________ ________ ________

2. trumpet flute drum harp oboe

________ ________ ________ ________ ________

Grammar 2 – Sentence Writing

Aim: Develop the children's understanding of what a sentence is. At this stage, they know that a sentence must make sense, and that it must start with a capital letter and end with a full stop (or question mark).

Introduction: Revise sentences. Ask the children to say the three things they have learnt about sentences. Write some incorrect sentences on the board and correct them with the children.

Examples: the girl played tennis.
Mum took us to the.
It is too late to go out

Main point: Look at the picture on the sheet. Go round the class, asking each child for a sentence about the picture. Make sure that the children give only one sentence each. They should not string several sentences together with the words 'and then'.

Grammar sheet 2: The children look at the picture on the sheet. They write as many sentences about it as they can. The Writing Master on page 176 may be photocopied onto the back of the grammar sheets for the children to write on.

Extension activity: The children read what they have written and make sure that it is correct. They should correct any mistakes they have made. They can do this in a different colour if preferred.

Rounding off: Go over the sheet with the class. Ask some children to share one of their sentences with the rest of the class.

Sentence Writing

Write some sentences about the picture.
Remember that each sentence must make sense, and must start with a capital letter and end with a full stop.

Spelling 3 – **silent ‹k›**

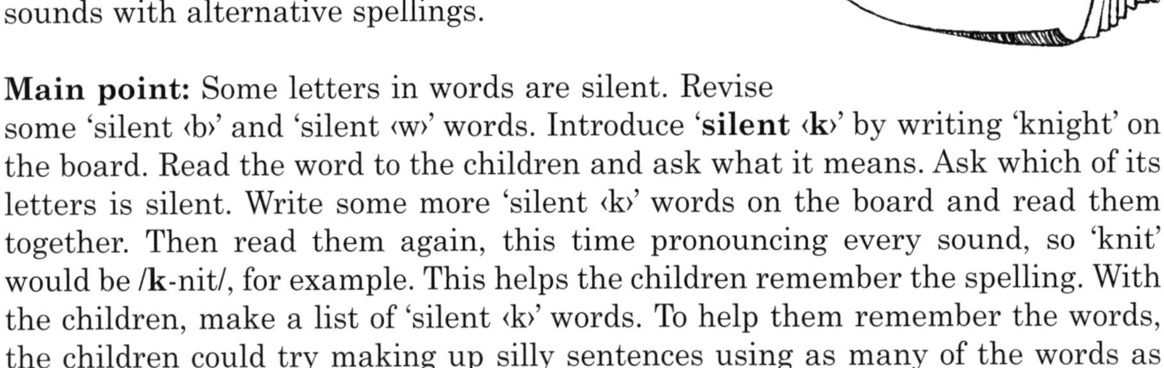

Revision: Revise some basic sounds. Go through the sounds with alternative spellings.

Main point: Some letters in words are silent. Revise some 'silent ‹b›' and 'silent ‹w›' words. Introduce '**silent ‹k›**' by writing 'knight' on the board. Read the word to the children and ask what it means. Ask which of its letters is silent. Write some more 'silent ‹k›' words on the board and read them together. Then read them again, this time pronouncing every sound, so 'knit' would be /**k**-nit/, for example. This helps the children remember the spelling. With the children, make a list of 'silent ‹k›' words. To help them remember the words, the children could try making up silly sentences using as many of the words as possible, e.g. 'I know the knitted knight's knees are knocking.'

Spelling sheet 3: As a class, read the spelling list and the sentences, without filling in the gaps. Revise sentences. The children complete the words in the spelling list by writing in the missing letter pattern. Then they work through the exercises on the sheet.

Dictation: Read the words and sentences for the children to write down. The Dictation Master on page 175 may be photocopied onto the back of the spelling sheets for the children to write on.

Spelling list: Read the spelling words with the children. Explain that the /oa/ sound in 'know' is spelt ‹ow›. Point out that the /ie/ sound in 'knight' is spelt ‹igh›, but that the /ie/ sound in 'penknife' is spelt ‹i_e›. Go over the family words '**grandma**' and '**grandpa**'. Remind the children that the /ar/ sound at the end of both words is spelt ‹a›. Tell the children to emphasise the ‹d› in both words, to help them remember to write it.

Dictation

1. knee
2. kneel
3. knelt
4. knit
5. knock
6. knife

1. She knelt to brush up the crumbs.
2. I knocked my knees as I climbed.
3. The knight killed the dragon with a sword.

Spelling List 3

1. song
2. trunk
3. knee
4. knit
5. know
6. knock
7. knight
8. penknife
9. **grandma**
10. **grandpa**

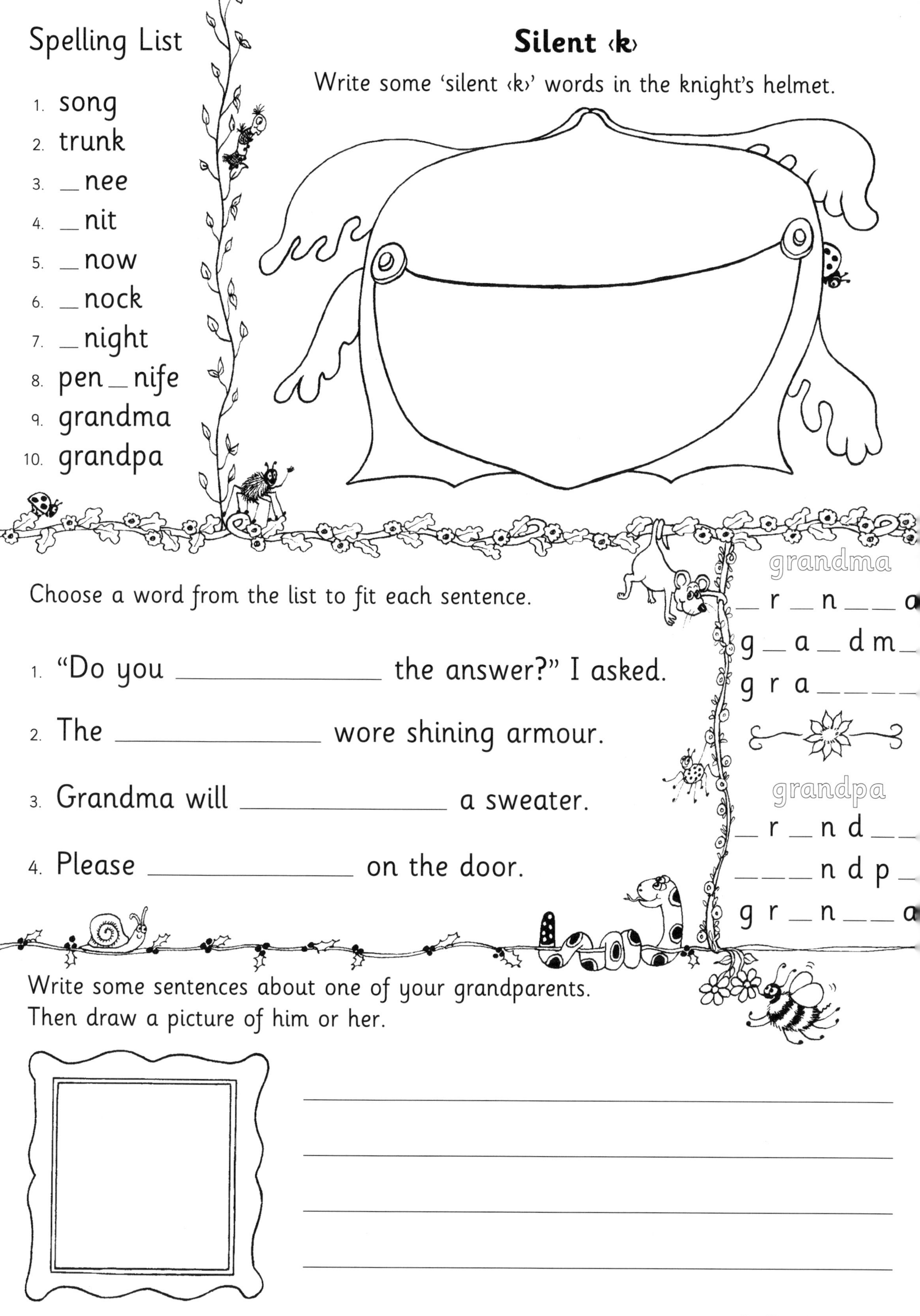

Spelling List

1. song
2. trunk
3. _nee
4. _nit
5. _now
6. _nock
7. _night
8. pen_nife
9. grandma
10. grandpa

Silent ‹k›

Write some 'silent ‹k›' words in the knight's helmet.

Choose a word from the list to fit each sentence.

1. "Do you ______________ the answer?" I asked.
2. The ______________ wore shining armour.
3. Grandma will ______________ a sweater.
4. Please ______________ on the door.

grandma

_ r _ n _ _ a

g _ a _ d m _

g r a _ _ _ _

grandpa

_ r _ n d _ _

_ _ _ _ n d p _

g r _ n _ _ a

Write some sentences about one of your grandparents.
Then draw a picture of him or her.

Grammar 3 – Speech Marks

Aim: Develop the children's ability to use speech marks.

Introduction: Show the children a comic or book which uses speech bubbles. Ask what the speech bubbles are for. Choose the words in one of the speech bubbles. Ask the children how they would show that these words were spoken, if they were writing a story. On the board, write the words in a sentence that explains who speaks them. Use speech marks around the words that are actually spoken. Remind the children how to write speech marks and where to position them above the line.

Example:	*Words in speech bubble:*	*Sentence on board:*
	I want to go home.	"I want to go home," said Karen.

Main point: Show the children Grammar sheet 3, which can be enlarged, using a photocopier. With the children, read the sentences at the top of the worksheet. Ask where the speech marks should be, to indicate which words were actually spoken. Then look at the picture and ask the children to suggest what each character might say next. Choose one of the suggestions and write it in the appropriate speech bubble.

Grammar sheet 3: The children write inside the outlined speech marks. Then they add speech marks to the sentences. Next they look at the picture, decide what each character says next and write it in the appropriate speech bubble. Finally they write out the words in the speech bubbles, in sentences. Remind the children to explain, in each case, which character is speaking, and to put in the speech marks. The Writing Master on page 176 may be photocopied onto the back of the grammar sheets for the children to write on.

Extension activity: The children continue the conversation, still using the back of their sheets.

Rounding off: Go over the sheet with the class, checking where the speech marks belong. Ask some of the children to read out what they wrote in the speech bubbles.

“ ” # “ Speech Marks ” “ ”

Add the speech marks to these sentences.

Hello Snake, said Inky .

We have been looking for you, buzzed Bee .

Sssss, hissed Snake . Well, here I am .

Snake looked at the letter in Inky's hand . Is that for me ? he asked .

Look at the picture. Think what the three friends might say next, and write the words in the speech bubbles.

Now write out the words in the speech bubbles as sentences. Remember to explain who speaks which words, and to include the speech marks.

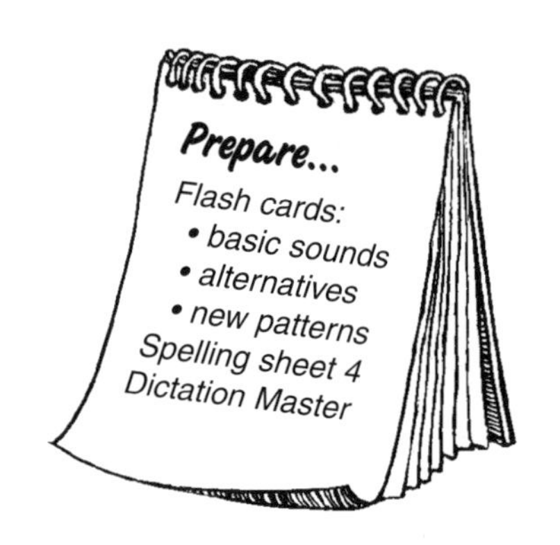

Spelling 4 – ‹**wh**›

Revision: Revise some basic sounds. Go through the sounds with alternative spellings and the new spelling patterns covered so far.

Main point: Revise the ‹**wh**› spelling of the /w/ sound. Remind the children that ‹wh› is used for many question words, including 'what', 'why', 'when', 'where', 'who', 'whose' and 'which'. (It helps the children to remember these words together, although 'who' and 'whose' are slightly different as their ‹w› is silent and their ‹h› sounded.) Most words with a /w/ sound take the ‹w› spelling, but there are a number of exceptions which take ‹wh›. These need to be learnt. In some regions, ‹w› and ‹wh› are pronounced differently, which makes this task easier. With the children, make a list of ‹wh› words. To help them remember the words, the children could try making up silly sentences using as many of the words as possible, e.g. 'The white whale whispered and whistled'.

Spelling sheet 4: As a class, read the spelling list and the sentences, without filling in the gaps. Revise speech marks. The children complete the words in the spelling list by writing in the missing letter pattern. Then they work through the exercises on the sheet.

Dictation: Read the words and sentences for the children to write down. The Dictation Master on page 175 may be photocopied onto the back of the spelling sheets for the children to write on.

Spelling list: Read the spelling words with the children. For 'whistle', tell them to emphasise the ‹t›, so they remember to write it. Point out that the swallowed /ool/ sound at the end of 'whistle' is spelt ‹le›. Go over the family words '**aunt**' and '**uncle**'. The children should practise saying the letter names for 'aunt'. For 'uncle', point out that the /nk/ sound is spelt ‹nc›, and the swallowed /ool/ sound at the end is spelt ‹le›.

Dictation

1. when
2. what
3. where
4. which
5. why
6. whenever

1. "When will I be seven?" asked Ben.
2. "Which thumb did you knock?" I whispered.
3. "Who wrote about the white lamb?" asked Jill.

Spelling List 4

1. this
2. that
3. while
4. wheat
5. whip
6. whistle
7. whiskers
8. whatever
9. **aunt**
10. **uncle**

Spelling List

1. this
2. that
3. _ _ile
4. _ _eat
5. _ _ip
6. _ _istle
7. _ _iskers
8. _ _atever
9. aunt
10. uncle

‹wh›

Write some ‹wh› words in the whale.

Choose a word from the list to fit each sentence.

1. ________________ grows in fields.
2. Becky's cat has white ________________.
3. You can wear ________________ you like.
4. I blew a ________________ to start the race.

aunt

a ___ n ___

___ u ___ t

a ___ ___ t

uncle

u ___ c ___ e

___ n ___ l ___

u ___ c ___ ___

Put the speech marks in these sentences.

1. The boy said, I rode my bike.
2. We like to go swimming, said the children.
3. Be careful, warned the policeman.
4. The librarian whispered, Please be quiet.

Grammar 4 – Questions

Aim: Develop the children's understanding of what a question is, and their ability to ask questions.

Introduction: Revise the question words and how to write a question mark. Ask the children for examples of questions starting with each of the words. Play '20 questions' with the children (or '10 questions' if preferred). Ask one of the children to choose an animal, without saying what sort it is. The others need to ask questions to find out as much as possible about the animal, until eventually they guess what it is. All the questions should be answerable with 'Yes', 'No' or 'I don't know'. Make sure the children think carefully about their questions, rather than guessing animal types at random. This is a good activity for any spare moments. Other word categories can also be used.

Main point: Remind the children that questions are usually asked to get information. Show them a picture of an animal that they are unlikely to know much about, such as an aardvark. Encourage the children to ask questions to find out as much as they can about the animal, e.g. 'Where does it live?', 'What does it eat?', 'What colour is it?' and 'How big is it?'.

Grammar sheet 4: The children read the sheet. First they write inside the outlined question marks and words. Then they decide what sort of animal they would like as a pet, and write its name. They explain why, and think of the sort of questions they would need to ask, to find out how to look after it. Remind the children to spell the question words carefully, and to use question marks. Finally the children draw a picture of the pet they would like.

Extension activity: The children look in books about animals, to try to answer their own questions.

Rounding off: Go over the sheet. Ask some children what sort of animal they chose as a pet, and what questions they asked about it.

? ? ? Questions ? ? ?

what why when where

who whose which how

What kind of animal would you like to have as a pet?

____

Why? ____

____

What questions could you ask to find out how to look after it properly?

1. ____

2. ____

3. ____

4. ____

Draw a picture of the pet you would like to have.

Spelling 5 – ‹**ph**›

Revision: Revise some basic sounds. Go through the sounds with alternative spellings and the new spelling patterns covered so far.

Main point: Most words with a /f/ sound take the ‹f› spelling, but there are a number of exceptions which take ‹**ph**›. These need to be learnt. Words which take the ‹ph› spelling of the /f/ sound are usually derived from Greek. With the children, make a list of ‹ph› words. To help them remember the words, the children could try making up silly sentences using as many of the words as possible, e.g. 'I photographed the orphan elephant learning the alphabet with the dolphin's nephew.'

Spelling sheet 5: As a class, read the spelling list and the sentences, without filling in the gaps. Revise questions and question marks. The children complete the words in the spelling list by writing in the missing letter pattern. Then they work through the exercises on the sheet.

Dictation: Read the words and sentences for the children to write down. The Dictation Master on page 175 may be photocopied onto the back of the spelling sheets for the children to write on.

Spelling list: Read the spelling words with the children. Point out that the /oa/ sound in 'phone' is spelt ‹o_e›, whereas both /oa/ sounds in 'photo' are spelt ‹o›. Explain that 'sphere' uses the unusual ‹e_e› spelling, like 'here'. Go over the family words '**nephew**' and '**niece**'. For 'nephew', point out that the /f/ sound is spelt ‹ph› and the /ue/ sound is spelt ‹ew›. The children should practise saying the letter names for 'niece'.

Dictation

1. graph
2. photo
3. phonic
4. nephew
5. phantom
6. saxophone

1. Whales and dolphins live in the sea.
2. I took a photograph of the elephant.
3. We know the alphabet.

Spelling List 5

1. club
2. flag
3. phone
4. photo
5. dolphin
6. elephant
7. sphere
8. alphabet
9. **nephew**
10. **niece**

Spelling List

1. club
2. flag
3. _ _ one
4. _ _ oto
5. dol _ _ in
6. ele _ _ ant
7. s _ _ ere
8. al _ _ abet
9. ne _ _ ew
10. niece

‹ph›

Write some ‹ph› words in the elephant.

Choose a word from the list to fit each sentence.

1. This is a ________________ of my baby sister.
2. We can say the ________________.
3. The ________________ swam by the boat.
4. "________________ me tomorrow," said Tom.

nephew

n _ p _ e _

_ e _ h _ w

n e _ _ e _

niece

n _ e _ e

n _ _ c _

_ i _ _ e

Finish each sentence correctly, by adding a question mark or a full stop.

1. What time do we have to go to bed ☐
2. An orphan is a child whose mother and father are dead ☐
3. How old is Grandma ☐
4. Whose is this photo album ☐

Grammar 5 – Commas in Lists

Aim: Develop the children's knowledge of what a comma is, and of how to use commas in lists.

Introduction: Revise full stops and question marks. Explain that punctuation is important because it helps us make sense of the words we read. A full stop shows where a sentence ends, which tells us when to pause and helps us make sense of the words. A question mark does this too, as well as showing that a sentence is a question. On the board, write the example sentences without any punctuation. With the children, read the text as it stands, and then add in the full stops and capital letters.

Example: the man sat down on his head was a black hat he was carrying an umbrella a briefcase and a newspaper two old ladies were sitting opposite him

Main point: Sometimes in the middle of a sentence, where it would be wrong to use a full stop, it is necessary to indicate a short pause. This helps the reader separate one idea from another. For this sort of pause we use a **comma**. Show the children how to write a comma, and where to position it on the line. Explain that we use commas to separate items in a list. Look again at the sentences on the board. Ask the children if they can see where a comma is needed. There should be one between 'an umbrella' and 'a briefcase'. Add it in. Ask the children what they bring to school each morning. Write these items on the board, with a comma after each one. Explain that before the last item on a list a comma is not used, but is replaced by the word 'and'.

Grammar sheet 5: The children read the sheet. They write inside the outlined commas (,). Then they insert commas between the items in the first three lists. Next they write their own lists to complete the sentences below, remembering to use commas and, before the last item, the word 'and'.

Extension activity: Write on the board 'I went shopping and I bought an apple, a boat, a crayon,'. The children complete this 'alphabetical shopping list' by adding one item beginning with each letter of the alphabet, in alphabetical order. The Writing Master on page 176 may be photocopied onto the back of the grammar sheets for the children to write on.

Rounding off: Go over the sheet with the class, checking where the commas belong. Ask some of the children to read one of their lists.

Commas in Lists

We use commas to separate words in a list. Add commas to these lists.

1. Red orange yellow green blue indigo and violet are the colours of the rainbow.
2. Oak elm holly fir beech apple and chestnut are all trees.
3. On the farm there are cows dogs pigs sheep and chickens.

Make lists to complete these sentences, remembering to use commas and the word 'and'.

The fruit stall sells ______________________________

____

My friends are called ______________________________

____

When it rains I wear ______________________________

____

My favourite games are ______________________________

____

In the zoo we saw ______________________________

____

Spelling 6 – ‹**ea**› for the **/e/** sound

Revision: Revise some basic sounds. Go through the sounds with alternative spellings and the new spelling patterns covered so far.

Main point: Most words with an /e/ sound take the ‹e› spelling, but there are a number of exceptions which take ‹**ea**›. These need to be learnt. With the children, make a list of words which use the ‹ea› spelling of the /e/ sound. To help them remember the words, the children could try making up silly sentences using as many of the words as possible, e.g. 'The deaf head teacher read the heavy leather book at breakfast.'

Spelling sheet 6: As a class, read the spelling list and the sentences, without filling in the gaps. Revise commas and how to use commas in lists. The children complete the words in the spelling list by writing in the missing letter pattern. Then they work through the exercises on the sheet.

Dictation: Read the words and sentences for the children to write down. The Dictation Master on page 175 may be photocopied onto the back of the spelling sheets for the children to write on.

Spelling list: Read the spelling words with the children. For 'treasure', the children could use the 'Say it as it sounds' method, pronouncing the second syllable to rhyme with 'pure'. Go over the family words '**cousin**' and '**friend**'. For 'cousin', the children could say the letter names to help them remember the spelling. For 'friends', the children could say that '*Friends* come on *Fri*day at the *end* of the week,' since ‹fri› + ‹end› = 'friend'!

Dictation

1. deaf
2. dead
3. heavy
4. breath
5. feather
6. leather

1. An elephant is heavy.
2. I cut bread with my knife.
3. He read the book in one night.

Spelling List 6

1. glad
2. plum
3. read
4. head
5. bread
6. weather
7. treasure
8. breakfast
9. **cousin**
10. **friend**

Spelling List

1. glad
2. plum
3. r _ _ d
4. h _ _ d
5. br _ _ d
6. w _ _ ther
7. tr _ _ sure
8. br _ _ kfast
9. cousin
10. friend

‹**ea**› for the /e/ sound

Write some ‹ea› words in the loaf of bread.

Choose a word from the list to fit each sentence.

1. The ______________ is sunny today.
2. Dad cooks ______________ in the morning.
3. She found some buried ______________.
4. I have ______________ that book already.

cousin

c _ u _ i _

_ o _ s _ n

_ _ u s _ _

friend

_ _ _ e n d

f r i _ _ _

f _ i _ n _

Add commas to these lists.

1. They went out to buy milk butter cheese and bread.
2. In my garden I grow carrots potatoes tomatoes beans and peas.
3. Squares circles triangles stars and rectangles are all shapes.

Grammar 6 – Exclamation Marks

Aim: Develop the children's knowledge of exclamations, and of when to use exclamation marks.

Introduction: Revise punctuation. Remind the children that punctuation is important because it helps us make sense of the words we read. Revise the punctuation covered so far: full stops, question marks, speech marks and commas in lists. On the board, write a sentence without any punctuation. Punctuate it with the children.

Example: do you need red blue or green paint asked dad

Main point: An **exclamation mark** is used at the end of a sentence instead of a full stop to show that the speaker or writer feels strongly about something. Explain that to exclaim means to cry out suddenly, especially in anger, surprise or pain. Show the children examples of exclamations with exclamation marks, in books. Ask what feelings these exclamations might express. With the children, think up other examples of feelings and situations, and of what these might make someone exclaim.

Examples: Help! How lovely! Oh dear! Ooh! Ouch! That hurt! Oh no! Stop! Go away! Wow! Gosh! Hello! Police! Great! I can't believe it!

Show the children how to write an exclamation mark. Tell them only to use one exclamation mark at a time, not two or three together, so 'Oh, no!' is correct, whereas 'Oh, no!!!' is wrong.

Grammar sheet 6: The children read the sheet. Discuss with them what each character is feeling and what they might exclaim. The children write inside the outlined exclamation marks. Then they decide what each character is exclaiming. They write this in the appropriate speech bubble, with an exclamation mark. Then they read the sentences at the bottom of the sheet and insert the missing punctuation marks in the boxes provided.

Extension activity: The children think of other words or phrases that someone might exclaim. They draw a face with a speech bubble for each idea. They write each exclamation in a speech bubble with an exclamation mark after it.

Rounding off: Go over the sheet with the class. Ask some of the children to read their exclamations. Go over the sentences at the bottom of the sheet, checking which punctuation mark belongs in each box.

Exclamation Marks

An exclamation mark shows that the person speaking or writing feels strongly about something.

! ! ! ! ! ! ! ! ! ! ! !

What might you exclaim if you had these strong feelings?

. ! " " Fill in the missing punctuation marks. " " ! .

1. ☐Stop☐☐ shouted the policeman☐

2. Tina went outside☐ ☐Brr☐ It is freezing☐☐ she said☐

3. ☐Brilliant☐ That is just what I wanted☐☐ exclaimed Seth☐

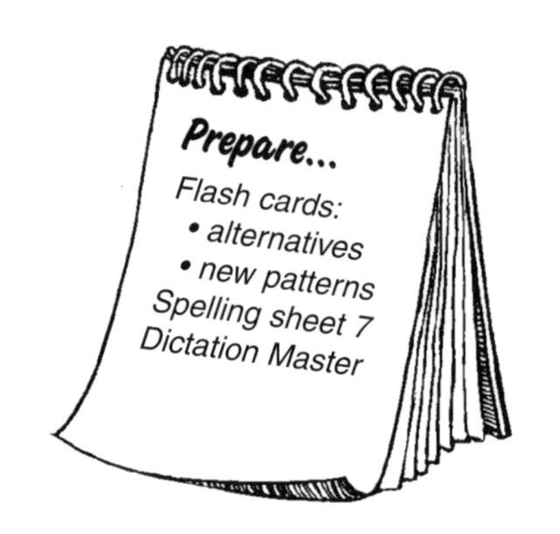

Spelling 7 – **soft ‹c›**

Revision: Revise the sounds with alternative spellings. As the children give the alternative spellings for each sound, write them on the board, e.g. ‹ai›, ‹ay› and ‹a_e›. Revise the new spelling patterns covered so far.

Main point: Introduce '**soft ‹c›**'. Explain that when the letter ‹c› is followed by the vowels ‹e›, ‹i› or ‹y›, its sound is usually changed from /k/ to /s/, as in 'ice', 'city' and 'cycle'. With the children, make a list of 'soft ‹c›' words. To help them remember the words, the children could try making up silly sentences using as many of the words as possible, e.g. 'The circus mice danced twice in a circle.'

Spelling sheet 7: As a class, read the spelling list and the sentences, without filling in the gaps. Revise exclamation marks and the other punctuation covered so far: full stops, question marks, speech marks and commas in lists. The children complete the words in the spelling list by writing in the missing letter pattern. Then they work through the exercises on the sheet.

Dictation: Read the words and sentences for the children to write down. The Dictation Master on page 175 may be photocopied onto the back of the spelling sheets for the children to write on.

Spelling list: Read the spelling words with the children. For 'circle', point out that the /er/ sound is spelt ‹ir› and that the swallowed /ool/ sound is spelt ‹le›. Explain that the /ee/ sound in 'police' is spelt ‹i_e›. Go over the month words '**January**' and '**February**'. Explain that both words have a 'toughy ‹y›' at the end. Tell the children to pronounce each syllable carefully to help them remember the spelling, i.e. 'Jan-**u**-ar-y' and 'Feb-**ru**-ar-y'.

Dictation

1. mice
2. face
3. slice
4. place
5. twice
6. pencil

1. They danced in a circle.
2. My aunt and uncle took me to the circus.
3. The police found the stolen treasure.

Spelling List 7

1. mill
2. tell
3. ice
4. dance
5. city
6. circle
7. police
8. cylinder
9. **January**
10. **February**

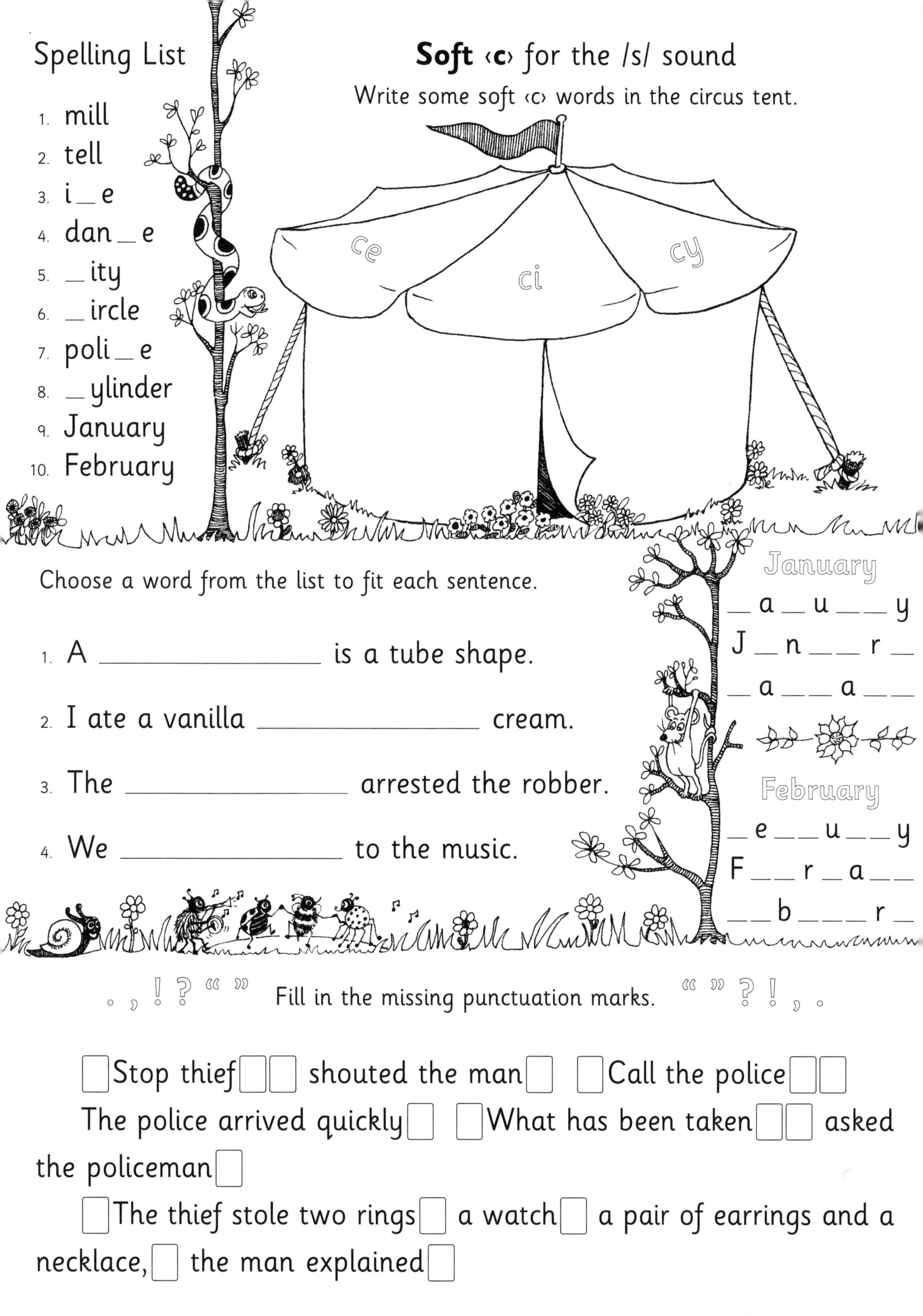
Spelling List
1. mill
2. tell
3. i _ e
4. dan _ e
5. _ ity
6. _ ircle
7. poli _ e
8. _ ylinder
9. January
10. February
Soft ‹c› for the /s/ sound
Write some soft ‹c› words in the circus tent.
ce
ci
cy
Choose a word from the list to fit each sentence.
1. A ______________ is a tube shape.
2. I ate a vanilla ______________ cream.
3. The ______________ arrested the robber.
4. We ______________ to the music.
January
_ a _ u _ _ y
J _ n _ _ r _
_ a _ _ a _ _
February
_ e _ _ u _ _ y
F _ _ r _ a _ _
_ _ b _ _ _ r _
. , ! ? " "
Fill in the missing punctuation marks.
" " ? ! , .
☐Stop thief☐☐ shouted the man☐ ☐Call the police☐☐
The police arrived quickly☐ ☐What has been taken☐☐ asked the policeman☐
☐The thief stole two rings☐ a watch☐ a pair of earrings and a necklace,☐ the man explained☐

Prepare...
Alphabet in four groups
(J. G. Big Book 2)
Dictionaries
Grammar sheet 7
(Extension activity, p. 206)

Grammar 7 – Alphabetical Order (2)

Aim: Develop the children's ability to put words into alphabetical order. Teach them that it may be necessary to look at the second letter of a word, to distinguish it from other words with the same first letter. This will improve their ability to find words in the dictionary.

Introduction: Revise the alphabet in the four dictionary groups. Call out a letter. Ask which letters come before and after it, and which group it belongs to. Repeat with other letters. Call out a letter and ask the children to try to open the dictionary in approximately the right place, e.g. for the letter ‹b› they should open it near the beginning. Repeat with other letters.

Main point: The children should already be able to put words into alphabetical order if each word begins with a different letter. Write the example words on the board. With the children, put them into alphabetical order.

Example: crab, starfish, octopus, shell, fish

Explain that since 'starfish' and 'shell' both begin with the letter ‹s›, we need to look at the letters which come next in order to put them into alphabetical order. The second letters of the two words are ‹t› and ‹h› respectively. As ‹h› comes before ‹t› in the alphabet, the word 'shell' comes before 'starfish'. Try some more examples on the board. Only two words are needed in each case.

Examples: boat, bike
purple, pink
horse, hedgehog

Grammar sheet 7: The children fill in the missing letters in the dictionary groups at the top of the sheet. Remind them to use capital letters. Then they put the words in each group into alphabetical order. The first group is the easiest as all the words begin with different letters. Each group is progressively harder, the last two consisting only of words beginning with the same letter.

Extension activity: The children put pairs of words into alphabetical order, using the extension activity on page 206.

Rounding off: Go over the sheet, with the class checking that their words are in the right order. Then go over the extension activity, with the class checking which word comes first in each pair.

Alphabetical Order

Fill in the missing letters.

1. A ___ C ___ ___

2. F G ___ I J ___ ___ M

3. N ___ ___ Q ___ S

4. T ___ ___ W ___ ___ ___

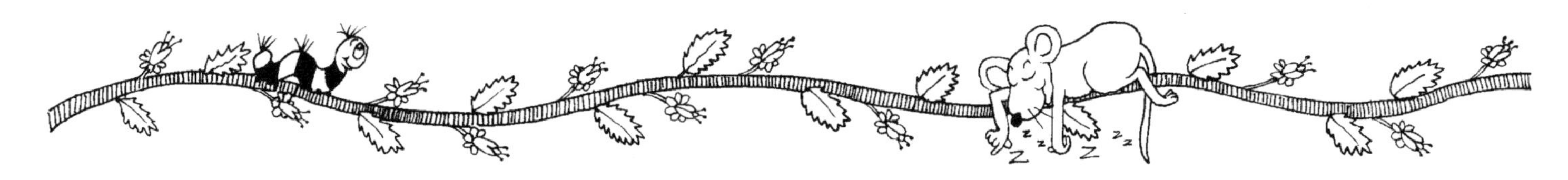

Put these words into alphabetical order. If more than one word starts with the same letter, look at the next letter in each word.

1. rabbit hamster dog cat

___ ___ ___ ___

2. swing bat bike toy

___ ___ ___ ___

3. Tyrone Sam Ted Billy Tom

___ ___ ___ ___ ___

4. avocado peach apple orange plum

___ ___ ___ ___ ___

5. chin clap cake cut coat crayon

___ ___ ___ ___ ___ ___

6. stop scar skin second sack shell

___ ___ ___ ___ ___ ___

Spelling 8 – **soft ‹g›**

Revision: Revise the sounds with alternative spellings. As the children give the alternative spellings for each sound, write them on the board, e.g. ‹ai›, ‹ay› and ‹a_e›. Revise the new spelling patterns covered so far.

Main point: Revise 'soft ‹c›'. Introduce '**soft ‹g›**'. Explain that when the letter ‹g› is followed by the vowels ‹e›, ‹i› or ‹y›, its sound is usually changed from /g/ to /j/, as in 'cabbage', 'giant' and 'gymnast'. With the children, make a list of 'soft ‹g›' words. To help them remember the words, the children could try making up silly sentences using as many of the words as possible, e.g. 'The dangerous giant made large magic cabbages and oranges.'

Spelling sheet 8: As a class, read the spelling list and the sentences, without filling in the gaps. Revise how to put words into alphabetical order by looking at the second letter. The children complete the words in the spelling list by writing in the missing letter pattern. Then they work through the exercises on the sheet.

Dictation: Read the words and sentences for the children to write down. The Dictation Master on page 175 may be photocopied onto the back of the spelling sheets for the children to write on.

Spelling list: Read the spelling words with the children. Point out that the /i/ sound in 'orange' is spelt ‹a›, and that 'vegetable' ends with the word 'table'. Go over the month words '**March**' and '**April**'. For 'April', the children could use the 'Say it as it sounds' method, pronouncing the first syllable to rhyme with 'tap'.

Dictation

1. gem
2. germ
3. large
4. margin
5. giant
6. urgent

1. Oranges grow on trees.
2. Leave a wide margin on the page.
3. There are large gems on the old sword.

Spelling List 8

1. miss
2. cross
3. giant
4. magic
5. large
6. danger
7. orange
8. vegetable
9. **March**
10. **April**

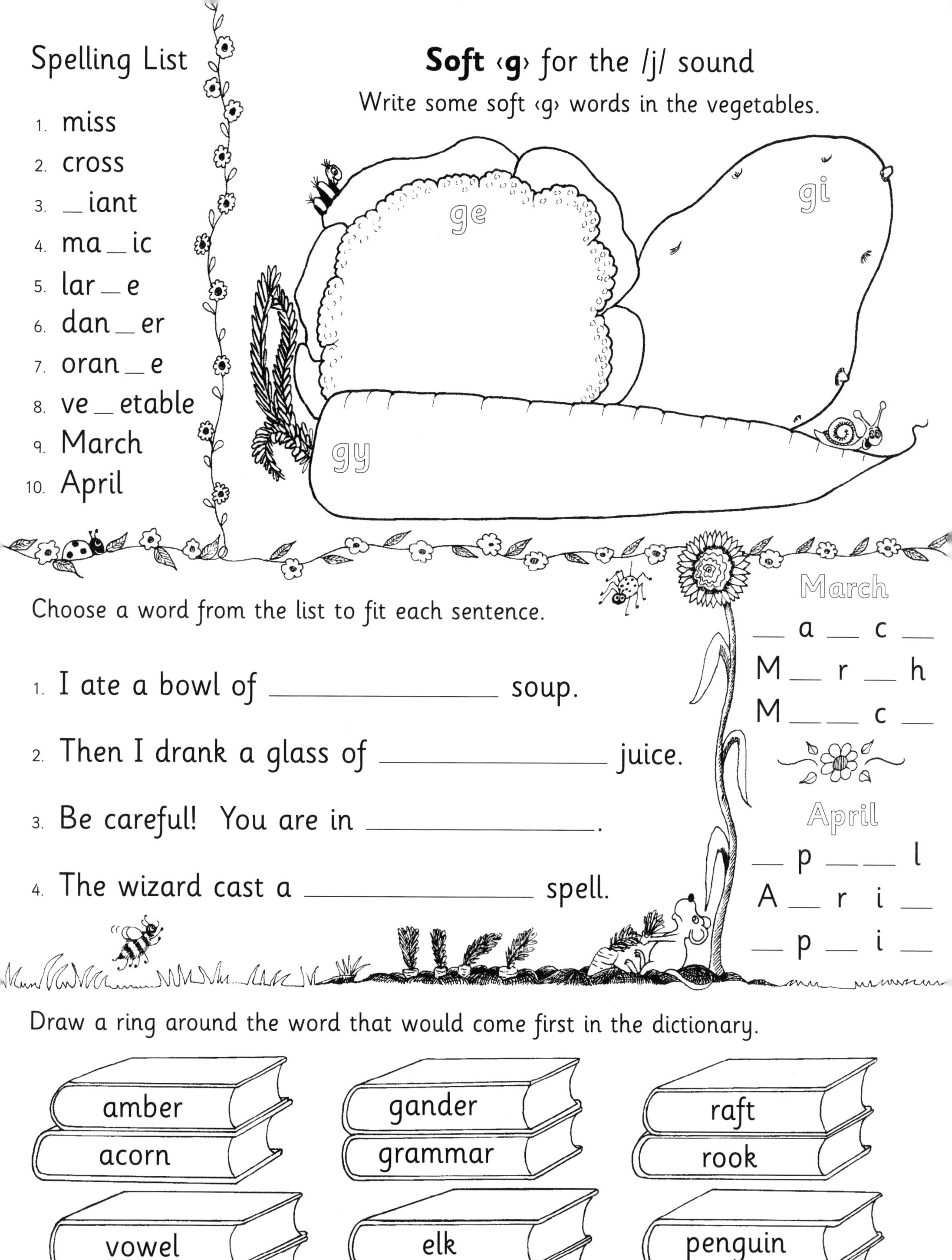

Spelling List

1. miss
2. cross
3. _ iant
4. ma _ ic
5. lar _ e
6. dan _ er
7. oran _ e
8. ve _ etable
9. March
10. April

Soft ‹g› for the /j/ sound

Write some soft ‹g› words in the vegetables.

ge

gi

gy

Choose a word from the list to fit each sentence.

1. I ate a bowl of ________________ soup.
2. Then I drank a glass of ________________ juice.
3. Be careful! You are in ________________.
4. The wizard cast a ________________ spell.

March

_ a _ c _

M _ r _ h

M _ _ c _

April

_ p _ _ l

A _ r i _

_ p _ i _

Draw a ring around the word that would come first in the dictionary.

amber / acorn

gander / grammar

raft / rook

vowel / vixen

elk / expel

penguin / plural

Grammar 8 – Proper Nouns

Aim: Develop the children's understanding of proper nouns.

Introduction: Revise nouns. Revise proper nouns, with the action. Proper nouns are the names given to particular people and places. Remind the children that because proper nouns are special they always start with a capital letter.

Main point: Explain that the names of months and days of the week are proper nouns, so they need capital letters. Revise the names and the order of the months. With the children, read and discuss a book or poem about the months. Revise the spelling of each month. Remind the children that they have already learnt the first four months in their spelling lists. They will learn the others in the next few weeks.

Grammar sheet 8: The children write inside the outlined words, Proper Nouns, using a black pencil. Then they write the names of the months in calendar order under the calendar picture frames, remembering to start each one with a capital letter. The children draw a picture for each month when they have finished.

Extension activity: The children either write a sentence for each month, or they write the months in alphabetical order. The Writing Master on page 176 may be photocopied onto the back of the grammar sheets for the children to write on.

Rounding off: Ask some children to show their work and read out any sentences they have written.

Action: The action for a proper noun is to touch one's forehead with the index and middle fingers.

Colour: The colour for nouns is black.

Proper Nouns

The names of the months are proper nouns. Write them in order under the calendar picture frames below, remembering to start each one with a capital letter. Then draw a picture for each month.

Prepare...
Flash cards:
• alternatives
• new patterns
Spelling sheet 9
Dictation Master

Spelling 9 – ‹**wa**› for the **/wo/** sound

Revision: Revise the sounds with alternative spellings. As the children give the alternative spellings for each sound, write them on the board, e.g. ‹ai›, ‹ay› and ‹a_e›. Revise the new spelling patterns covered so far.

Main point: Some words with a /wo/ sound take the ‹wo› spelling, but there are many which take ‹**wa**›. These need to be learnt. With the children, make a list of words which use the ‹wa› spelling of the /wo/ sound. To help them remember the words, the children could try making up silly sentences, using as many of the words as possible, e.g. 'The waddling swan was watching the wasp washing.'

Spelling sheet 9: As a class, read the spelling list and the sentences, without filling in the gaps. Revise the difference between proper and common nouns. The children complete the words in the spelling list by writing in the missing letter pattern. Then they work through the exercises on the sheet.

Dictation: Read the words and sentences for the children to write down. The Dictation Master on page 175 may be photocopied onto the back of the spelling sheets for the children to write on.

Spelling list: Read the spelling words with the children. Tell them to emphasise the ‹t› in 'watch', to help them remember to write it. Point out that the /oa/ sound in 'swallow' is spelt ‹ow›. Go over the month words '**May**' and '**June**'. Point out that the /ai/ sound in 'May' is spelt ‹ay› and the /oo/ sound in 'June' is spelt ‹u_e›.

Dictation

1. wasp
2. wash
3. wand
4. wallet
5. wallow
6. swamp

1. A wasp stung me on the thumb.
2. The wizard waved his magic wand.
3. The swan was made of ice.

Spelling List 9

1. luck
2. click
3. was
4. wash
5. wasp
6. swan
7. watch
8. swallow
9. **May**
10. **June**

Spelling List
1. luck
2. click
3. _ _ s
4. _ _ sh
5. _ _ sp
6. s _ _ n
7. _ _ tch
8. s _ _ llow
9. May
10. June
‹wa› for the /wo/ sound
Write some ‹wa› words in the swan.
Choose a word from the list to fit each sentence.
1. My ________ says two o'clock.
2. She was stung by a ________.
3. We must ________ our hands.
4. A ________ is a big, white bird.
May
_ a _
M _ y
_ _ _
June
_ u _ e
J _ n _
_ _ n _
Read these nouns, and give each proper noun a capital letter.
england
michael
mrs swan
monday
wand
chair
pig
fire
new zealand
september
inky
flower
mr brown
house
watch
hannah

Grammar 9 – Adjectives

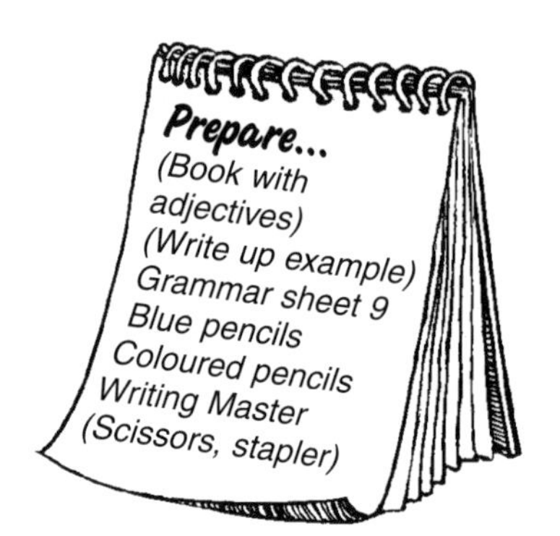

Prepare...
(Book with
adjectives)
(Write up example)
Grammar sheet 9
Blue pencils
Coloured pencils
Writing Master
(Scissors, stapler)

Aim: Develop the children's understanding of adjectives. Encourage them to think about using adjectives when writing descriptions.

Introduction: Revise proper nouns, common nouns and **adjectives**. An adjective is a word which describes a noun (or pronoun). Write some nouns on the board and ask the children for adjectives to describe them. Find a passage with examples of adjectives in a book, or write the example passage on the board. Read it to the class, with the children identifying the adjectives.

Example: Ricky was **glad** to take off his **sweaty** shoes, although the sand was **hot** for his **bare** feet. He ran to paddle in the **cool**, **green** water. A **big** wave made his shorts **wet**, so it was **lucky** that they were already **old** and **ragged**.

Main point: Talk about the planets. Explain that the names of the planets are proper nouns, so they need capital letters. Talk about aliens and ask the children to think of adjectives that might describe them. Remind the children that colours are adjectives. Ask them for adjectives to describe an alien's texture, like 'scaly', 'smooth', 'slimy', 'lumpy' or 'wrinkled'. Then ask the children to think of other ways they might describe an alien. For example, they might describe its age as 'old' or 'young', its face as 'friendly' or 'fierce' and its mood as 'happy', 'angry' or 'sad'.

Grammar sheet 9: The children write inside the outlined word, Adjectives, using a blue pencil. They choose a planet and write its name on the line at the top. Then they imagine an alien and write an adjective to describe it in each box. Their first adjective can describe it in any way they choose. Their second should describe the texture of its body and their third the colour of its legs and feet. Next the children each draw and colour an alien to fit their adjectives. Their sheets are divided into sections with dotted lines. Make sure the children draw the alien's head in the top section, its body in the middle and its legs and feet at the bottom.

Extension activity: The children write a description of their alien. The Writing Master on page 176 may be photocopied onto the back of the grammar sheets for them to write on. The finished sheets can also be put together and stapled at the side, to make a class book. Alternatively, the children can each complete several sheets and make individual books. The books can be divided into three sections by cutting along the dotted lines, taking care to leave the stapled edge intact. Now the sections can be turned over like separate pages, to show different sorts of aliens.

Rounding off: If the children have written descriptions, ask some of them to read their work. If they have made a class book or individual books, ask some children to read their adjectives and show the different aliens they can make.

Action: Touch side of temple with fist.

Colour: The colour for adjectives is blue.

Adjectives

Choose a name for a planet, and write it on the line.

____

Think of an alien and write an adjective to describe it in each box. Then draw the alien in three sections.

head

[ ]
(any adjective)

---

body

[ ]
(texture adjective)

---

feet

[ ]
(colour adjective)

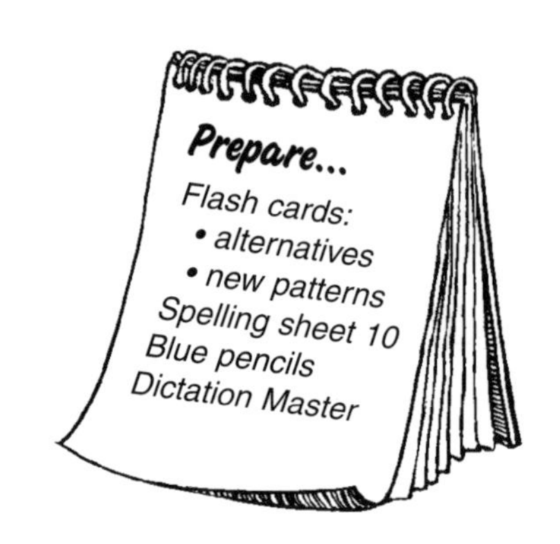

Spelling 10 – ‹**ou**› for the **/u/** sound

Revision: Revise the sounds with alternative spellings. As the children give the alternative spellings for each sound, write them on the board, e.g. ‹ai›, ‹ay› and ‹a_e›. Revise the new spelling patterns covered so far.

Main point: Most words with an /u/ sound take the ‹u› spelling, but there are a number of exceptions which take ‹**ou**›. These need to be learnt. With the children, make a list of words which use the ‹ou› spelling of the /u/ sound. To help them remember the words, the children could try making up silly sentences using as many of the words as possible, e.g. 'The young couple were double trouble for their country cousins.'

Spelling sheet 10: As a class, read the spelling list and the sentences, without filling in the gaps. Revise adjectives. Point out that an adjective does not have to be next to the noun it is describing. The children complete the words in the spelling list by writing in the missing letter pattern. Then they work through the exercises on the sheet.

Dictation: Read the words and sentences for the children to write down. The Dictation Master on page 175 may be photocopied onto the back of the spelling sheets for the children to write on.

Spelling list: Read the spelling words with the children. Point out that the swallowed /ool/ sound at the end of both 'double' and 'trouble' is spelt ‹le›. Explain that there is a 'toughy ‹y›' at the end of 'country'. Go over the month words '**July**' and '**August**'. The children should practise saying the letter names for 'July'. Point out that the /or/ sound in 'August' is spelt ‹au›.

Dictation

1. touch
2. young
3. trouble
4. cousin
5. nourish
6. flourish

1. My cousins live in the country.
2. I ate a couple of slices of bread.
3. He watched the young whale swim over the wreck.

Spelling List 10

1. thin
2. thick
3. touch
4. young
5. double
6. trouble
7. country
8. nourish
9. **July**
10. **August**

Spelling List

1. thin
2. thick
3. t __ __ ch
4. y __ __ ng
5. d __ __ ble
6. tr __ __ ble
7. c __ __ ntry
8. n __ __ rish
9. July
10. August

‹**ou**› for the /u/ sound

Write some ‹ou› words in the young birds.

July

__ u __ y
J __ l __
__ u __ __

August

A __ __ u __ t
__ u __ u __ t
__ __ g __ s __

Choose a word from the list to fit each sentence.

1. Is he from the town or the ____________?
2. A kitten is a ____________ cat.
3. Oh dear! We shall be in ____________.
4. The oven is hot! Do not ____________ it.

Write an adjective in each space. Then underline each adjective in blue.

1. I have a ____________ dog with a ____________ bark.
2. The ____________, ____________ child played football.
3. The tree was ____________ and ____________.
4. My hair is ____________ and my eyes are ____________.

Grammar 10 – Plurals: ‹-s› and ‹-es›

Aim: Develop the children's understanding of plurals.
Revise the plural endings ‹-s› and ‹-es›.

Introduction: Revise the concepts of singular and plural. Look at pictures showing items both singly and in groups. The children decide whether each picture shows the singular or the plural.

Main point: Remind the children that the simplest way of making a plural is by adding an ‹-s› to the end of a noun. Ask if they can remember another ending that can be added to a noun to give its plural. Revise how to add ‹-es›. Words ending in ‹sh›, ‹ch› for the /ch/ sound, ‹s› and ‹x› make the plural by adding ‹-es›. Ask the children for examples of nouns that end with these sounds. Practise making plurals for the nouns they suggest.

Grammar sheet 10: The children draw more pictures in the boxes to make each item plural. Then they write the appropriate plural noun underneath each box. Next they look at the pictures in the second exercise. They write the noun for each picture, remembering that if it shows more than one item, they must add ‹-s› or ‹-es› to make the plural.

Extension activity: The children write a sentence containing each of the nouns on the sheet, first in singular and then in plural form. The Writing Master on page 176 may be photocopied onto the back of the grammar sheets for the children to write on.

Rounding off: Go over the sheet with the class, checking which nouns need the ‹-es› ending to form the plural, and which of the words in the second section are singular and which plural. Ask some of the children who wrote sentences to share them with the class.

Plurals – ‹-s› and ‹-es›

Draw more of each to make the pictures show plurals. Write the plural nouns underneath.

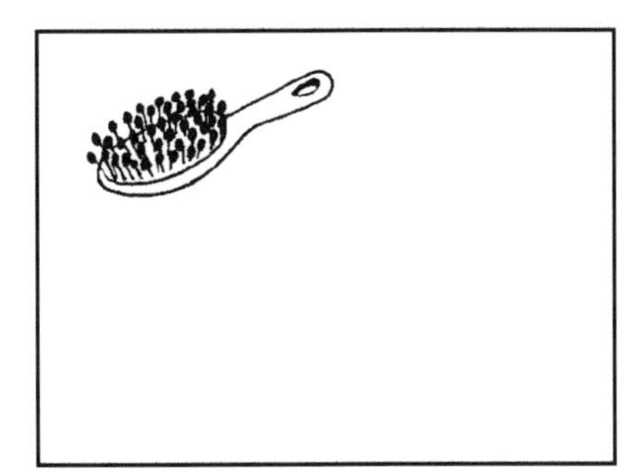

Write the word for each picture.

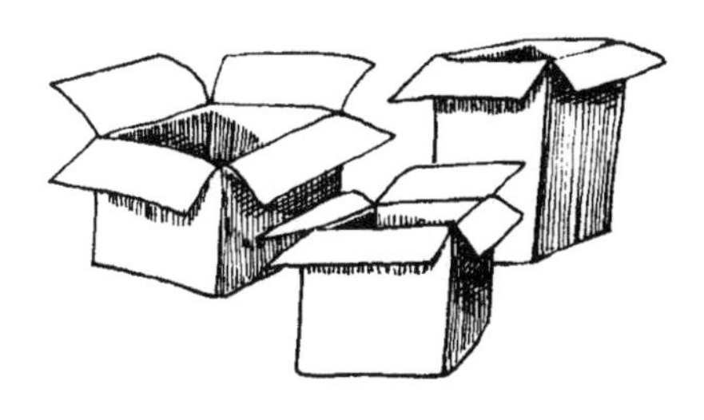

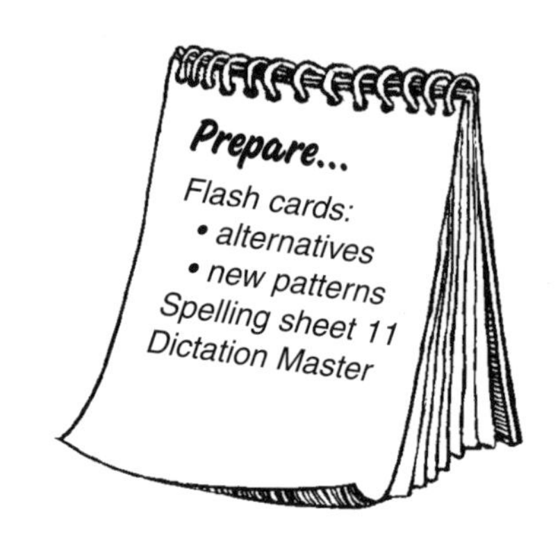

Spelling 11 – ‹**air**›

Revision: Revise the sounds with alternative spellings. As the children give the alternative spellings for each sound, write them on the board, e.g. ‹ai›, ‹ay› and ‹a_e›. Revise the new spelling patterns covered so far.

Main point: Introduce the ‹**air**› spelling of the /air/ sound. This sound is new to the children since, as it is relatively unusual, it was not included in *The Phonics Handbook*. The main ways of writing the /air/ sound are ‹air›, ‹are› and ‹ear›. The ‹are› and ‹ear› spellings will be covered later. With the children, make a list of words which use the ‹air› spelling of the /air/ sound. To help them remember the words, the children could try making up silly sentences using as many of the words as possible, e.g. 'The airy fairy chair flew down the stairs.'

Spelling sheet 11: As a class, read the spelling list and the sentences, without filling in the gaps. Revise plurals, and the plural endings ‹-s› and ‹-es›. The children complete the words in the spelling list by writing in the missing letter pattern. Then they work through the exercises on the sheet.

Dictation: Read the words and sentences for the children to write down. The Dictation Master on page 175 may be photocopied onto the back of the spelling sheets for the children to write on.

Spelling list: Read the spelling words with the children. Go over the month words '**September**' and '**October**'. Tell the children to pronounce each syllable carefully to help them remember the spelling, i.e. 'Sep-tem-ber' and 'Oc-to-ber'.

Dictation

1. fair
2. pair
3. stair
4. dairy
5. fairy
6. repair

1. The place was hot and airless.
2. "That is unfair!" cried the boy.
3. My young cousin has orange hair.

Spelling List 11

1. cliff
2. off
3. air
4. hair
5. pair
6. stair
7. chair
8. hairbrush
9. **September**
10. **October**

Spelling List

1. cliff
2. off
3. _ _ _
4. h _ _ _
5. p _ _ _
6. st _ _ _
7. ch _ _ _
8. h _ _ _ brush
9. September
10. October

‹**air**› for the /air/ sound

Write some ‹air› words in the hair.

Choose a word from the list to fit each sentence.

1. Her balloon floated up in the ______________.
2. I brush my ____________ with a ______________.
3. The baby sits on a high ______________.
4. He has a new ______________ of shoes.

September

_ e _ t _ m _ e _

S _ p _ e _ b _ r

_ _ _ t _ _ _ e _

October

_ c _ o _ e _

O _ t _ b _ r

_ _ _ o _ _ _

Give the plural for each of these nouns by adding ‹-s› or ‹-es›.

______________ ______________ ______________ ______________

Grammar 11 – Possessive Adjectives

Aim: Develop the children's understanding of possessive adjectives. A possessive adjective describes a noun, by saying whose it is.

Introduction: Revise adjectives. Adjectives are words that describe nouns (or pronouns). Revise the personal pronouns: 'I', 'you', 'he', 'she', 'it', 'we', 'you' and 'they'. Remind the children that the first 'you' is singular, and the second plural.

Main point: Write the personal pronouns ('I', 'you', 'he', 'she', 'it', 'we', 'you' and 'they') as a list on the board. Explain that a **possessive adjective** describes a noun by saying who it belongs to. There is one possessive adjective for each personal pronoun. Ask the children to think what the possessive adjective might be for each personal pronoun on the board. Next to the personal pronouns, write the possessive adjectives: 'my', 'your', 'his', 'her', 'its', 'our', 'your' and 'their'. The Possessive Adjective Poem on page 215 may be enlarged, using a photocopier. Read it with the children. Explain that the possessive adjective 'its' never has an apostrophe between the letters ‹t› and ‹s›. Tell the children to emphasise the /ou/ sound in 'our', to avoid confusing it with 'are'. 'Their' sounds the same as 'there' but has a different meaning, so the children must be careful to choose the correct spelling for the word they mean.

Grammar sheet 11: The children write inside the outlined words, using a blue pencil. They match up each personal pronoun with its possessive adjective. Then they choose the right possessive adjective to complete each sentence. Finally they think of a different noun for each of the possessive adjectives.

Extension activity: On the board, write a passage with lots of possessive adjectives.

Example: Ben's friend, Sarah, came to visit. She brought her colouring books and pencils.
"Your books have lovely pictures in them," said Ben.
"This is my favourite book," replied Sarah. "If we share our coloured pencils, we will have plenty of colours for that picture."
Ben fetched his coloured pencils. He took them out of their box.

The children copy the passage onto the back of their sheets, and then underline the possessive adjectives in blue. The Writing Master on page 176 may be photocopied onto the back of the grammar sheets for the children to write on.

Rounding off: Go over the sheet, with the class checking their answers.

Action: Touch side of temple with fist.

Colour: The colour for adjectives is blue.

Possessive Adjectives

Blue

Match each pronoun to its possessive adjective.

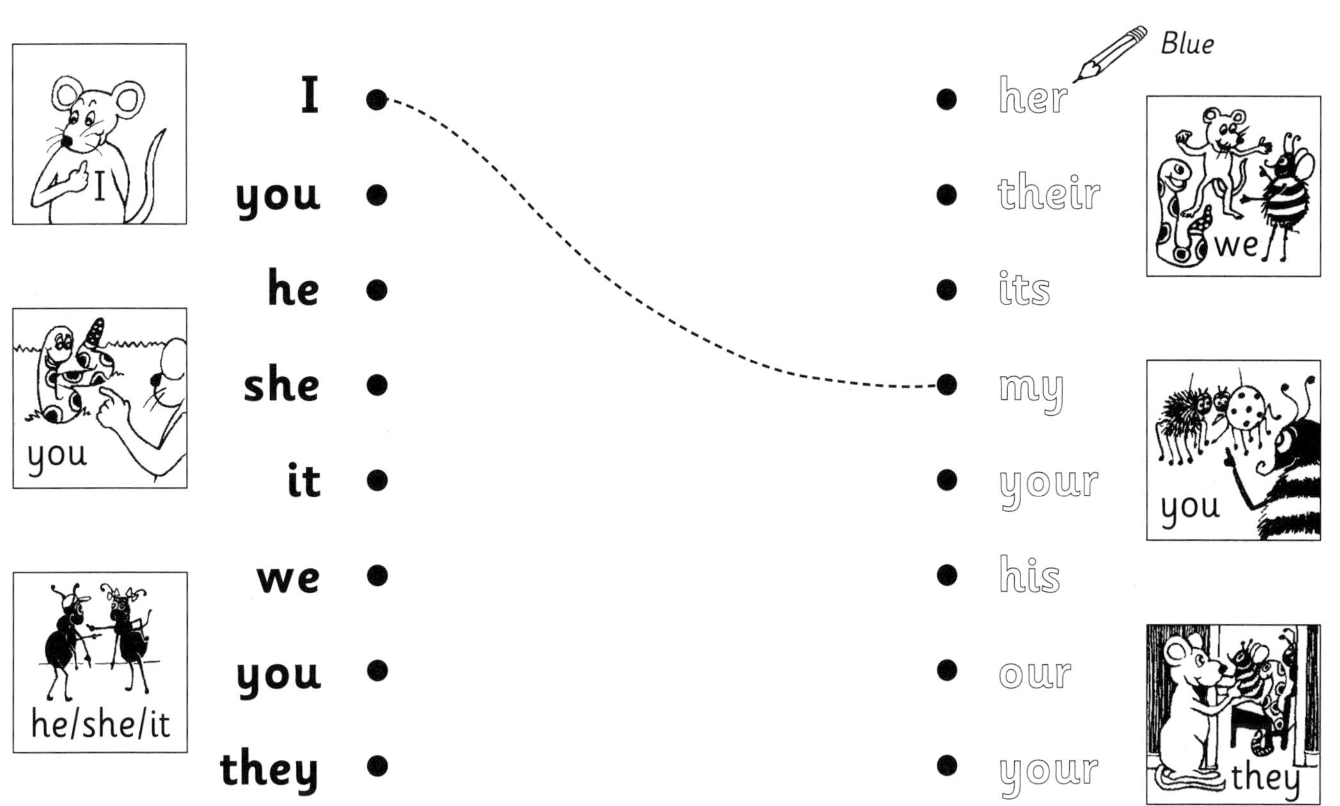

Choose the right possessive adjective for each sentence.

They put on ____________ coats.

I put on ____________ coat.

He puts on ____________ coat.

We put on ____________ coats.

She puts on ____________ coat.

You put on ____________ coat.

You put on ____________ coats.

Choose a noun for each possessive adjective.

my ____________

your ____________

his ____________

her ____________

its ____________

our ____________

your ____________

their ____________

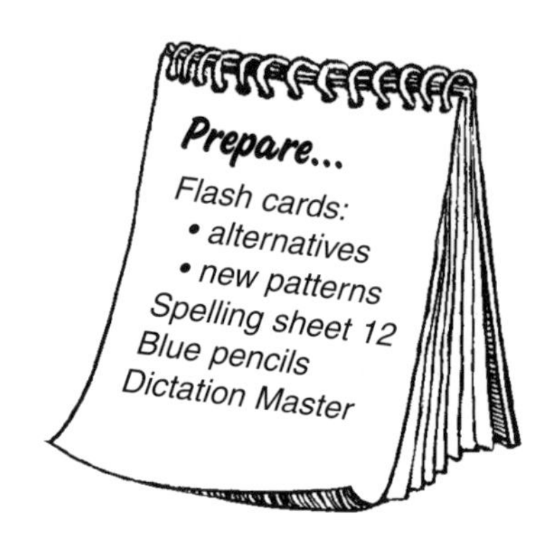

Spelling 12 – **‹ch›** for the **/k/** sound

Revision: Revise the sounds with alternative spellings. As the children give the alternative spellings for each sound, write them on the board, e.g. ‹ai›, ‹ay› and ‹a_e›. Revise the new spelling patterns covered so far.

Main point: Although ‹ch› normally makes a /ch/ sound, as in 'chop', in some words it makes a /k/ sound instead. Most words with a /k/ sound take the ‹k›, ‹c› or ‹ck› spellings, but there are a number of exceptions which take **‹ch›**. Words which take the ‹ch› spelling of the /k/ sound are usually derived from Greek. These need to be learnt. With the children, make a list of words which use the ‹ch› spelling of the /k/ sound. To help them remember the words, the children could try making up silly sentences using as many of the words as possible, e.g. 'The orchestra echoed the choir's Christmas chorus.'

Spelling sheet 12: As a class, read the spelling list and the sentences, without filling in the gaps. Revise possessive adjectives. The children complete the words in the spelling list by writing in the missing letter pattern. Then they work through the exercises on the sheet.

Dictation: Read the words and sentences for the children to write down. The Dictation Master on page 175 may be photocopied onto the back of the spelling sheets for the children to write on.

Spelling list: Read the spelling words with the children. Point out that the /oa/ sound in 'echo' is spelt ‹o› and the /u/ sound in 'stomach' is spelt ‹o›. The children should practise saying the letter names for 'choir'. Go over the month words '**November**' and '**December**'. Tell the children to pronounce each syllable carefully to help them remember the spelling, i.e. 'No-vem-ber' and 'De-cem-ber'. Point out that the /s/ sound in 'December' is spelt with a 'soft ‹c›'.

Dictation

1. chord
2. chorus
3. echo
4. chemist
5. orchestra
6. character

1. The orchestra played chords.
2. Our cousin is a mechanic.
3. The choir boy had fair hair.

Spelling List 12

1. buzz
2. fizz
3. echo
4. choir
5. chemist
6. stomach
7. Christmas
8. character
9. **November**
10. **December**

Spelling List

1. buzz
2. fizz
3. e _ _ o
4. _ _ oir
5. _ _ emist
6. stoma _ _
7. _ _ ristmas
8. _ _ aracter
9. November
10. December

‹**ch**› for the /k/ sound

In the choir, write some words with ‹ch› for the /k/ sound.

Choose a word from the list to fit each sentence.

1. I sing in the ________________.
2. December 25th is ________________ Day.
3. She was ill with a ________________ ache.
4. The ________________ sells medicine.

November

N _ v _ m _ e _

_ o _ e _ b _ r

_ _ _ e _ _ e _

December

_ e _ e _ b _ r

D _ c _ m _ e _

_ _ _ em _ _ _

Complete each sentence with a possessive adjective. *Blue*

my your his her its our your their

1. The children took out ________________ pencil cases.
2. The boy read ________________ book.
3. My sister played ________________ recorder.
4. We sang ________________ favourite song.

Grammar 12 – Homophone Mix-ups

Aim: Develop the children's awareness of similar-sounding words, and their ability to choose between them in their writing.

Introduction: Revise the possessive adjectives, 'my', 'your', 'his', 'her', 'its', 'our', 'your' and 'their'. Ask the children for sentences using each of the possessive adjectives.

Main point: Introduce **homophones**. Homophones are words that sound similar to one another despite having different meanings and spellings. This makes it easy to get confused and use the wrong word when writing. If the children use the wrong word, their writing will not make sense.

Ask if the children can think of two ways of spelling the word 'there'/'their'. Write both words on the board. Tell the children that 'there' is a word relating to place, whereas 'their' is a possessive adjective. The children need to be able to choose between 'there' and 'their' in their writing, in order to spell the word they really mean. Ask them for examples of sentences using 'there' and 'their'.

'Are' and 'our' are not really homophones, since they do not sound quite alike. However, in some areas they are often pronounced so as to sound the same or very similar. Write both words on the board. Tell the children that 'are' is part of the verb 'to be', whereas 'our' is a possessive adjective. The children need to be able to choose between 'are' and 'our' in their writing, in order to spell the word they really mean. Ask them for examples of sentences using 'are' and 'our'.

Grammar sheet 12: The children read the sentences. They choose between 'there' and 'their' to complete each of the first five sentences. Then they choose between 'are' and 'our' to complete the next five sentences.

Extension activity: The children write more sentences containing the words. The Writing Master on page 176 may be photocopied onto the back of the grammar sheets for the children to write on.

Rounding off: Go over the sheet with the class. Ask some of the children who wrote sentences to share them and to say which spellings they chose.

Homophone Mix-ups

there or **their ?**

Choose the right word to complete each sentence.

1. They put on ______________ hats.
2. Leave the parcel over ______________.
3. ______________ he is, behind the tree.
4. The children rode ______________ bikes.
5. ______________ is no-one at home.

are or **our ?**

Choose the right word to complete each sentence.

1. You ______________ very tall.
2. ______________ house has a red door.
3. They ______________ all going to a party.
4. We put on ______________ boots to go outside.
5. He likes ______________ cat.

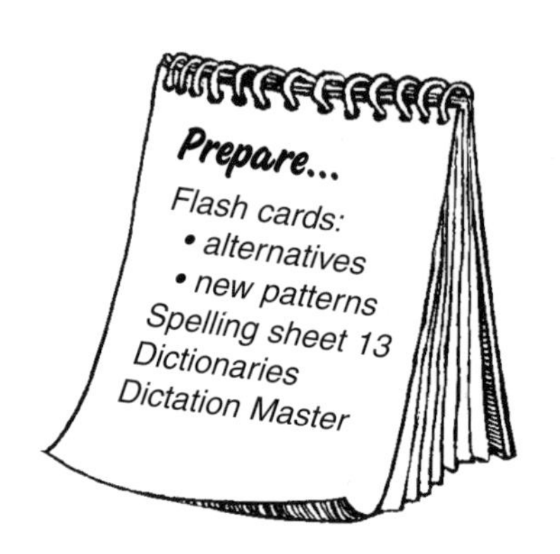

Prepare...
Flash cards:
• alternatives
• new patterns
Spelling sheet 13
Dictionaries
Dictation Master

Spelling 13 – the **/ai/** sound

Revision: Revise the sounds with alternative spellings. As the children give the alternative spellings for each sound, write them on the board, e.g. ‹ai›, ‹ay› and ‹a_e›. Revise the new spelling patterns covered so far.

Main point: Revise the main ways of writing the **/ai/** sound, which are ‹ai›, ‹ay› and ‹a_e›. Now that these spellings are familiar, the children need to start memorising which words take each one. Remind them that the ‹ay› spelling is usually used when the /ai/ sound is found at the end of a word, where 'toughy ‹y›' takes the place of 'shy ‹i›'. With the children, make a list of words for each spelling of the /ai/ sound. To help them remember the words, the children could try making up silly sentences for each spelling, using as many of the words as possible, e.g. 'The vain painter complained about the rain.'

Spelling sheet 13: As a class, read the spelling list and the sentences, without filling in the gaps. Revise 'there' and 'their', and 'are' and 'our'. The children complete the words in the spelling list by writing in the missing letter patterns. Then they work through the exercises on the sheet.

Dictation: Read the words and sentences for the children to write down. The Dictation Master on page 175 may be photocopied onto the back of the spelling sheets for the children to write on.

Spelling list: Read the spelling words with the children. Remind them that they need to remember how the /ai/ sound is spelt in each of the relevant words. The longer word 'rainstorm' is a compound word. It has two syllables and can be remembered as 'rain' and 'storm' for spelling. Go over the number words '**half**' and '**quarter**'. For both words the children could use the 'Say as it sounds' method, pronouncing 'half' to rhyme with 'Alf' and the first two sounds of 'quarter' like those of 'qualm'.

Dictation

1. name
2. day
3. rain
4. play
5. paint
6. mistake

1. Stay and wait for the train.
2. The circus came on Monday.
3. The choir boys ate slices of cake.

Spelling List 13

1. next
2. quit
3. make
4. pay
5. main
6. clay
7. waist
8. rainstorm
9. **half**
10. **quarter**

Spelling List

1. next
2. quit
3. m _ k _
4. p _ _
5. m _ _ n
6. cl _ _
7. w _ _ st
8. r _ _ nstorm
9. half
10. quarter

the /ai/ sound: ‹ai›, ‹ay› or ‹a_e›

Underline the spelling you think is correct. Then use a dictionary to check your answer, and tick the right spelling.

ate ait ayt	wate wait wayt	day dai daye
naym naim name	snaik snake snayk	traye trai tray

Choose a word from the list to fit each sentence.

1. She made a model from ________________.
2. Is it free or do we have to ________________?
3. I got wet in the ________________.
4. My jeans have a tight ________________.

half (1/2)

h _ l _

_ a _ f

h _ _ _

quarter (1/4)

q _ a _ t e _

_ u _ r _ _ r

_ _ _ _ t _ r

'there' or 'their'?

1. ________________ they are! Up ________________.
2. ________________ toys are over ________________.

'are' or 'our'?

1. We ________________ going to visit ________________ grandma.
2. They ________________ all coming to ________________ school.

Grammar 13 – Alphabetical Order (3)

Aim: Develop the children's ability to put words into alphabetical order. Teach them that it may be necessary to look at the third letter of a word, to distinguish it from other words with the same first two letters. This will improve their ability to find words in the dictionary.

Introduction: Revise the alphabet in the four dictionary groups. Call out a letter. Ask which letters come before and after it, and which group it belongs to. Repeat with other letters. Call out a letter and ask the children to try to open the dictionary in approximately the right place, e.g. for the letter ‹w› they should open it near the end. Repeat with other letters. Write two words on the board which have the same first letter. Ask which word would come first in the dictionary, and why.

Example: bread, butter

Main point: Write two words on the board which have the same first two letters. Ask the children which would come first in the dictionary.

Example: house, home

Explain that since 'house' and 'home' both begin with ‹ho›, we need to look at the letters which come next in order to put them into alphabetical order. The third letters of the two words are ‹u› and ‹m› respectively. As ‹m› comes before ‹u› in the alphabet, the word 'home' comes before 'house'. Try some more examples on the board. Use groups of three words, and decide which would come first, second and third in each case. Teach the spelling of the contractions '1st', '2nd' and '3rd'.

Examples: bowl, box, bottle
penguin, peacock, pelican
chocolate, chip, cherry

Grammar sheet 13: The children fill in the missing letters in the dictionary groups at the top of the page. Remind them to use capital letters. Then they look at the groups of words. In each case they decide which word would come first, which second and which third in the dictionary. They write '1st', '2nd' and 3rd' next to the appropriate words.

Extension activity: The children put more groups of three words into alphabetical order, using the extension activity on page 208.

Rounding off: Go over the sheet, with the class checking that their words are in the right order. Then go over the extension exercise.

Alphabetical Order

Write the four dictionary groups.

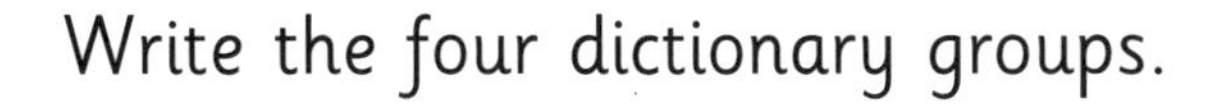

1. ____ ____ ____ ____ ____ 2. ____ ____ ____ ____ ____ ____ ____ ____

3. ____ ____ ____ ____ ____ ____ 4. ____ ____ ____ ____ ____ ____ ____

In each group of three, decide which word comes first (1st), which word comes second (2nd) and which word comes third (3rd). If the words start with the same two letters, remember to look at the third letter of each word.

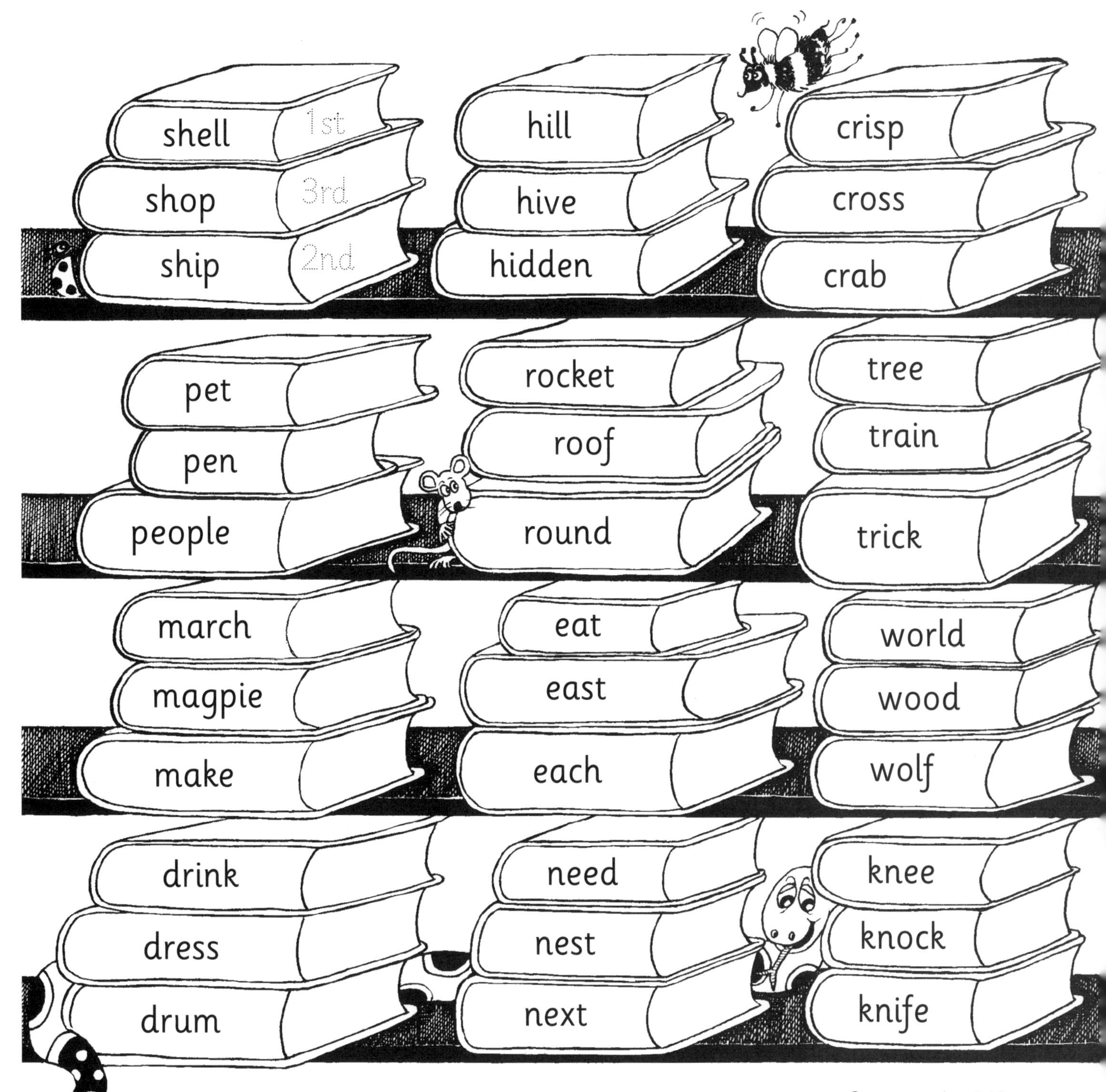

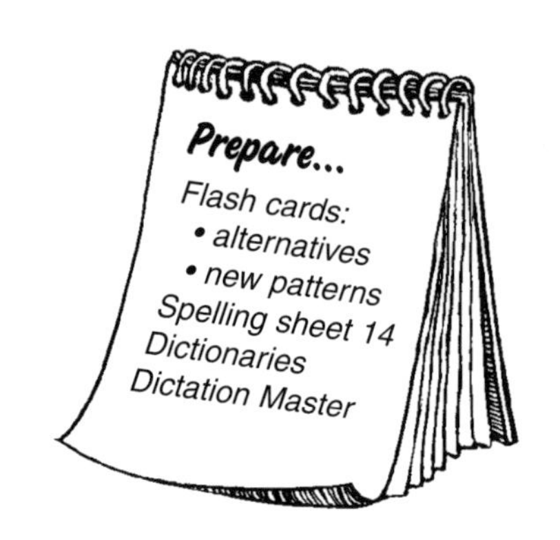

Spelling 14 – the /ee/ sound

Revision: Revise the sounds with alternative spellings. As the children give the alternative spellings for each sound, write them on the board, e.g. ‹ai›, ‹ay› and ‹a_e›. Revise the new spelling patterns covered so far.

Main point: Revise the main ways of writing the **/ee/** sound, which are ‹ee› and ‹ea›. Now that these spellings are familiar, the children need to start memorising which words take each one. With the children, make a list of words for each spelling of the /ee/ sound. To help them remember the words, the children could try making up silly sentences for each spelling, using as many of the words as possible, e.g. 'Have you seen the sweet, green queen bee?'

Spelling sheet 14: As a class, read the spelling list and the sentences, without filling in the gaps. Revise how to put words into alphabetical order by looking at the third letter. The children complete the words in the spelling list by writing in the missing letter patterns. Then they work through the exercises on the sheet.

Dictation: Read the words and sentences for the children to write down. The Dictation Master on page 175 may be photocopied onto the back of the spelling sheets for the children to write on.

Spelling list: Read the spelling words with the children. Remind them that they need to remember how the /ee/ sound is spelt in each of the relevant words. Point out that the /j/ sound in 'teenager' is spelt with a 'soft ‹g›'. Go over the number words '**eleven**' and '**twelve**'. For 'eleven', tell the children to emphasise the last syllable so that it rhymes with 'pen'. Explain that the ‹e› is needed at the end of 'twelve', since English words do not end with the letter ‹v›.

Dictation

1. tea
2. each
3. bee
4. leaf
5. sweet
6. feet

1. A young swan was seen on the sea.
2. We climbed the large green tree.
3. "A cup of weak tea, please," said Tim.

Spelling List 14

1. arm
2. shark
3. seen
4. three
5. seat
6. cream
7. please
8. teenager
9. **eleven**
10. **twelve**

Spelling List

1. arm
2. shark
3. s _ _ n
4. thr _ _
5. s _ _ t
6. cr _ _ m
7. pl _ _ se
8. t _ _ nager
9. eleven
10. twelve

the /ee/ sound: ‹ee› or ‹ea›

Underline the spelling you think is correct. Then use a dictionary to check your answer, and tick the right spelling.

bee / bea
leef / leaf
cheese / chease
streat / street
dream / dreem
eest / east

Choose a word from the list to fit each sentence.

1. I like strawberries and ______________.
2. Eight plus ______________ makes eleven.
3. We have ______________ the new film.
4. ______________ take care of my rabbit.

eleven (11)

e _ e _ e _
_ l _ v _ n
e _ _ v _ _

twelve (12)

_ w _ l v _
t _ e _ _ e
t _ _ l _ _

Which word would come 1st, which 2nd and which 3rd in a dictionary?

green, grass (1st), grin
smile, smell, small
allow, also, along
blue, black, block
skin, skunk, skate
parrot, paper, paint

Grammar 14 – Sentences and Verbs

Aim: Develop the children's understanding of what a sentence is. At this stage, they know that a sentence must make sense, and that it must start with a capital letter and end with a full stop, question mark or exclamation mark. Teach them that a sentence must also contain a verb.

Introduction: Revise verbs, with the action (see page 8). Ask the children for examples of verbs. Revise the personal pronouns: 'I', 'you', 'he', 'she', 'it', 'we', 'you' and 'they', with the actions (see page 6). Remind the children that the first 'you' is singular, and the second plural. Conjugate a verb in the present tense, e.g. 'to play':

Present: I play, you play, he/she/it plays, we play, you play, they play

Knowing how to conjugate verbs will be very useful for the children when they learn other languages. Choose a different verb and conjugate it with the children. Remind them that a verb can describe past, present or future time. Conjugate a verb in the simple past tense and then in the future, e.g. 'to play':

Past: I played, you played, he/she/it played, we played, you played, they played

Future: I shall play, you will play, he/she/it will play, we shall play, you will play, they will play

Main point: Write the following text on the board, and ask whether it is a sentence.

Text: a dog ran across the

Ask the children how this text might be made into a sentence. It needs a capital letter, a full stop and more word(s) in order to make sense. Explain that sentences also have to contain a verb. With the children, find the verb in the sentence and underline it in red chalk. Then write the following text on the board, and ask whether it is a sentence. If not, ask why not. Explain that as there is no verb, it is not a sentence.

Text: Fish and chips.

Grammar sheet 14: The children read each line of writing. If it contains a verb, they underline the verb in red and mark the sentence right with a tick. If there is no verb the children write a cross to show that the words are not a sentence.

Extension activity: The children write some sentences of their own about the picture. The Writing Master on page 176 may be photocopied onto the back of the grammar sheets for them to write on. Remind them to make sure that their sentences make sense, start with a capital letter, end with a full stop, and contain a verb. Tell the children to underline the verbs in red. Encourage them to proofread (i.e. check) their work.

Rounding off: Go over the sheet with the class. Ask some children to share one of their sentences with the rest of the class.

Are These Sentences?

Read each line. If there is a verb, underline it in red, and mark the sentence right with a tick. If there is no verb, mark the writing wrong with a cross.

1. The ducks swim on the pond. ________
2. The cat watches the birds. ________
3. A spotty dog. ________
4. The boys play bat and ball. ________
5. The tall tree. ________
6. The park keeper sweeps up the leaves. ________
7. The rabbit hides from the fox. ________
8. A wooden boat with a blue sail. ________
9. A bird sings. ________
10. A spotty dog has a stick in his mouth. ________

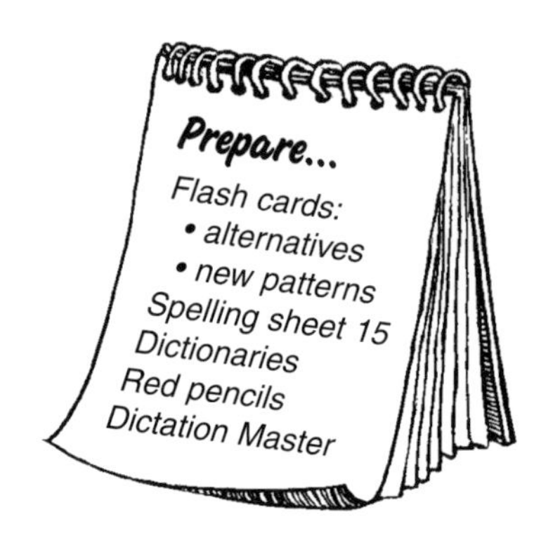

Prepare...
Flash cards:
• alternatives
• new patterns
Spelling sheet 15
Dictionaries
Red pencils
Dictation Master

Spelling 15 – the **/ie/** sound

Revision: Revise the sounds with alternative spellings. As the children give the alternative spellings for each sound, write them on the board, e.g. ‹ai›, ‹ay› and ‹a_e›. Revise the new spelling patterns covered so far.

Main point: Revise the main ways of writing the **/ie/** sound, which are ‹ie›, ‹igh›, ‹y› and ‹i_e›. Now that these spellings are familiar, the children need to start memorising which words take each one. With the children, make a list of words for each spelling of the /ie/ sound. To help them remember the words, the children could try making up silly sentences for each spelling, using as many of the words as possible, e.g. 'If you lie about the tie you will get no pie!'

Spelling sheet 15: As a class, read the spelling list and the sentences, without filling in the gaps. Revise sentences, and the fact that a sentence must contain a verb. The children complete the words in the spelling list by writing in the missing letter patterns. Then they work through the exercises on the sheet.

Dictation: Read the words and sentences for the children to write down. The Dictation Master on page 175 may be photocopied onto the back of the spelling sheets for the children to write on.

Spelling list: Read the spelling words with the children. Remind them that they need to remember how the /ie/ sound is spelt in each of the relevant words. Go over the number words '**thirteen**' and '**fourteen**'. Remind the children that the /er/ sound in 'thirteen' is spelt ‹ir›, as in other number words such as 'first', 'third', 'thirty' and 'thirtieth'. Tell the children to think of 'fourteen' as the two syllables 'four' and 'teen'.

Dictation

1. try
2. mine
3. my
4. pie
5. sight
6. daytime

1. She gave a nice wide smile.
2. I like to ride my bike.
3. The lights shine brightly at night.

Spelling List 15

1. club
2. flex
3. flying
4. sight
5. side
6. die
7. bright
8. sunshine
9. **thirteen**
10. **fourteen**

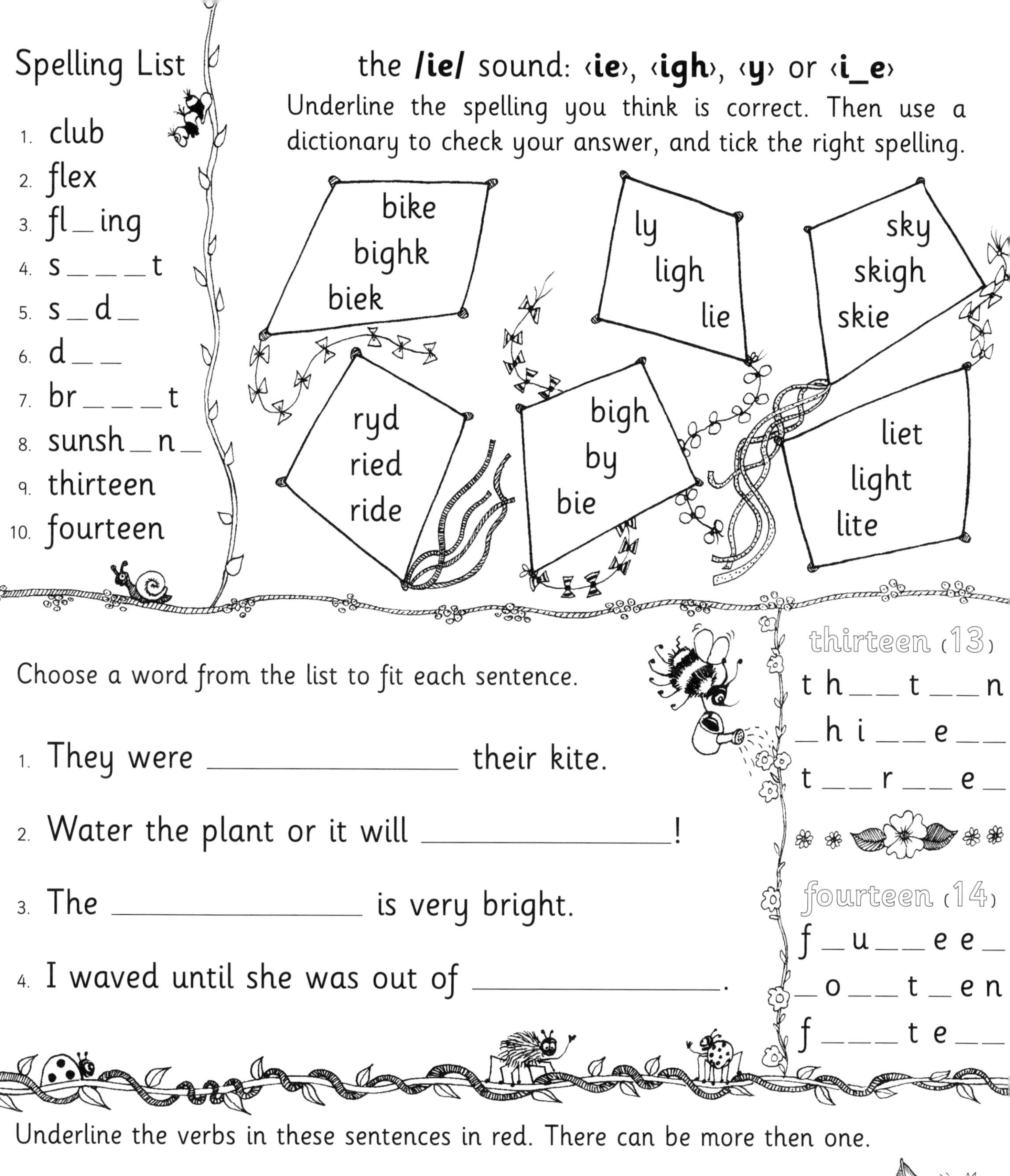

Spelling List

1. club
2. flex
3. fl_ing
4. s _ _ _ t
5. s _ d _
6. d _ _
7. br _ _ _ t
8. sunsh _ n _
9. thirteen
10. fourteen

the /ie/ sound: ‹ie›, ‹igh›, ‹y› or ‹i_e›

Underline the spelling you think is correct. Then use a dictionary to check your answer, and tick the right spelling.

bike
bighk
biek

ly
ligh
lie

sky
skigh
skie

ryd
ried
ride

bigh
by
bie

liet
light
lite

Choose a word from the list to fit each sentence.

1. They were ______________ their kite.
2. Water the plant or it will ______________!
3. The ______________ is very bright.
4. I waved until she was out of ______________.

thirteen (13)

t h _ _ t _ _ n

_ h i _ _ e _ _

t _ _ r _ _ e _

fourteen (14)

f _ u _ _ e e _

_ o _ _ t _ e n

f _ _ _ t e _ _

Underline the verbs in these sentences in red. There can be more then one.

1. I fly my kite.
2. The big boat sails across the sea.
3. The dog barks and runs after the ball.
4. The children hop, skip and jump.

Grammar 15 – Adverbs

Aim: Revise and develop the children's understanding of adverbs.

Introduction: Revise proper and common nouns, pronouns, adjectives, possessive adjectives, and verbs. Do the action for one of the pronouns (see page 6), and then mime a verb, e.g. point to self and then pretend to sleep. See if the children can guess what the actions mean, in this case 'I sleep'. Ask several children to act out pronouns with verbs for the others to guess.

Main point: Revise adverbs. Remind the children that an adverb describes a verb. It tells us how, when or where an action is performed. Many adverbs end with the suffix ‹-ly›, though not all do. Choose a verb, e.g. 'to speak'. Ask the children for adverbs to describe it, e.g. 'loudly', 'softly', 'fast', 'clearly', 'slowly', 'huskily', 'sweetly', 'angrily'. The children can also play the adverb game. One child thinks of, or is given, an adverb, e.g. 'quickly'. The other children take turns to suggest activities, and the chosen child pretends to act them out in the manner suggested by the adverb. For 'eating an ice cream,' for example, the chosen child would pretend to eat an ice cream quickly. The other children continue to suggest activities until they can guess what the adverb is. Once they have done so another child has a turn. The Adverb Poem on page 216 may be enlarged, using a photocopier. Read it with the children.

Grammar sheet 15: As a class, read through the sheet. Ask the children to suggest adverbs to describe each verb. The children write inside the outlined word, Adverbs, using an orange pencil. Then they write an adverb for each of the day's activities, trying not to use the same one more than once.

Extension activity: The children turn their 'adverb day' poems into comic strips. They choose lines from their poem and illustrate them. Then under each picture they write the appropriate line.

Rounding off: Ask some of the children to share lines from their 'adverb day' poems with the class.

Action: The action for an adverb is to bang one fist on top of the other.

Colour: The colour for adverbs is orange.

Think of an adverb to describe each verb.

My Day

I wake ________________,

I stretch ________________,

I get out of bed ________________,

I eat my breakfast ________________,

I go to school ________________,

I work ________________,

I listen ________________,

I play ________________,

I speak ________________,

I go home ________________,

I watch television ________________,

I wash ________________,

I go to bed ________________,

I sleep ________________ and

I dream ________________.

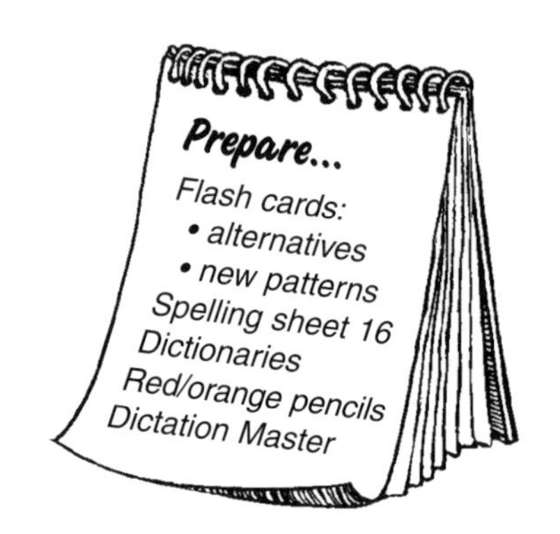

Spelling 16 – the /oa/ sound

Revision: Revise the sounds with alternative spellings. As the children give the alternative spellings for each sound, write them on the board, e.g. ‹ai›, ‹ay› and ‹a_e›. Revise the new spelling patterns covered so far.

Main point: Revise the main ways of writing the **/oa/** sound, which are ‹oa›, ‹ow› and ‹o_e›. Now that these spellings are familiar, the children need to start memorising which words take each one. With the children, make a list of words for each spelling of the /oa/ sound. To help them remember the words, the children could try making up silly sentences for each spelling, using as many of the words as possible, e.g. 'The goats and toads wore coats on the boat as they toasted a loaf.'

Spelling sheet 16: As a class, read the spelling list and the sentences, without filling in the gaps. Revise adverbs. The children complete the words in the spelling list by writing in the missing letter patterns. Then they work through the exercises on the sheet.

Dictation: Read the words and sentences for the children to write down. The Dictation Master on page 175 may be photocopied onto the back of the spelling sheets for the children to write on.

Spelling list: Read the spelling words with the children. Remind them that they need to remember how the /oa/ sound is spelt in each of the relevant words. Point out that the /or/ sound in 'snowball' is spelt ‹al›. Go over the number words '**fifteen**' and '**sixteen**'. Tell the children to pronounce each syllable carefully to help them remember the spelling, i.e. 'fif-teen' and 'six-teen'.

Dictation

1. oat
2. note
3. crow
4. road
5. stove
6. toadstool

1. Smoke came from the fireplace.
2. I ate ice cream in a cone.
3. We made toast for breakfast.

Spelling List 16

1. such
2. luck
3. home
4. froze
5. foal
6. stone
7. toast
8. snowball
9. **fifteen**
10. **sixteen**

Spelling List

1. such
2. luck
3. h _ m _
4. fr _ z _
5. f _ _ l
6. st _ n _
7. t _ _ st
8. sn _ _ ball
9. fifteen
10. sixteen

the **/oa/** sound: ‹**oa**›, ‹**ow**› or ‹**o_e**›

Underline the spelling you think is correct. Then use a dictionary to check your answer, and tick the right spelling.

broak
browk
broke

toad
tode
towd

bloa
blow
bloe

nose
nows
noas

coste
cowst
coast

elboa
elbow
elboe

Choose a word from the list to fit each sentence.

1. A ________________ is a baby horse.
2. They ate buttered ________________.
3. I went ________________ after school.
4. We had a ________________ fight.

fifteen (15)

_ i f _ e e _
f _ _ t _ _ n
_ i f _ e _ _

sixteen (16)

s _ x _ e e _
_ i _ t _ _ n
s _ _ t e _ _

Underline the verbs in these sentences in red.
Write an adverb to describe each verb. Underline your adverbs in orange.

1. She sings ________________.
2. He dresses ________________.
3. The cat plays ________________.
4. We cut out the pictures ________________.

Grammar 16 – Irregular Verb 'to be' (Simple present tense)

Aim: Teach the simple present tense of the irregular verb 'to be'.

Introduction: Revise verbs. Remind the children that the infinitive, or name, of a verb begins with the word 'to', as in 'to hop', 'to smile' and 'to write'. Ask for examples of verbs. It may help to show the irregular verbs picture in the *Jolly Grammar Big Book 2*. Encourage the children to give the infinitive form of each verb they suggest, e.g. 'to jump'. Choose one of the verbs and conjugate it in the simple present tense:

Present: I jump, you jump, he/she/it jumps, we jump, you jump, they jump

Write up this conjugation, on the board or on the plastic sheet over the bee hives in the *Big Book 2*. Remind the children that the first three are singular and the second three plural. ('I' is the first person singular; 'you' is the second person singular; 'he', 'she' and 'it' are the third person singular; 'we' is the first person plural; 'you' is the second person plural and 'they' is the third person plural.) Remind the children to add an ‹s› to the verb root for the third person singular. As a class, conjugate some of the other verbs. Remind the children that these verbs are all being conjugated in the present tense.

Main point: Explain that not all verbs follow this regular pattern. Some verbs are irregular or 'tricky'. The verb **'to be'** is very irregular. When parts of 'to be' occur in sentences, children often find them difficult to identify as verbs. It is important to overcome this problem, as the verb 'to be' is used so frequently. Familiarity with it will also help the children later, since 'to be' is used to form other tenses like the present continuous, as in 'I am running'. Conjugate the verb 'to be' in the simple present tense, and write it on the board:

Present: I am, you are, he/she/it is, we are, you are , they are

As a class, practise conjugating the verb 'to be' in the simple present tense.

Grammar sheet 16: As a class, read through the sheet. The children write inside the outlined word, Verb, using a red pencil. Then they fill in the parts of the verb 'to be' in the present tense. Next they write in the missing parts of the verb 'to be' to complete the first set of sentences. Then they read the next set of sentences. In each one, the children identify the part of the verb 'to be' and draw a bee shape around it.

Extension activity: The children write out the verb 'to be' on a large piece of paper. Then they draw a bee shape around their writing.

Rounding off: Go over the sheet, with the class identifying the parts of the verb 'to be'.

'to be'

Fill in the verb 'to be' in the present tense.

I ______________

you ______________

he/she/it ______________

we ______________

you ______________

they ______________

Write in the missing parts of the verb 'to be'.

1. You ______________ very tall.
2. She ______________ a girl.
3. Today they ______________ happy.
4. Ben said, "I ______________ six years old."
5. The car ______________ red.
6. We ______________ in the race.

Draw a bee around the part of the verb 'to be' in each sentence.

1. It is a lovely day today .
2. She is in the choir .
3. The bees are busy .
4. The tree is tall .
5. " I am sorry ," he said .
6. You are good at dancing .

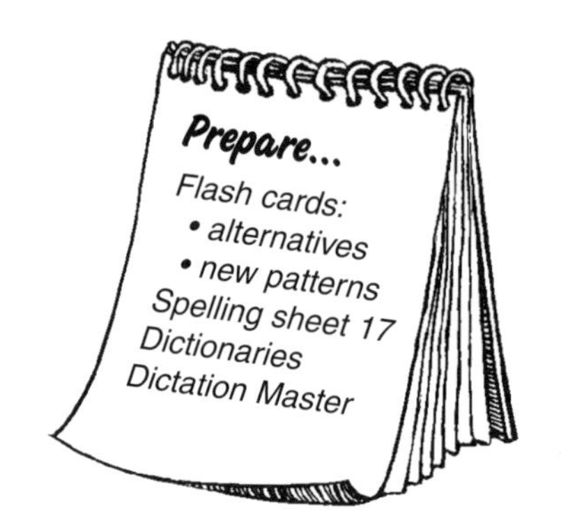

Spelling 17 – the /ue/ sound

Revision: Revise the sounds with alternative spellings. As the children give the alternative spellings for each sound, write them on the board, e.g. ‹ai›, ‹ay› and ‹a_e›. Revise the new spelling patterns covered so far.

Main point: Revise the main ways of writing the **/ue/** sound, which are ‹ue›, ‹ew› and ‹u_e›. Now that these spellings are familiar, the children need to start memorising which words take each one. With the children, make a list of words for each spelling of the /ue/ sound. To help them remember the words, the children could try making up silly sentences for each spelling, using as many of the words as possible, e.g. 'They continued to argue although they were due to be rescued.'

Spelling sheet 17: As a class, read the spelling list and the sentences, without filling in the gaps. Revise the simple present tense of the irregular verb 'to be'. The children complete the words in the spelling list by writing in the missing letter patterns. Then they work through the exercises on the sheet.

Dictation: Read the words and sentences for the children to write down. The Dictation Master on page 175 may be photocopied onto the back of the spelling sheets for the children to write on.

Spelling list: Read the spelling words with the children. Remind them that they need to remember how the /ue/ sound is spelt in each of the relevant words. Point out that the /j/ sound in 'huge' is spelt with a 'soft ‹g›'. For 'queue', explain that the ‹qu› makes a /k/ sound, and that the extra ‹e› is needed to separate the first ‹u› from the second. Point out the extra ‹e› at the end of 'ewe'. Go over the number words '**seventeen**' and '**eighteen**'. For 'eighteen', explain that the /ai/ sound is spelt ‹eigh›, and that it has only one ‹t› in the middle.

Dictation

1. use
2. few
3. tune
4. pew
5. due
6. mule

1. The plug needed a new fuse.
2. The couple used to argue.
3. The foal is due to be born in April.

Spelling List 17

1. sunk
2. book
3. huge
4. fuse
5. rescue
6. queue
7. ewe
8. useful
9. **seventeen**
10. **eighteen**

Spelling List

1. sunk
2. book
3. h _ g _
4. f _ s _
5. resc _ _
6. que _ _
7. _ _ _ e
8. _ s _ ful
9. seventeen
10. eighteen

the /ue/ sound: ‹ue›, ‹ew› or ‹u_e›

Underline the spelling you think is correct. Then use a dictionary to check your answer, and tick the right spelling.

cube cueb cewb	nues news nuse	argew argue
fue few	refews refues refuse	tube tewb tueb

Choose a word from the list to fit each sentence.

1. A female sheep is called a ______________.
2. They had to wait in a ______________.
3. A fireman came to ______________ us.
4. That whale is ______________!

seventeen (17)

s _ v _ _ t _ _ n

_ e _ e _ _ e e _

_ e v _ n _ _ _ _

eighteen (18)

e _ g h t _ _ n

e i _ _ _ _ e e _

_ _ _ _ _ t e _ _

Write out the verb 'to be'.

I ________	you ________	he/she/it ________
we ________	you ________	they ________

Draw a bee around the part of the verb 'to be' in each sentence.

1. Today we are playing outside.
2. That elephant is very big.
3. "I am so tired," said Sam.
4. It is quite cold today.

Grammar 17 – Regular Past Tense

Prepare...
(J. G. Big Book 2)
Grammar sheet 17
Red pencils
(Scissors, glue)
(Extension activity, p. 195)

Aim: Develop the children's understanding of the past tense, and their ability to form correctly the simple past tense of regular verbs.

Introduction: Revise verbs and remind the children that verb roots often change to show when the action takes place. Revise the present and past tenses with their actions. (See page 8.) Say some words and sentences. The children decide which tense they are in, and do the appropriate action.

Examples:	'I brush my hair': (Present tense)	Action:	Point towards the floor with the palm of the hand.
	'I brushed my hair': (Past tense)	Action:	Point backwards over the shoulder with a thumb.

Conjugate a verb, e.g. 'to walk', in the present and past tenses.

Main point: Remind the children that the simple past tense of a regular verb is made by adding ‹-ed› to the root. However, this suffix may be added in one of three different ways, depending on how the verb root is spelt:

a) If the verb root ends with a consonant which is not immediately after a short, stressed vowel sound, simply add ‹-ed›, e.g. 'hook' becomes 'hooked'.
b) If the verb root ends with the letter ‹e›, remove it before adding ‹-ed›, e.g. 'bake' becomes 'baked'.
c) If the verb root ends with a consonant immediately after a short, stressed vowel sound, double the final consonant before adding ‹-ed›, e.g. 'hop' becomes 'hopped'. Remind the children that the two consonants are needed to make a wall, to prevent 'magic' from the final ‹e› jumping over to change the short vowel sound. (See picture on page 23.)

Write some verbs on the board. As a class, decide how to form each past tense.

Examples:							
	a)	to pick	to rush	to lift	to cook	to join	to start
	b)	to skate	to free	to like	to hope	to use	to sneeze
	c)	to grab	to beg	to fit	to stop	to hum	to clap

Grammar sheet 17: As a class, look at the clocks and see which past tense ending belongs on each one. Then read through the verb roots on the mice. The children write inside the outlined word, Verbs, using a red pencil. They decide how to make the past tense for each verb root. Then they cut out the mice and place each one on the appropriate clock. When the children are confident that their answers are correct, they stick down the mice. Alternatively, they can simply write each past tense verb in the appropriate clock.

Extension activity: The children put more verbs into the past, using the extension activity on page 195.

Rounding off: Go over the sheet, with the class checking where each mouse belongs. Go over the extension activity, with the class checking their answers.

Red

Verbs

Regular Past Tense

Which clock does each mouse run up?

+ed

e̸ +ed

double +ed

Verb roots

Add the past tense ending.

batted

chew____

look____

wipe____

hate____

walk____

hug____

please____

rip____

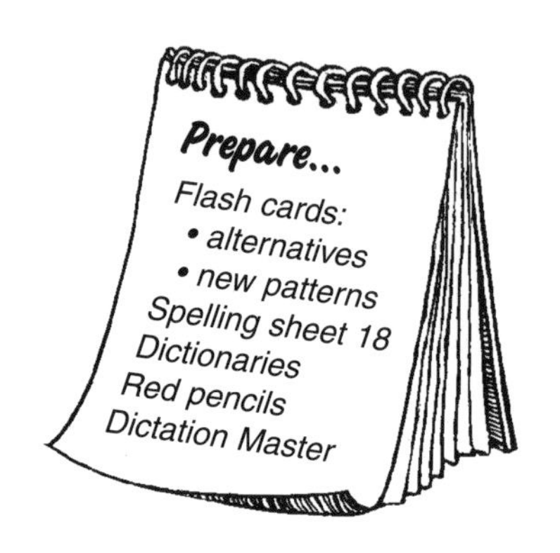

Spelling 18 – the /k/ sound

Revision: Revise the sounds with alternative spellings. As the children give the alternative spellings for each sound, write them on the board, e.g. ‹ai›, ‹ay› and ‹a_e›. Revise the new spelling patterns covered so far.

Main point: Revise the main ways of writing the **/k/** sound, which are ‹c›, ‹ck› and ‹k›. Now that these spellings are familiar, the children need to start memorising which words take each one. At the end of a one-syllable word with a short vowel, a ‹c› is usually doubled by adding a 'kicking ‹k›', as in 'sack', 'neck', 'quick', 'clock' and 'truck'. At the end of a one-syllable word which does not have a short vowel sound, a /k/ sound is usually made by ‹k›, as in 'look', 'beak', 'hawk', 'talk' and 'work'. In order to understand this, the children must be able to hear the syllables as well as the short vowel sounds in words. Use 'Chin Bumps' as a fun way to teach syllables (see page 21). Revise the short vowel sounds, /a/, /e/, /i/, /o/ and /u/, with their actions (see picture on page 22).

Spelling sheet 18: As a class, read the spelling list and the sentences, without filling in the gaps. Revise the three ways of making the simple past tense with ‹-ed›. The children complete the words in the spelling list by writing in the missing letter patterns. Then they work through the exercises on the sheet.

Dictation: Read the words and sentences for the children to write down. The Dictation Master on page 175 may be photocopied onto the back of the spelling sheets for the children to write on.

Spelling list: Read the spelling words with the children. Remind them that after a short vowel in a one-syllable word, they need ‹ck› to spell the /k/ sound. Go over the number words '**nineteen**' and '**twenty**'. Point out that the /ie/ sound in 'nineteen' is spelt ‹i_e›, and that 'twenty' has a 'toughy ‹y›' at the end.

Dictation

1. duck
2. peck
3. bike
4. clock
5. book
6. trick

1. Stack the bricks up over there.
2. The ducks quacked as they pecked at the loaf.
3. Our cousin parked his bike by the truck.

Spelling List 18

1. hook
2. fork
3. back
4. brick
5. deck
6. flock
7. struck
8. rucksack
9. **nineteen**
10. **twenty**

Spelling List

1. hoo _
2. for _
3. ba _ _
4. bri _ _
5. de _ _
6. flo _ _
7. stru _ _
8. ru _ _ sa _ _
9. nineteen
10. twenty

nineteen (19)

n _ n _ t _ _ n

_ i _ e _ e e _

n i _ _ t _ _ n

twenty (20)

t w _ n _ y

t _ e _ t _

_ w _ _ t _

the /k/ sound: ‹k› or ‹ck›

Underline the spelling you think is correct. Then use a dictionary to check your answer, and tick the right spelling.

duck duk	sack sak	forck fork
sharck shark	oack oak	chick chik
neck nek	boock book	rocket roket
bicke bike	black blak	cacke cake

Underline the verbs in these sentences in red.
Then re-write the sentences in the past tense.

1. I zip up my coat.
   Yesterday ______________________________

2. He talks to his friend.
   Last week ______________________________

Grammar 18 – Irregular Past Tense ('Tricky Pasts')

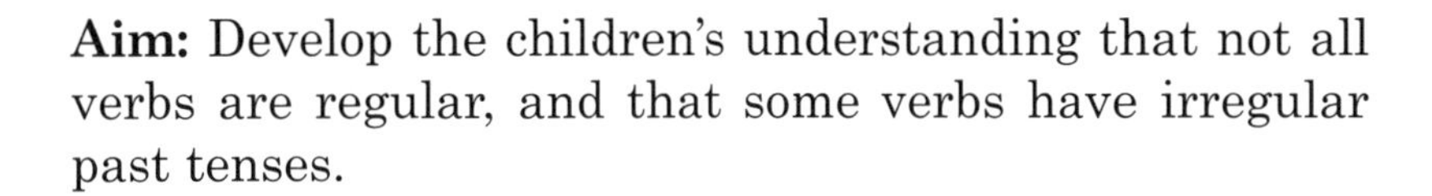

Aim: Develop the children's understanding that not all verbs are regular, and that some verbs have irregular past tenses.

Introduction: Revise verbs and how to form the past tense of regular verbs. Do the action for the present or past tense, followed by the action for one of the pronouns. Then mime a verb. See if the children can guess what the actions mean.

Examples:	For 'I clap':	Point towards the floor with the palm of the hand, point to self, and clap.
	For 'I clapped':	Point backwards over the shoulder with a thumb, point to self, and clap.

Main point: Explain that some verbs do not form the past tense by adding ‹-ed› to the root. The roots of these verbs change when they are put into the past. We call them 'tricky pasts'. The children will already know many 'tricky pasts'. Ask them to think of as many examples as they can. Write some of their suggestions onto paper hexagons.

Examples:	'come' and 'came'	'dig' and 'dug'
	'drink' and 'drank'	'draw' and 'drew'
	'get' and 'got'	'give' and 'gave'
	'have' and 'had'	'hide' and 'hid'
	'lose' and 'lost'	'make' and 'made'
	'ride' and 'rode'	'run' and 'ran'
	'say' and 'said'	'sing' and 'sang'
	'speak' and 'spoke'	'swim' and 'swam'
	'take' and 'took'	'throw' and 'threw'
	'win' and 'won'	'write' and 'wrote'

The hexagons may then be fitted together to make a honeycomb, for display. As more 'tricky pasts' are discovered, these can be added to the honeycomb too.

Grammar sheet 18: As a class, read through the sheet. The children write inside the outlined word, Verbs, using a red pencil. Then they match each verb root with its 'tricky past'. Next they read the sentences underneath and rewrite them in the past tense on the lines provided.

Extension activity: The children put more verbs into the past, using the extension activity on page 197. Alternatively they use the template on page 198 to copy 'tricky pasts' from the honeycomb display, and see if they can add any examples of their own.

Rounding off: Go over the sheet, with the class checking their answers. See if any children have thought of additional 'tricky pasts'. If so, these may be added to the honeycomb display. Go over the extension activity, with the class checking their answers.

Irregular Past Tense

Not all verbs make the past tense by adding ‹-ed›. Some verb roots change when they are put into the past. These are the 'tricky pasts'.

e.g. Today I **swim** Yesterday I **swam**

Match the present and past tenses of these verbs.

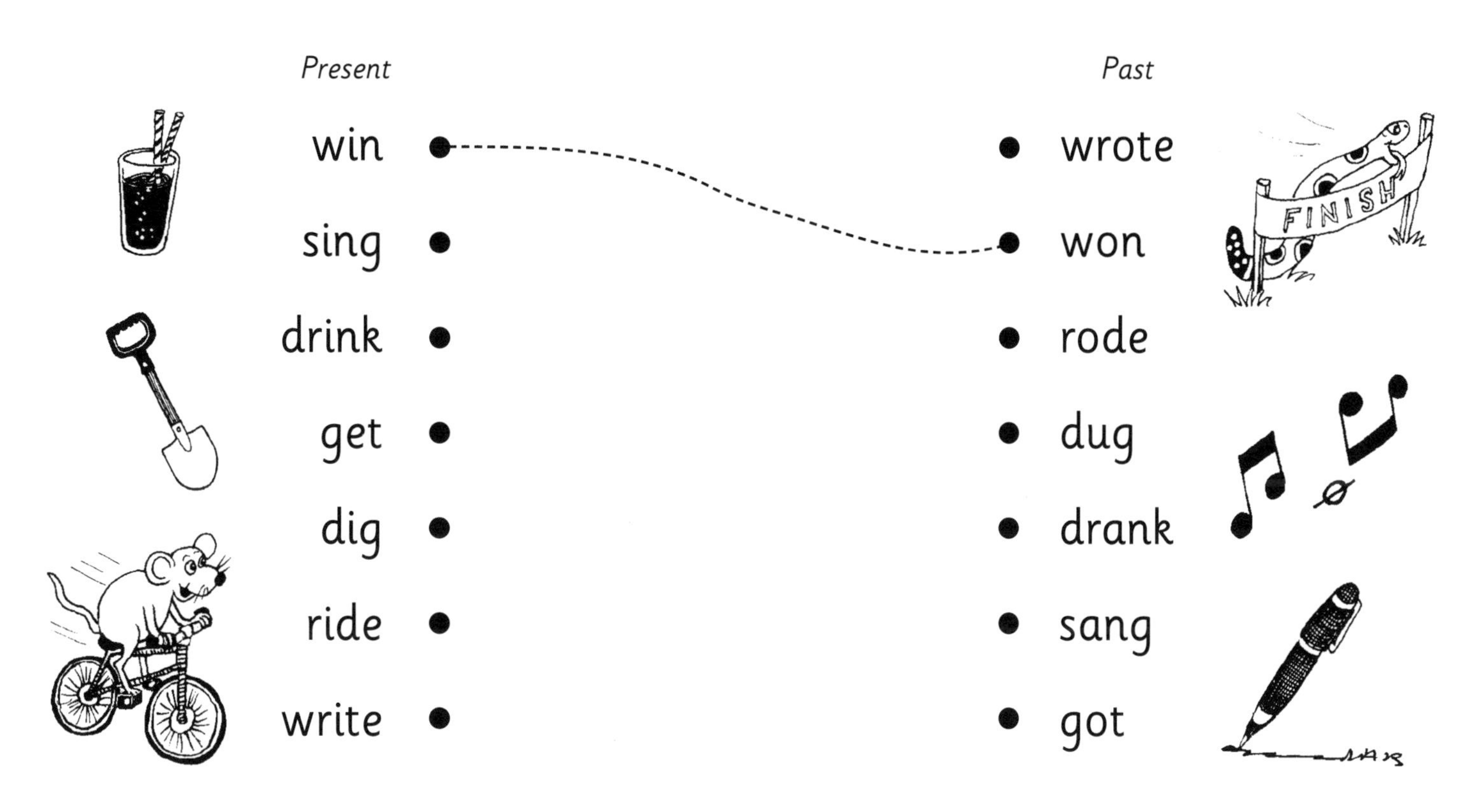

Present	*Past*
win •	• wrote
sing •	• won
drink •	• rode
get •	• dug
dig •	• drank
ride •	• sang
write •	• got

Re-write these sentences in the past tense.

1. We sing a song. ____________________

2. He rides his bike. ____________________

3. I write a letter. ____________________

4. You win a prize. ____________________

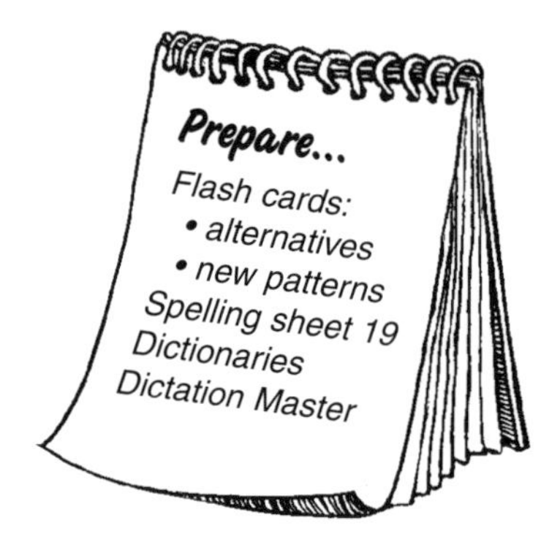

Prepare...
Flash cards:
• alternatives
• new patterns
Spelling sheet 19
Dictionaries
Dictation Master

Spelling 19 – the /er/ sound

Revision: Revise some of the spelling patterns and tricky words covered so far this year.

Main point: Revise the main ways of writing the **/er/** sound, which are ‹er›, ‹ir› and ‹ur›. Now that these spellings are familiar, the children need to start memorising which words take each one. The ‹er› spelling often comes at the end of words, where it makes a slightly shorter sound. The ‹ir› spelling is often found in number words, e.g. 'first', 'third', 'thirteen' and 'thirty'. The ‹ur› spelling is found in two days of the week: 'Thursday' and 'Saturday'. With the children, make a list of words for each spelling of the /er/ sound. To help them remember the words, the children could try making up silly sentences for each spelling, using as many of the words as possible, e.g. 'Her sister served herbs and pepper on a silver salver for supper in winter.'

Spelling sheet 19: As a class, read the spelling list and the sentences, without filling in the gaps. Revise 'tricky pasts'. The children complete the words in the spelling list by writing in the missing letter patterns. Then they work through the exercises on the sheet.

Dictation: Read the words and sentences for the children to write down. The Dictation Master on page 175 may be photocopied onto the back of the spelling sheets for the children to write on.

Spelling list: Read the spelling words with the children. Remind them that they need to remember how the /er/ sound is spelt in each of the relevant words. Go over the number words '**thirty**' and '**forty**'. Explain that both words have a 'toughy ‹y›' at the end. Point out that the /or/ sound in 'forty' is spelt regularly, unlike the /or/ sound in 'four'.

Dictation

1. girl
2. skirt
3. summer
4. Thursday
5. hurt
6. number

1. He came first in the sack race.
2. She had a purple shirt and skirt.
3. Turn the page over to see the third number.

Spelling List 19

1. drip
2. plug
3. third
4. winter
5. bird
6. over
7. hurt
8. butterfly
9. **thirty**
10. **forty**

Spelling List
1. drip
2. plug
3. th _ _ d
4. wint _ _
5. b _ _ d
6. ov _ _
7. h _ _ t
8. butt _ _ fly
9. th _ _ ty
10. forty
the /er/ sound: ‹er›, ‹ir› or ‹ur›
Underline the spelling you think is correct. Then use a dictionary to check your answer, and tick the right spelling.
gingir
gingur
ginger
pirple
purple
perple
girl
gerl
gurl
furst
ferst
first
bern
burn
birn
hirb
herb
hurb
Choose a word from the list to fit each sentence.
1. She fell and ________ her knee.
2. A ________ is a beautiful insect.
3. The snow was deep last ________.
4. I finished the race in ________ place.
thirty (30)
_ _ i _ _ y
t _ _ r _ _
_ h _ _ t _
forty (40)
f _ r _ y
_ o _ t _
_ _ _ t y
Each of these verb roots has a tricky past. Write each past tense in the honeycomb.
run
sing
swim
dig
ride
win
HONEY
Spelling sheet 19 (GH2)

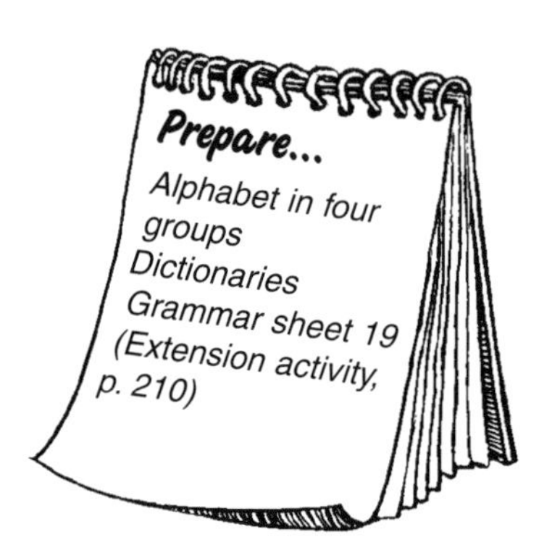

Prepare...
Alphabet in four groups
Dictionaries
Grammar sheet 19
(Extension activity, p. 210)

Grammar 19 – Using a Dictionary

Aim: Develop the children's ability to use a dictionary to find the correct spelling and meaning of words.

Introduction: Revise the alphabet in the four dictionary groups. Call out a letter. Ask which letters come before and after it, and which group it belongs to. Repeat with other letters. Call out a letter and ask the children to try to open the dictionary in approximately the right place, e.g. for the letter ‹m› they should open it near the middle. Repeat with other letters. Write two words on the board which have the same first letter. Ask which word would come first in the dictionary, and why. Then write up two more words which have the same first three or four letters, to extend the teaching.

Examples: sunny, Sunday
thirty, thirteen

Main point: One reason why the children need to know the order of the alphabet is that it will enable them to find words in a dictionary. Explain that a dictionary can help in two ways. Firstly, it shows how a word is spelt. Write some misspelt words on the board, such as 'dolfin', 'streem' and 'retern'. Ask the children whether each word is spelt correctly and how they could use a dictionary to find out. First they look up the given spelling to see if it is correct. If this spelling is not in the dictionary, the children need to think how else the sounds in the word might be spelt. They look up alternative spellings until they find the word. The second way a dictionary can help is in showing what a word means. When the children come across an unfamiliar word in their reading, they can look up its meaning in a dictionary, rather than asking for help or ignoring the word altogether.

Grammar sheet 19: The children read the words at the top of the sheet, which are all spelt incorrectly. They think how each word might be spelt instead, and look up alternative spellings in the dictionary until they find the word. They write each word correctly on the line below, and draw a picture for it. Then they read the words in the books. They look each word up in the dictionary, and draw a picture to show what it means.

Extension activity: The children look up more words and draw pictures for them, using the extension activity on page 210.

Rounding off: Go over the sheet, with the class checking the spellings of the words in the first section, and the meanings of the words in the books. Then go over the meanings of the words in the extension activity.

Using a Dictionary

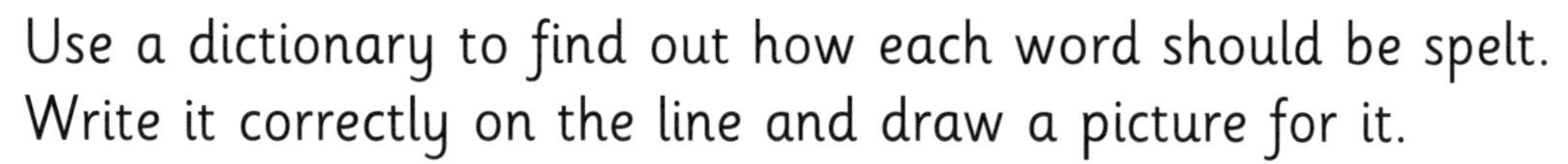

Use a dictionary to find out how each word should be spelt.
Write it correctly on the line and draw a picture for it.

catapiller	bananar	kangeroo
____________	____________	____________

ambulense	tortoss	calcuelaiter
____________	____________	____________

Look up each word in the dictionary. Read the meaning and draw a picture for it.

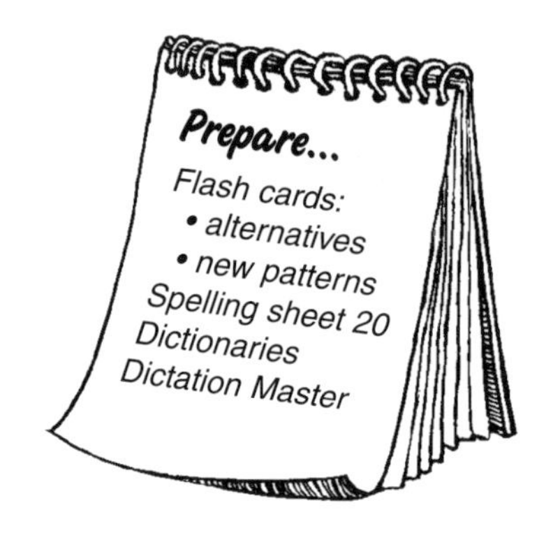

Spelling 20 – the **/oi/** sound

Revision: Revise some of the spelling patterns and tricky words covered so far this year.

Main point: Revise the main ways of writing the **/oi/** sound, which are ‹oi› and ‹oy›. Now that these spellings are familiar, the children need to start memorising which words take each one. Remind them that the ‹oy› spelling is usually found at the end of a word, where 'toughy ‹y›' takes the place of 'shy ‹i›'. With the children, make a list of words for each spelling of the /oi/ sound. To help them remember the words, the children could try making up silly sentences for each spelling, using as many of the words as possible, e.g. 'Boiling the oil spoiled the moist ointment.'

Spelling sheet 20: As a class, read the spelling list and the sentences, without filling in the gaps. Revise how to use the dictionary. The children complete the words in the spelling list by writing in the missing letter patterns. Then they work through the exercises on the sheet.

Dictation: Read the words and sentences for the children to write down. The Dictation Master on page 175 may be photocopied onto the back of the spelling sheets for the children to write on.

Spelling list: Read the spelling words with the children. Remind them that they need to remember how the /oi/ sound is spelt in each of the relevant words. Point out that that the /oi/ sound in 'royal' is spelt ‹oy›, although it is not at the end of the word. Go over the number words '**fifty**' and '**sixty**'. Explain that both words have a 'toughy ‹y›' at the end.

Dictation

1. oil
2. coin
3. boy
4. joint
5. annoy
6. toilet

1. The weather was boiling hot.
2. We enjoyed our day in the country.
3. My sister destroyed her toy clock.

Spelling List 20

1. drag
2. trip
3. join
4. spoil
5. point
6. joy
7. royal
8. ointment
9. **fifty**
10. **sixty**

Spelling List

1. drag
2. trip
3. j _ _ n
4. sp _ _ l
5. p _ _ nt
6. j _ _
7. r _ _ al
8. _ _ ntment
9. fifty
10. sixty

the /oi/ sound: ‹oi› or ‹oy›

Underline the spelling you think is correct. Then use a dictionary to check your answer, and tick the right spelling.

coin / coyn

boi / boy

noise / noyse

annoi / annoy

loial / loyal

toilet / toylet

Choose a word from the list to fit each sentence.

1. Her pencil has a sharp ______________.
2. Can we ______________ your club?
3. The rain may ______________ our picnic.
4. The nurse put ______________ on his burn.

fifty (50)

_ i _ t _

f _ f _ y

_ _ _ t y

sixty (60)

s _ x _ y

_ i _ t _

_ _ _ t _

Look through the dictionary. Find two words that you did not know before. Copy each word with its meaning.

1. ______________ ______________________________

____

2. ______________ ______________________________

____

Grammar 20 – Proofreading Sentences

Aim: Develop the children's ability to proofread text, looking for spelling and punctuation mistakes.

Introduction: Revise sentences, and the punctuation covered so far: full stops, question marks, exclamation marks, speech marks, and commas in lists. On the board, write some sentences without any punctuation. Punctuate them with the children.

Examples: Oh It is just what I always wanted exclaimed the little girl
Would you like to come to my house asked Matthew
At the aquarium there were sharks rays eels and an octopus

Main point: Tell the children that once they finish a piece of writing, it is a good idea to read it through to make sure there are not any mistakes. This is called proofreading. When people are thinking hard about what they are writing, they sometimes forget about spelling and punctuation. Proofreading gives the children a chance to find and correct their own mistakes.

Grammar sheet 20: The children proofread each sentence on the sheet. Using a coloured pencil, they correct the spelling and punctuation where necessary. The correctly-spelt words can be written above the misspelt ones. The children can use dictionaries to help them if they are not sure how a word is spelt.

Extension activity: The children exchange sheets or confer with a neighbour, to see whether they found all the mistakes.

Rounding off: Go over sentences from the sheet, with the class identifying the mistakes.

Proofreading Sentences

Proofread these sentences. Write out the correct spelling above each misspelt word. Then add in the missing punctuation.

1. Dolfins and wales live in the sea.

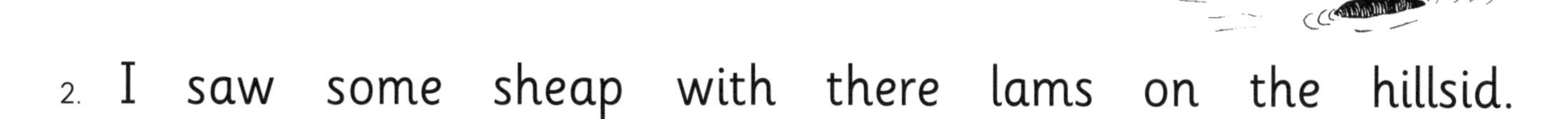

2. I saw some sheap with there lams on the hillsid.

3. it was mie berthday party

4. The dog ait the duc.

5. i wet on holiday with my muther father sister brother granma and grampa

6. Could I have a drinck pleas askt meg.

7. Whot is your naim sed the litle gerl.

8. Ouch i hit my thum wiv the hamer.

9. their are three yung Berds in the nest in are tree.

10. at the zoo we sor jiraffes elefants penguins and aardvarks.

Spelling 21 – the /ou/ sound

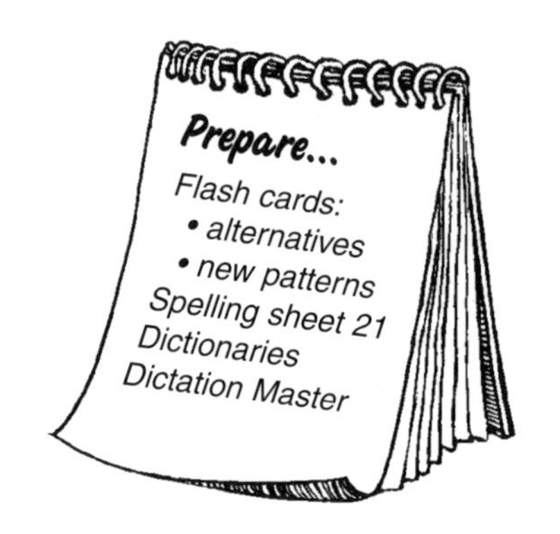

Revision: Revise some of the spelling patterns and tricky words covered so far this year.

Main point: Revise the main ways of writing the **/ou/** sound, which are ‹ou› and ‹ow›. Now that these spellings are familiar, the children need to start memorising which words take each one. With the children, make a list of words for each spelling of the /ou/ sound. To help them remember the words, the children could try making up silly sentences for each spelling, using as many of the words as possible, e.g. 'Our proud mouse shouted loudly about his counting house.'

Spelling sheet 21: As a class, read the spelling list and the sentences, without filling in the gaps. Revise how to proofread sentences. The children complete the words in the spelling list by writing in the missing letter patterns. Then they work through the exercises on the sheet.

Dictation: Read the words and sentences for the children to write down. The Dictation Master on page 175 may be photocopied onto the back of the spelling sheets for the children to write on.

Spelling list: Read the spelling words with the children. Remind them that they need to remember how the /ou/ sound is spelt in each of the relevant words. Go over the number words '**seventy**' and '**eighty**'. Explain that both words have a 'toughy ‹y›' at the end. For 'eighty', point out that the /ai/ sound is spelt ‹eigh›, and that it has only one ‹t› in the middle.

Dictation

1. out
2. owl
3. mouth
4. clown
5. mouse
6. flower

1. I saw a pair of barn owls.
2. We rode our bikes around the town.
3. He rescued the brown mouse.

Spelling List 21

1. snap
2. swam
3. loud
4. cloud
5. found
6. now
7. crowd
8. sunflower
9. **seventy**
10. **eighty**

Spelling List

1. snap
2. swam
3. l _ _ d
4. cl _ _ d
5. f _ _ nd
6. n _ _
7. cr _ _ d
8. sunfl _ _ er
9. seventy
10. eighty

the /ou/ sound: ‹ou› or ‹ow›

Underline the spelling you think is correct. Then use a dictionary to check your answer, and tick the right spelling.

out / owt

broun / brown

shout / showt

toun / town

mouth / mowth

croun / crown

seventy (70)

_ e _ e _ t _

s _ v _ n _ y

_ _ _ _ _ _ t y

eighty (80)

e _ g _ t _

_ i _ h _ y

_ _ _ _ _ _ y

Choose a word from the list to fit each sentence.

1. She grew a tall, yellow ______________.
2. He ______________ my lost watch.
3. A big ______________ gathered to watch.
4. The music was very ______________.

Proofread these sentences.

1. I have made a caik for yor berthday said mum .
2. Can you see the wite swon He asked .
3. the duks kwacked lowdly as i threw them some bred .
4. She swimmed with dolfins last summir

Grammar 21 – Irregular Verb 'to be' (Simple past tense)

Aim: Teach the simple past tense of the irregular verb 'to be'.

Introduction: Revise the past tense of verbs which have 'tricky pasts', such as 'rode' for 'to ride', and 'drank' for 'to drink'. Remind the children that the infinitive, or name, of a verb begins with the word 'to', as in 'to swim', 'to climb' and 'to think'. Call out examples of 'tricky pasts', and see if the children can give the infinitives for them, e.g. for 'I ran,' the children respond, 'to run'. After several examples, call out 'I was'. It is unlikely that any of the children will realise that this is the past tense of the verb 'to be', as it is so irregular.

Main point: The verb **'to be'** is very irregular. When parts of 'to be' occur in sentences, children often find them difficult to identify as verbs. It is important to overcome this problem, as the verb 'to be' is used so frequently. Familiarity with it will also help the children later, since the verb 'to be' is used to form other tenses like the imperfect tense, as in 'They were talking'. Conjugate the verb 'to be' in the simple present tense, and write it on the board. Now see if the children can give each part of the verb 'to be' in the simple past tense. Write each part on the board as they work it out.

Present:	*Past:*
I am	I was
you are	you were
he/she/it is	he/she/it was
we are	we were
you are	you were
they are	they were

As a class, practise conjugating the verb 'to be' in the simple past tense.

Grammar sheet 21: As a class, read through the sheet. The children write inside the outlined word, Verb, using a red pencil. Then they fill in the parts of the verb 'to be' in the simple present and past tenses. Next they identify the part of the verb 'to be' in each sentence, and draw a bee shape around it. They re-write each sentence in the simple past tense, using the lines provided. Finally they underline each past tense part of the verb 'to be' in red.

Extension activity: On the board, write more sentences which use the verb 'to be' in the simple present tense. The children identify the part of the verb 'to be'. Then they re-write each sentence in the simple past tense. The Writing Master on page 176 may be photocopied onto the back of the grammar sheets for the children to write on.

Rounding off: Go over the sheet, with the class identifying the parts of the verb 'to be', and checking that they re-wrote the sentences correctly in the past tense.

'to be'

Conjugate the verb 'to be' in the present and past tenses.

Present		Past	
I	________	I	________
you	________	you	________
he/she/it	________	he/she/it	________
we	________	we	________
you	________	you	________
they	________	they	________

Draw a bee around the part of the verb 'to be' in each sentence.
Then re-write each sentence in the past tense. Underline each past tense part of the verb 'to be' in red.

1. I am at school.
   Yesterday ____________________
2. It is a beautiful sunny day.
   Last Monday ____________________
3. We are happy.
   Last week ____________________
4. They are good at football.
   Last year ____________________

Prepare...
Flash cards:
• alternatives
• new patterns
Spelling sheet 22
Dictionaries
Dictation Master

Spelling 22 – the **/or/** sound

Revision: Revise some of the spelling patterns and tricky words covered so far this year.

Main point: Revise the main ways of writing the **/or/** sound, which are ‹or›, ‹al›, ‹au› and ‹aw›. Now that these spellings are familiar, the children need to start memorising which words take each one. With the children, make a list of words for each spelling of the /or/ sound. To help them remember the words, the children could try making up silly sentences for each spelling, using as many of the words as possible, e.g. 'One stormy morning forty horses snorted.'

Spelling sheet 22: As a class, read the spelling list and the sentences, without filling in the gaps. Revise the present and past tenses of the verb 'to be'. The children complete the words in the spelling list by writing in the missing letter patterns. Then they work through the exercises on the sheet.

Dictation: Read the words and sentences for the children to write down. The Dictation Master on page 175 may be photocopied onto the back of the spelling sheets for the children to write on.

Spelling list: Read the spelling words with the children. Remind them that they need to remember how the /or/ sound is spelt in each of the relevant words. Point out that the second /s/ sound in 'saucepan' is spelt with a 'soft ‹c›', followed by a 'silent ‹e›'. Go over the number words '**ninety**' and '**hundred**'. Explain that there is a 'toughy ‹y›' at the end of 'ninety'.

Dictation

1. fork
2. talk
3. storm
4. saw
5. walk
6. August

1. The brown horse ran forty races.
2. The boy climbed down the beanstalk.
3. It was dawn on an autumn morning.

Spelling List 22

1. twig
2. from
3. pork
4. walk
5. jaw
6. north
7. straw
8. saucepan
9. **ninety**
10. **hundred**

Spelling List

1. twig
2. from
3. p _ _ k
4. w _ _ k
5. j _ _
6. n _ _ th
7. str _ _
8. s _ _ cepan
9. ninety
10. hundred

the **/or/** sound: ‹**or**›, ‹**al**›, ‹**au**› or ‹**aw**›

Underline the spelling you think is correct. Then use a dictionary to check your answer, and tick the right spelling.

sor
sau
saw

forlt
fault
fawlt

tork
tauk
talk

storm
staum
stalm

borl
baul
ball

fork
fauk
fawk

Choose a word from the list to fit each sentence.

1. She always drinks through a ______________.
2. We went for a ______________ in the park.
3. He cooked rice in a big ______________.
4. Shall we drive ______________ or south?

ninety (90)

n _ n _ t _

_ i _ e _ y

_ _ _ _ _ _ y

hundred (100)

h _ n _ r _ d

_ u _ d _ e _

h _ _ _ _ _ _

Conjugate the verb 'to be' in the present and the past.

	Present	*Past*
I		
you		
he/she/it		
we		
you		
they		

Grammar 22 – Expanding a Sentence

Aim: Develop the children's ability to write interesting sentences by thinking carefully about the words they use.

Introduction: Revise sentences. Remind the children that a sentence must make sense, and that it must start with a capital letter, end with a full stop, question mark or exclamation mark, and contain a verb. Revise proper and common nouns, verbs, adjectives and adverbs. Revise the colours for the different parts of speech: black for nouns, red for verbs, blue for adjectives and orange for adverbs.

Main point: On the board, write the sentence 'The cat ran.' Read this sentence with the children, and underline the noun in black and the verb in red. (If using a blackboard, explain that as there is no black chalk, white chalk is used instead.) Point out that the sentence is rather boring. Ask the children how they might make it more interesting and informative. Encourage them to think of ways of adding to the sentence. Ask them for words to describe the cat, such as 'black', 'small' or 'fluffy'. Choose one of the children's suggestions and add it to the sentence. Ask which part of speech the new word is. It is an adjective, so underline it in blue. Now ask the children for words to describe how the cat ran, such as 'quickly', 'silently' or 'happily'. Choose one of their suggestions and add it to the sentence. Ask which part of speech this new word is. It is an adverb, so underline it in orange. Now ask the children for more ideas, such as where or when the cat ran. Choose some of their suggestions and add them to the sentence. Some of these words may also be adverbs, such as 'away' and 'today'. Now ask why the cat ran, and choose from the children's suggestions to add to the sentence. Compare the new sentence with the original.

Grammar sheet 22: As a class, read the sentence at the top of the sheet. The children underline the noun in black and the verb in red. They write inside the outlined words in the appropriate colours. Then they expand the sentence by adding adjectives, an adverb, and some more detail. They write out the new sentence and underline the noun(s) in black, the verb in red, the adjectives in blue and the adverb in orange.

Extension activity: The children expand the additional sentences from the bottom of the sheet. The Writing Master on page 176 may be photocopied onto the back of the grammar sheets for the children to write on.

Rounding off: Ask some of the children to share their expanded sentences with the class.

Expanding a Sentence

A sentence can be made more interesting by adding extra information to it.

Read this simple sentence. Underline the noun in black and the verb in red.

The dog barked.

Now add an adjective to describe the noun.

The ____________ dog barked.

Now add another adjective.

The ____________, ____________ dog barked.

Now add an adverb to describe the verb.

The dog barked ____________.

Adding details can make a sentence more interesting.
What was the dog barking at?

The dog barked at ________________________.

Now write out the sentence, adding in all the details.

The ____________, ____________ dog barked ____________ at ________________________.

Now the sentence is much more interesting!

Expand these sentences on the back of the sheet.

1. The boy laughed.
2. The rabbit hopped.

Prepare...
Flash cards:
• alternatives
• new patterns
Spelling sheet 23
Blue pencils
Orange pencils
Dictation Master

Spelling 23 – **‹ey›**

Revision: Revise some of the spelling patterns and tricky words covered so far this year.

Main point: Most words with an /ee/ sound take the ‹ee› or ‹ea› spellings, but at the end of a word, the /ee/ sound is often spelt **‹ey›**. These exceptions need to be learnt. With the children, make a list of words which use ‹ey›. To help them remember these words, the children could try making up silly sentences using as many of the words as possible, e.g. 'Honey the donkey had keys and money for the journey.'

Spelling sheet 23: As a class, read the spelling list and the sentences, without filling in the gaps. Revise how to use adjectives and adverbs to expand a sentence. The children complete the words in the spelling list by writing in the missing letter pattern. Then they work through the exercises on the sheet.

Dictation: Read the words and sentences for the children to write down. The Dictation Master on page 175 may be photocopied onto the back of the spelling sheets for the children to write on.

Spelling list: Read the spelling words with the children. Point out that the /u/ sound in 'honey' and 'money' is spelt ‹o›. For 'journey', the children could use the 'Say it as it sounds' method, pronouncing the first syllable to rhyme with 'flour'. Go over the number words '**thousand**' and '**million**'. It helps the children remember the spelling of 'thousand' if they emphasise the /a/ sound in the second syllable, pronouncing it to rhyme with 'band'. Similarly it helps them remember the spelling of 'million' if they emphasise the /o/ sound in the third syllable, pronouncing it to rhyme with 'gone'.

Dictation

1. key
2. turkey
3. barley
4. pulley
5. monkey
6. keyhole

1. Here is money to buy chalk.
2. She rode a donkey this morning.
3. They say the chimney is haunted.

Spelling List 23

1. film
2. kept
3. key
4. honey
5. money
6. donkey
7. chimney
8. journey
9. **thousand**
10. **million**

Spelling List

1. film
2. kept
3. k _ _
4. hon _ _
5. mon _ _
6. donk _ _
7. chimn _ _
8. journ _ _
9. thousand
10. million

‹ey›

Write some ‹ey› words in the honey pot.

thousand (1,000)

t _ o _ s _ n _

_ h _ u _ a _ d

t h _ _ s _ _ _

million (1,000,000)

_ i _ l _ o _

m _ l _ i _ n

m i l _ _ _ _

Choose a word from the list to fit each sentence.

1. She set off on a long ________________.
2. He locked the door with his ________________.
3. Bees collect pollen to make ________________.
4. I saved up my ________________ to buy a toy.

Adjective — *Blue*

Expand these sentences.

Adverb — *Orange*

1. The ________________ horse jumped ________________ over ________________.
2. Our ________________ cousin played ________________ in the ________________.

Grammar 23 – Conjunctions

Aim: Develop the children's knowledge of conjunctions.
A conjunction joins parts of a sentence together.

Introduction: Revise sentences. Read the example story. With the children, find the verbs.

Example: Rob went to the zoo. It was his birthday. He took his friend. He was not lonely. They looked at the animals. They walked around. They saw snakes. They saw monkeys. It was cold. They had fun.
"Shall we go home? Shall we look at more animals?" asked Rob.

Main point: Explain that it can be boring to read one short simple sentence after another. Joining short sentences together can make them more interesting to read. A **conjunction** is a word that joins other words or groups of words together. If possible, show the children the conjunctions page in the *Jolly Grammar Big Book 2.*

Action: The action for conjunctions is to hold hands apart with palms facing up. Move both hands so one is on top of the other.

Colour: The colour for conjunctions is purple.

Six of the most useful conjunctions are **and**, **but**, **because**, **or**, **so**, and **while**. Write them on the board and ask the children to try using them to join pairs of sentences from the story. Use some of the children's suggestions to turn each pair of short sentences into one longer one. In each case, remember to remove the full stop at the end of the first sentence and the capital letter at the start of the second one. Sometimes using a conjunction can avoid the need to repeat words. In the fourth sentence below, for instance, it is not necessary to repeat the words 'they saw'.

Example: Rob went to the zoo **because** it was his birthday. He took his friend **so** he was not lonely. They looked at the animals **while** they walked around. They saw snakes **and** monkeys. It was cold **but** they had fun.
"Shall we go home **or** shall we look at more animals?" asked Rob.

Grammar sheet 23: Using a purple pencil, the children write inside the outlined words and underline the conjunctions in the first exercise. Then they read the sentence parts underneath. They match each sentence part on the left with one on the right. They choose a conjunction to join each pair, and write it on the line.

Extension activity: The children choose the right conjunction to complete each sentence in the extension activity on page 199.

Rounding off: Go over the sheet with the class. Then go over the extension activity.

Conjunctions

Purple

There are many conjunctions, but these are six of the most useful ones.

and　but　because　or　so　while

Underline the conjunctions in purple.

1. Would you like an apple or an orange?
2. I did not tell anyone the news because it was a secret.
3. He fell over but he did not hurt himself.
4. We played games while we waited.
5. cats and dogs
6. It rained so she took her umbrella.

Match each sentence part on the left to one on the right. Choose a conjunction to join them together, and write it on the line.

I was late for school	________ the band played.
We went to the country	________ is it too late?
Kim ran fast in the race	because I overslept.
Is there time to play	________ he ate some oats.
The horse was hungry	________ had a picnic.
They listened quietly	________ she did not win.

Action: Hold hands apart with palms facing up. Move both hands so one is on top of the other.

Colour: Purple

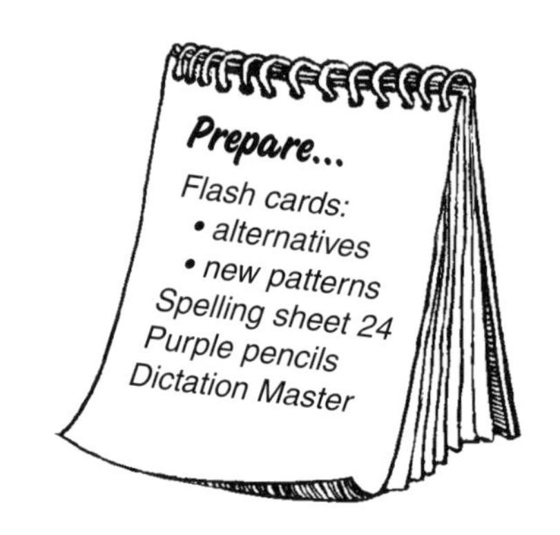

Spelling 24 – ‹**y**› as the final syllable

Revision: Revise some of the spelling patterns and tricky words covered so far this year.

Main point: Most words with an /ee/ sound take the ‹ee› or ‹ea› spellings, but at the end of a multi-syllabic word, the /ee/ sound is often spelt ‹y›. Introduce the ‹**y**› spelling of the /ee/ sound, as the final syllable of multi-syllabic words. Use 'Chin Bumps' as a fun way to teach syllables (see page 21). With the children, make a list of words with ‹y› as the final syllable. To help them remember these words, the children could try making up silly sentences using as many of the words as possible, e.g. 'The fancy lady's tiny baby was happy about the silly, funny story.'

Spelling sheet 24: As a class, read the spelling list and the sentences, without filling in the gaps. Revise the conjunctions 'and', 'but', 'because', 'or', 'so' and 'while'. The children complete the words in the spelling list by writing in the missing letter pattern. Then they work through the exercises on the sheet.

Dictation: Read the words and sentences for the children to write down. The Dictation Master on page 175 may be photocopied onto the back of the spelling sheets for the children to write on.

Spelling list: Read the spelling words with the children. Point out that the /ai/ sound in 'baby' and 'lady' is spelt ‹a›. Go over the number words '**zero**' and '**equals**'. Point out that the /oa/ sound in 'zero' is spelt ‹o›. It helps the children remember the spelling of 'equals' if they emphasise the /a/ sound in the second syllable, pronouncing it to rhyme with 'pals'.

Dictation

1. silly
2. hurry
3. cherry
4. puppy
5. lazy
6. history

1. Their baby was noisy but happy.
2. I am sorry I used your lucky penny.
3. Our teacher read us a funny fairy story.

Spelling List 24

1. grip
2. milk
3. baby
4. lady
5. holly
6. fairy
7. happy
8. family
9. **zero**
10. **equals**

Spelling List

1. grip
2. milk
3. bab _
4. lad _
5. holl _
6. fair _
7. happ _
8. famil _
9. zero
10. equals

‹**y**› at the end

Write some words with ‹y› at the end, in the holly leaves.

Choose a word from the list to fit each sentence.

1. The ______________ sat on a toadstool.
2. She smiled because she was ______________.
3. The ______________ is asleep in his pram.
4. There are two children in my ______________.

zero (0)

z __ r __

__ e __ o

__ __ __ o

equals (=)

e __ u __ l __

__ q __ a __ s

e __ __ __ __ s

Complete each sentence with a conjunction. *Purple*

and   but   because   or   so   while

1. We went indoors ______________ it started to rain.
2. I tried to catch the ball ______________ I missed it.
3. Would you rather have cake ______________ ice cream?
4. I would like apple pie ______________ cream, please.

Grammar 24 – Plurals: ‹-s› and ‹-ies›

Aim: Develop the children's knowledge of plurals. If a noun ends with the letter ‹y› after a vowel, the plural is made by adding ‹-s›. If a noun ends with the letter ‹y› after a consonant, the plural is made by replacing the ‹y› with ‹i› and adding ‹-es›.

Introduction: Revise vowels and consonants. Revise the concept of singular and plural. Revise the plural endings covered so far. Remind the children that the simplest way of making a plural is by adding an ‹-s› to the end of the noun. Words ending in ‹sh›, ‹ch› for the /ch/ sound, ‹s› and ‹x› make the plural by adding ‹-es›. With the children, think of some examples and write them on the board.

Main point: Explain that some words make the plural differently. Tell the children to be careful when making the plural of a noun which ends with the letter ‹y›. If the letter before the ‹y› is a vowel, then the plural is made by adding ‹-s›, e.g. 'boy' becomes 'boys'. However, if the letter before the ‹y› is a consonant, then the plural is made by first replacing the ‹y› with ‹i›, and then adding ‹-es›, e.g. 'daisy' becomes 'daisies'. In these cases, because in the plural the 'shy ‹i›' is not at the very end of the word, it no longer needs to be replaced by 'toughy ‹y›'.

Examples:	'day' becomes 'days'	'fly' becomes 'flies'
	'key' becomes 'keys'	'puppy' becomes 'puppies'
	'toy' becomes 'toys'	'party' becomes 'parties'
	'turkey' becomes 'turkeys'	'mystery' becomes 'mysteries'

Grammar sheet 24: The children read each noun and decide how to make its plural. They write the plural on the line. Then they draw a picture for it in the daisy, remembering to show more than one item.

Extension activity: Write some singular nouns on the board. Use words with ‹-s›, ‹-es› and ‹-ies› plurals. Ask the children to write the plural for each word. The Writing Master on page 176 may be photocopied onto the back of the grammar sheets for the children to write on.

Rounding off: Go over the sheet with the class.

Plurals – ‹-s› and ‹-ies›

Write the plural for each word in the leaf. Then draw a picture for it in the daisy.

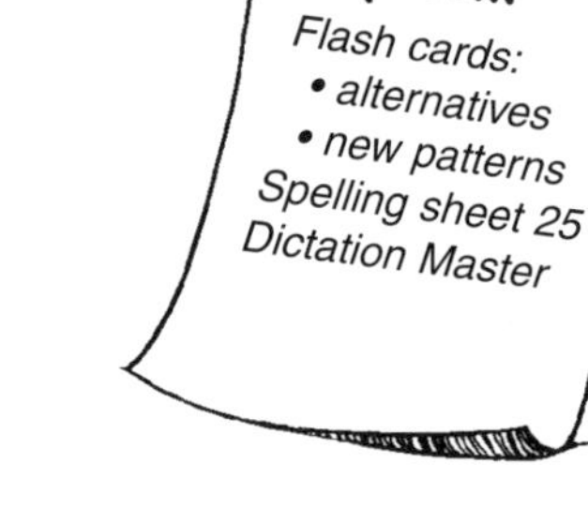

Spelling 25 – **silent ‹h›**

Revision: Revise some of the spelling patterns and tricky words covered so far this year.

Main point: Some letters in words are silent. Revise some 'silent ‹b›' words (e.g. 'lamb'), 'silent ‹w›' words (e.g. 'wreck') and 'silent ‹k›' words (e.g. 'knight'). Introduce '**silent ‹h›**' by writing 'rhinoceros' on the board. Read the word to the children and ask what it means. Ask which of its letters is silent. Write some more 'silent ‹h›' words on the board and read them together. Then read them again, this time pronouncing every sound, so 'rhubarb' would be /r-**h**oobarb/, for example. This helps the children remember the spelling. With the children, make a list of 'silent ‹h›' words. To help them remember the words, the children could try making up silly sentences using as many of the words as possible, e.g. 'John the honest ghost liked rhythm and rhyme.'

Spelling sheet 25: As a class, read the spelling list and the sentences, without filling in the gaps. Revise the plural endings ‹-s› and ‹-ies›. The children complete the words in the spelling list by writing in the missing letter pattern. Then they work through the exercises on the sheet.

Dictation: Read the words and sentences for the children to write down. The Dictation Master on page 175 may be photocopied onto the back of the spelling sheets for the children to write on.

Spelling list: Read the spelling words with the children. Point out that the /oa/ sound in 'ghost' is spelt ‹o›; the /ie/ sound in 'rhyme' is spelt ‹**y_e**›; 'rhythm' has no vowel except ‹y›; and the /s/ sound in 'rhinoceros' is spelt with a 'soft ‹c›'. Go over the measurement words '**centimetre**' and '**metre**', which are only slightly irregular. Point out that the /er/ sound at the end of each word is spelt ‹re›, and that the /s/ sound in 'centimetre' is spelt with a 'soft ‹c›'. The prefix 'centi-' comes from the Latin word for a hundredth, because there are a hundred centimetres in a metre.

Dictation

1. John
2. hour
3. honest
4. rhubarb
5. ghastly
6. rhombus

1. The keys are by the hourglass.
2. That house is haunted by a ghost!
3. My family likes poems with rhythm and rhyme.

Spelling List 25

1. belt
2. farm
3. hour
4. ghost
5. rhyme
6. rhythm
7. honest
8. rhinoceros
9. **centimetre**
10. **metre**

Spelling List
1. belt
2. farm
3. _ our
4. g _ ost
5. r _ yme
6. r _ ythm
7. _ onest
8. r _ inoceros
9. centimetre
10. metre
Silent ‹h›
Write some 'silent ‹h›' words in the rhinoceros.
Choose a word from the list to fit each sentence.
1. Poems often ________________.
2. The train leaves in one ________________.
3. I trust John because he is ________________.
4. A ________________ is a wild animal.
centimetre
c_n_i_e_r_
_e_t_m_t_e
_ent__et__
metre
m __ t __ e
__ e __ r __
m __ t ____
Each daisy has a noun in it. Write the plural of each noun on the leaf, and draw a picture for it in the daisy.
star
pony
toy
fairy
Spelling sheet 25 (GH2)

Grammar 25 – Word Webs

Aim: Develop the children's ability to use a thesaurus, and encourage them to think carefully about the words they use.

Introduction: Revise the alphabet in the four dictionary groups. Write two sentences on the board which feature commonly overused words.

Examples: "It is my birthday," said Hannah.
The mountain view was nice.

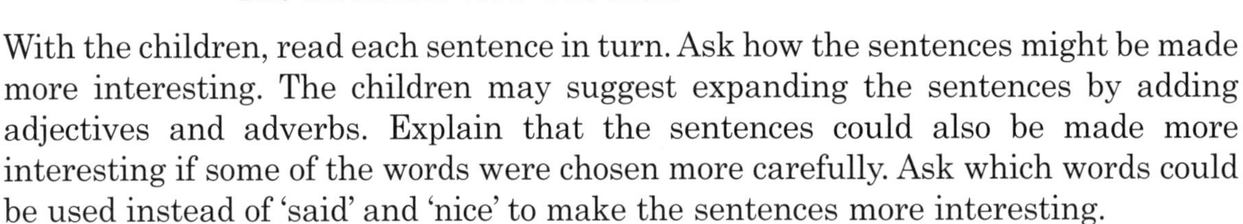

With the children, read each sentence in turn. Ask how the sentences might be made more interesting. The children may suggest expanding the sentences by adding adjectives and adverbs. Explain that the sentences could also be made more interesting if some of the words were chosen more carefully. Ask which words could be used instead of 'said' and 'nice' to make the sentences more interesting.

Word:	*Some possible alternatives:*
said	cried, exclaimed, whispered, announced, replied
nice	pretty, beautiful, glorious, stunning, magnificent

Main point: Show the children a thesaurus. Explain that it lists words with similar meanings. Show the children how to a find a word in it, e.g. 'pretty'. Explain that to find a verb they should look up its root, so for 'said', which is a tricky past, they would look up 'say'. With the children, think of more overused words. These could be written in the middle of the word webs in the *Jolly Grammar Big Book 2.* Make up a sentence for each word. Use a thesaurus to find alternatives for the words. Encourage the children to think about the meaning of the words they find, and about how these words sound in the sentences. Some words will not work in the sentences. If the children come across an unfamiliar word, they can look up its meaning in a dictionary. This will help increase their vocabulary.

Grammar sheet 25: The children read the words in the middle of the word webs. For each word, they write alternatives in the sections of the web. First they write any words they can think of by themselves. Then they use the thesaurus to add to their words.

Word:	*Some possible alternatives:*
angry	furious, enraged, annoyed, irritated, grumpy
quick	fast, rapid, speedy, swift, hasty
pretty	beautiful, attractive, good-looking, lovely, gorgeous

Extension activity: The children find alternatives to more words, using the extension activity on page 212. Possible answers for 'hot' include 'boiling', 'baking' and 'warm'; for 'little': 'small', 'tiny' and 'wee'; and for 'rush': 'hurry', 'dash' and 'race'.

Rounding off: Go over the sheet with the class. See how many different words the children have thought of, or found. Then go over the extension activity.

Word Webs

In the spaces of each word web, write words which could be used instead of the word in the middle.

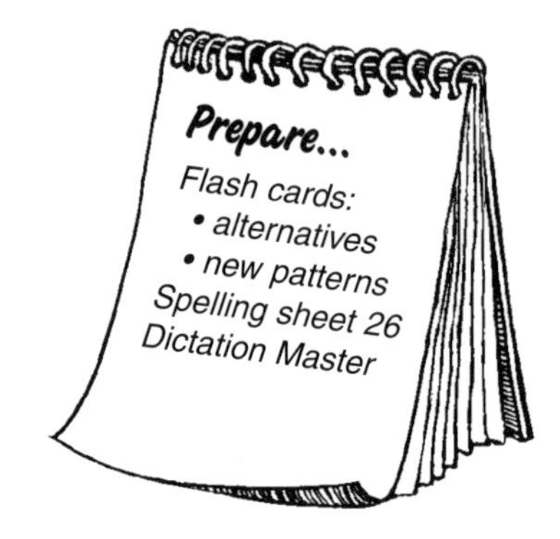

Spelling 26 – **silent ‹c›**

Revision: Revise some of the spelling patterns and tricky words covered so far this year.

Main point: Some letters in words are silent. Revise some 'silent ‹b›' words (e.g. 'lamb'), 'silent ‹w›' words (e.g. 'wreck'), 'silent ‹k›' words (e.g. 'knight') and 'silent ‹h›' words (e.g. 'rhinoceros'). Introduce '**silent ‹c›**' by writing 'crescent' on the board. Read the word to the children and ask what it means. Ask which of its letters is silent. Write some more 'silent ‹c›' words on the board and read them together. Then read them again, this time pronouncing every sound, so 'scent' would be /s**k**ent/, for example. This helps the children remember the spelling. With the children, make a list of 'silent ‹c›' words. To help them remember the words, the children could try making up silly sentences using as many of the words as possible, e.g. 'The muscled scientist cut the scenery with scissors.'

Spelling sheet 26: As a class, read the spelling list and the sentences, without filling in the gaps. Revise word webs. The children complete the words in the spelling list by writing in the missing letter pattern. Then they work through the exercises on the sheet.

Dictation: Read the words and sentences for the children to write down. The Dictation Master on page 175 may be photocopied onto the back of the spelling sheets for the children to write on.

Spelling list: Read the spelling words with the children. Point out that 'scene' takes the unusual ‹e_e› spelling of the /ee/ sound, and that the /ool/ sound in 'muscle' is spelt ‹le›. Explain that the second /s/ sound in 'science' is spelt with a 'soft ‹c›', followed by a 'silent ‹e›'. For 'scissors', point out that the /z/ sound is spelt ‹ss› and the /er/ sound is spelt ‹or›. Go over the measurement words '**gram**' and '**kilogram**'. The prefix 'kilo-' comes from the Greek word for a thousand, because there are a thousand grams in a kilogram.

Dictation

1. scent
2. scenic
3. scenery
4. crescent
5. scissors
6. scimitar

1. We act in the third scene.
2. I honestly like the scent of cherries.
3. Our science homework took hours.

Spelling List 26

1. land
2. quiz
3. scene
4. scent
5. muscle
6. science
7. scissors
8. crescent
9. **gram**
10. **kilogram**

Spelling List

1. land
2. quiz
3. s _ ene
4. s _ ent
5. mus _ le
6. s _ ience
7. s _ issors
8. cres _ ent
9. gram
10. kilogram

Silent ‹c›

Write some 'silent ‹c›' words in the crescent moon.

Choose a word from the list to fit each sentence.

1. A new moon is a ______________ shape.
2. I cut the paper with my ______________.
3. Those flowers have a lovely ______________.
4. We do experiments in ______________.

gram

g __ a __
__ r __ m
g __ __ __

kilogram

_ i _ _ g _ _ m
k _ _ o _ r _ _
_ _ l _ g _ a _

In the spaces of each word web, write words which could be used instead of the word in the middle.

cold

sad

happy

Grammar 26 – Proofreading a Story

Aim: Develop the children's ability to proofread text, paying particular attention to punctuation.

Introduction: Revise sentences, and the punctuation covered so far: full stops, question marks, exclamation marks, speech marks, and commas in lists. Remind the children that punctuation is important because it helps us make sense of the words we read. Without punctuation, writing can be hard to understand. On the board, write some sentences without any punctuation. Punctuate them with the children.

Examples:
Do you know what the time is asked Belinda
My presents were a kite a book a paintbox and a box of chocolates
Oh no I told you not to do that yelled the furious man

Main point: As a class, either read and punctuate the story on Grammar sheet 26, or write a passage on the board to punctuate together.

Example:
aunt carol was going shopping she decided to take her umbrella when she arrived at the shop she put her umbrella in a stand she hurried as she chose soap cornflakes eggs and bread then she rushed home later that day she remembered that she had left her umbrella in the shop oh dear she exclaimed i shall have to go back and get it

Grammar sheet 26: The children proofread the passage on the sheet. Using coloured pencils, they correct the spelling and add in the punctuation where necessary. The correctly-spelt words can be written above the misspelt ones. The children use the checklist to help them find the right number of mistakes.

Extension activity: The children imagine what might happen next and continue the story. The Writing Master on page 176 may be photocopied onto the back of the grammar sheets for the children to write on.

Rounding off: Go over the sheet, with the class identifying the mistakes. (See corrected passage below, with corrections marked in bold.)

Farmer **B**rown has lots of animals on his farm**. H**e has rab**b**its**,** pigs**,** cows**,** horses**,** a donke**y** and a goat**. T**he goat has a very bad temper and butts his horns against the tree trun**k** w**h**en he is angry**. I**t w**a**s **Mo**nday morning and **F**armer **B**rown was fe**e**ding his animals**.**

"Good morning**,"** he called to the horses**. "H**ere is your ha**y." H**e gave the goat a big bag of oats**. J**ust then a little robin flew down and started pec**k**ing at them**.**

"Those are mine**!"** sho**u**ted the goat**.**

Proofreading a Story

After writing something, it is a good idea to read it through, to make sure there are not any mistakes.

This is the beginning of a story. Read it through, correcting the spelling mistakes, and adding in punctuation and capital letters.

farmer brown has lots of animals on his farm he has rabits pigs cows horses a donkee and a goat the goat has a very bad temper and butts his horns against the tree trunc wen he is angry it wos munday morning and farmer brown was feding his animals good morning, he called to the horses here is your hai he gave the goat a big bag of oats just then a little robin flew down and started peking at them those are mine showted the goat

There are 13 missing capital letters, 9 missing full stops, 4 missing commas, 6 missing speech marks, 1 missing exclamation mark and 10 spelling mistakes.

What do you think might happen next?

Continue the story on the back of the sheet, remembering to proof-read your work when you have finished.

Spelling 27 – ‹**are**› for the **/air/** sound

Revision: Revise some of the spelling patterns and tricky words covered so far this year.

Main point: Introduce the ‹**are**› spelling of the /air/ sound. The /air/ sound was first introduced in Spelling 11 since it is relatively unusual. The main ways of writing the /air/ sound are ‹air›, ‹are› and ‹ear›. With the children, make a list of words which use the ‹are› spelling of the /air/ sound. To help them remember the words, the children could try making up silly sentences using as many of the words as possible, e.g. 'I dare you to scare the spare mare in the square.'

Spelling sheet 27: As a class, read the spelling list and the sentences, without filling in the gaps. Revise how to proofread a story. The children complete the words in the spelling list by writing in the missing letter pattern. Then they work through the exercises on the sheet.

Dictation: Read the words and sentences for the children to write down. The Dictation Master on page 175 may be photocopied onto the back of the spelling sheets for the children to write on.

Spelling list: Read the spelling words with the children. Point out that the /k/ sound in 'scare' is spelt with a ‹c›. Go over the measurement words '**millilitre**' and '**litre**'. Point out that the /er/ sound at the end of each word is spelt ‹re›. The prefix 'milli-' comes from the Latin word for a thousandth, because there are a thousand millilitres in a litre.

Dictation

1. fare
2. bare
3. share
4. flare
5. dare
6. compare

1. This story is about hares.
2. The mare had a foal last winter.
3. The spare wheel is in the back of the truck.

Spelling List 27

1. film
2. kept
3. hare
4. care
5. share
6. scare
7. square
8. nightmare
9. **millilitre**
10. **litre**

Spelling List

1. film
2. kept
3. h_ _ _
4. c_ _ _
5. sh_ _ _
6. sc_ _ _
7. squ_ _ _
8. nightm_ _ _
9. millilitre
10. litre

‹**are**› for the /air/ sound

Write some ‹are› words in the hare.

Choose a word from the list to fit each sentence.

1. Tim takes ________________ of his pets.
2. We must ________________ the sweets fairly.
3. A ________________ is bigger than a rabbit.
4. She woke from a frightening ________________.

millilitre

m_l_i_i_r_

_i_l_l_t_e

_ill_l_t_ _

litre

l __ t __ e

__ i __ r __

l __ t __ __

Proofread this story.

the goat wos very angry that the robin had stolen sum of his brekfast he snorted and stamped his hooves the robin floo up into the oak tree and started singin the goat was so angry that he charged the tree Crash a larje branch fell on top ov him oh dear exclaimed farmer brown i shal have to go and get my tractor to get you owt.

Grammar 27 – Prefixes

Aim: Develop the children's understanding of prefixes. A prefix is one or more syllables added at the beginning of a word to change its meaning.

Introduction: Revise using the dictionary to find out what a word means. Think of some words which have meanings that the children are unlikely to know, and write them on the board. If preferred, the words might all be related to a particular topic. Make sure the words are included in the dictionary being used. This can be either an individual or a class activity.

Main point: Explain that a **prefix** is one or more syllables added at the beginning of a word to change its meaning, such as ‹un-› in 'unhappy', 'unkind' and 'unlike'. On the board, write the base words 'happy', 'kind' and 'like'. Read each word with the children, and ask them what it means. Explain that 'like' has more than one meaning. It can function either as a verb, meaning 'to enjoy' or 'to be fond of', or as an adjective, meaning 'similar to' or 'such as'. Write the prefix ‹un-› at the beginning of each of the three base words. Read each new word with the children, and ask them what it means. Now write the base word 'like' again. This time write the prefix ‹dis-› before it. Read the new word 'dislike' with the children, and ask them what it means. Explain that there are many prefixes. Four of the most useful ones are **‹un-›**, **‹dis-›**, **‹mis-›** and **‹im-›**. Write these four prefixes on the board and ask the children for any words that start with them. Write some of the children's suggestions on the board. Erase the prefixes and read each new word with the children. Explain that the word remaining is called the 'base word'.

Grammar sheet 27: As a class, read the prefixes at the top of the sheet. The children choose a prefix to complete each of the sentences, and write it on the line before the base word. Then they choose a prefix to go before each of the base words in the fish bodies, and write it in the fish head.

Extension activity: The children look up their words in the dictionary to see whether the prefixes they chose were correct. Alternatively they match more prefixes with base words, using the extension activity on page 200. The extension activity introduces five more useful prefixes, which are ‹de-›, ‹mid-›, ‹non-›, ‹semi-› and ‹re-›.

Rounding off: Go over the sheet with the class. Then go over the extension activity.

Prefixes

There are many prefixes, but these are four of the most useful ones.

Choose a prefix to go in front of each of the base words, and write it on the line. Then see how the meaning of the words and sentences has changed.

1. It was _____possible to walk along the path.
2. I really _____like writing stories in school.
3. Mum _____packed the holiday suitcases.
4. Jason _____understood what he had to do.

Choose a prefix to go in front of each of the base words in the fish bodies, and write it on the line in the fish's head.

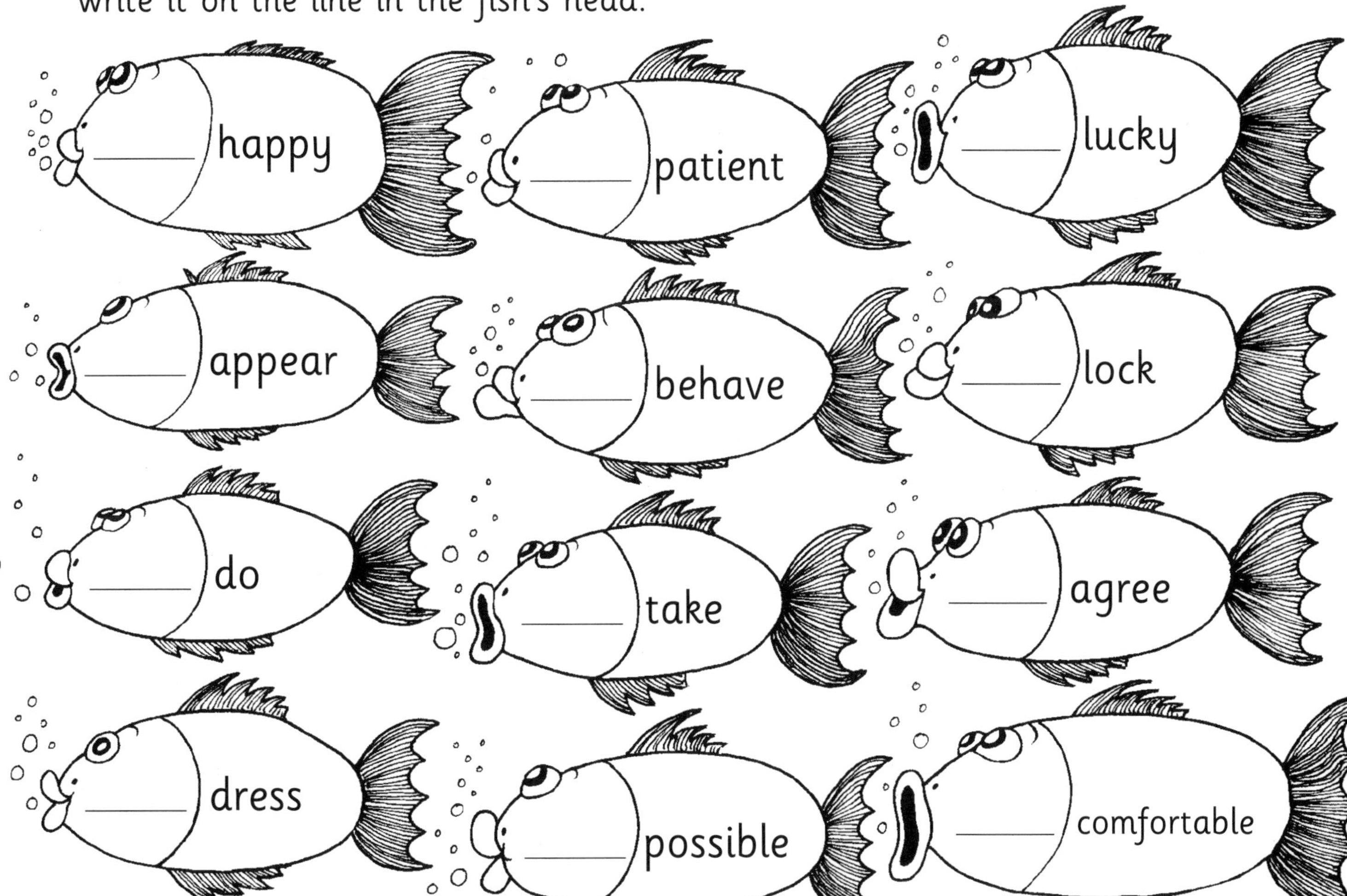

You can use a dictionary to check whether you have chosen the right prefixes.

Prepare...
Flash cards:
• alternatives
• new patterns
Spelling sheet 28
Dictation Master

Spelling 28 – ‹**ear**› for the **/air/** sound

Revision: Revise some of the spelling patterns and tricky words covered so far this year.

Main point: Introduce the ‹**ear**› spelling of the /air/ sound. The /air/ sound was first introduced in Spelling 11. The main ways of writing it are ‹air›, ‹are› and ‹ear›. With the children, make a list of words which use the ‹ear› spelling of the /air/ sound. The four most common words are 'bear', 'tear', 'wear' and 'pear'. To help them remember these words, the children could try making up silly sentences using as many of the words as possible, e.g. 'The bear eats pears in his underwear.'

Spelling sheet 28: As a class, read the spelling list and the sentences, without filling in the gaps. Revise prefixes, and introduce the prefixes ‹tri-› and ‹tele-›. The children complete the words in the spelling list by writing in the missing letter pattern. Then they work through the exercises on the sheet.

Dictation: Read the words and sentences for the children to write down. The Dictation Master on page 175 may be photocopied onto the back of the spelling sheets for the children to write on.

Spelling list: Read the spelling words with the children. Go over the measurement words '**weight**' and '**volume**'. Point out that the /ai/ sound in 'weight' is spelt ‹eigh› and that the /ue/ sound in 'volume' is spelt ‹u_e›.

Dictation

1. wear
2. bear
3. pear
4. tearing
5. wearing
6. bearing

1. She ate pears with honey.
2. I cannot bear the way he swears.
3. The orchestra wears orange.

Spelling List 28

1. grip
2. milk
3. bear
4. tear
5. pear
6. wear
7. swear
8. underwear
9. **weight**
10. **volume**

Spelling List

1. grip
2. milk
3. b _ _ _
4. t _ _ _
5. p _ _ _
6. w _ _ _
7. sw _ _ _
8. underw _ _ _
9. weight
10. volume

‹**ear**› for the /air/ sound

Write some ‹ear› words in the bear.

Choose a word from the list to fit each sentence.

1. I shall ______________ my new shoes.
2. The ______________ was green and juicy.
3. Be careful not to ______________ the paper!
4. I like to cuddle my teddy ______________.

weight

_ e _ g _ t

w _ i _ h _

w _ _ _ _ t

volume

_ o _ u _ e

v _ l _ m _

v _ _ _ _ _

Make new words by joining the prefixes and base words below.

tri   tele

scope   angle   cycle   vision

______________   ______________   ______________   ______________

Prepare...
(J.G. Big Book 2)
(Poem, p. 217)
Grammar sheet 28
Writing Master

Grammar 28 – Apostrophe ‹s›

Aim: Develop the children's knowledge of what an apostrophe is, and of how to use an apostrophe with the letter ‹s›, to indicate possession.

Introduction: Revise the punctuation covered so far: full stops, question marks, exclamation marks, speech marks, and commas in lists. Remind the children that punctuation is important because it helps us make sense of the words we read.

Main point: To show that something belongs to someone, we add an **apostrophe** with the letter **‹s›** after their name, as in 'Tiffany's bike' and 'Luke's sister'. The apostrophe is needed to show that the ‹s› is not being used to make the plural. Show the children how to write an apostrophe, and where to position it above the line. Use the children's own possessions to give them examples, such as 'This is Rebecca's lunch box', 'These are Danny's shoes', or 'This is Jeremy's toy'. Write some of these examples on the board, pointing out each apostrophe ‹s›. Explain that the word 'this' is used when the possession is singular, and 'these' is used when the possessions are plural. The Apostrophe ‹s› Poem on page 217 may be enlarged, using a photocopier. Read it with the children.

Grammar sheet 28: The children write inside each apostrophe ‹s› at the top of the sheet. Then they complete the 'Belonging Poem'. First they think of a person's name for each letter of the alphabet. Then, after each name, the children write an apostrophe ‹s›, followed by something that person might own. Each possession should begin with the same letter as its owner's name. Tell the children to write a comma at the end of every line except the last one, where they write a full stop.

Extension activity: The children choose items from their 'Belonging Poem' and write sentences to describe them. In each case, they try to think of an adjective beginning with the same letter as the person's name. Alternatively they could try writing another 'Belonging Poem' in rhyming couplets.

Examples:	Anna's apple is awful.	Anna's cat,
	Ben's book is brilliant.	Ben's bat,
	Claire's cats are clever.	Claire's hair,
	Dan's dad is daring.	Dan's chair,

The Writing Master on page 176 may be photocopied onto the back of the grammar sheets for the children to write on.

Rounding off: Go over the sheet with the class. Ask each child to share one line from their 'Belonging Poem' with the rest of the class.

Apostrophe ‹s›

An apostrophe ‹s› shows that something belongs to someone.
Write inside each outlined apostrophe ‹s›.

's 's 's 's 's 's 's 's 's

Belonging Poem

Think of a person's name for each letter of the alphabet. Then think of something that person might own, that begins with the same letter as their name. Remember to use an apostrophe ‹s› after each name, to show that the next word is something belonging to the person.

Anna's apple,
Ben's book,
Claire's
D
E
F
G
H
I
J
K
L
M

N
O
P
Quentin's
R
S
T
U
V
W
Xander's
Y
Zoe's

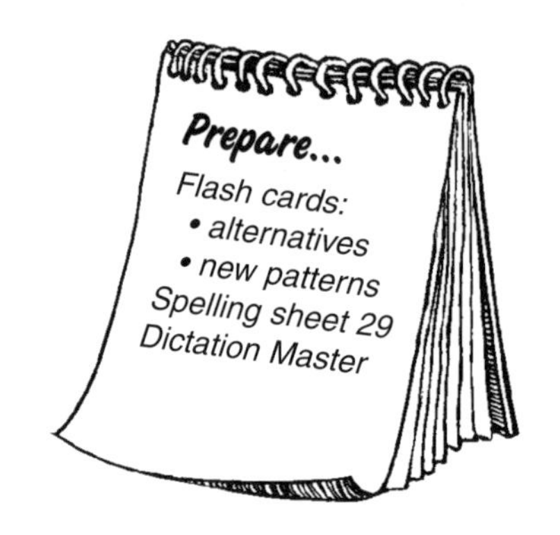

Spelling 29 – ‹**tion**›

Revision: Revise some of the spelling patterns and tricky words covered so far this year.

Main point: Introduce the ‹**tion**› spelling. At the end of a multi-syllabic word, this sounds something like /shun/. The /u/ sound in the middle is a swallowed sound, known as a 'schwa', as made by ‹er› in 'butter', for example. Although this sounds complicated, the children should have no problem with the ‹tion› spelling in context. They should listen to the sounds at the end of a word like 'station', and use analogy to spell these sounds in other words. With the children, make a list of words which use the ‹tion› spelling. To help them remember the words, the children could try making up silly sentences using as many of the words as possible, e.g. 'My relation went in the direction of the station junction.'

Spelling sheet 29: As a class, read the spelling list and the sentences, without filling in the gaps. Revise how to use apostrophe ‹s›. The children complete the words in the spelling list by writing in the missing letter pattern. Then they work through the exercises on the sheet.

Dictation: Read the words and sentences for the children to write down. The Dictation Master on page 175 may be photocopied onto the back of the spelling sheets for the children to write on.

Spelling list: Read the spelling words with the children. Point out that the /ai/ sounds in 'nation', 'station' and 'relation' are spelt ‹a›. Go over the time measurement words '**minute**' and '**second**'. It helps the children remember the spelling of 'minute' if they emphasise the 'long /ue/' sound in the second syllable, pronouncing it to rhyme with 'cute'. Similarly, it helps them remember the spelling of 'second' if they emphasise the 'short /o/' in the second syllable, pronouncing it to rhyme with 'pond'.

Dictation

1. lotion
2. infection
3. mention
4. direction
5. invention
6. collection

1. He swears he can see his reflection.
2. There is a junction near the station.
3. Shall I mention the Christmas decorations?

Spelling List 29

1. must
2. stuck
3. nation
4. station
5. relation
6. action
7. fiction
8. dictionary
9. **minute**
10. **second**

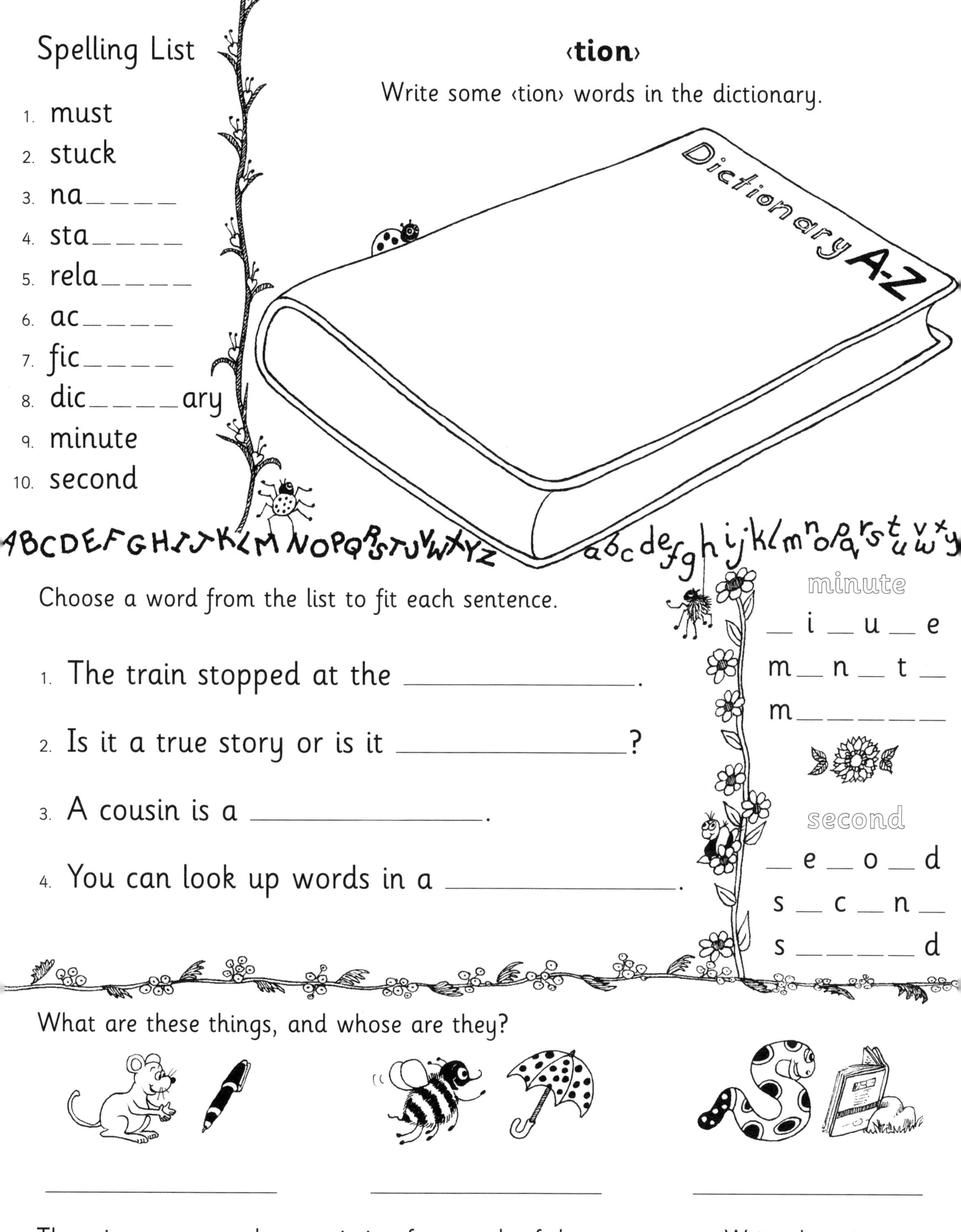

Spelling List

1. must
2. stuck
3. na_ _ _ _
4. sta_ _ _ _
5. rela_ _ _ _
6. ac_ _ _ _
7. fic_ _ _ _
8. dic_ _ _ _ary
9. minute
10. second

‹tion›

Write some ‹tion› words in the dictionary.

Choose a word from the list to fit each sentence.

1. The train stopped at the ______________.
2. Is it a true story or is it ______________?
3. A cousin is a ______________.
4. You can look up words in a ______________.

minute

_ i _ u _ e

m _ n _ t _

m _ _ _ _ _

second

_ e _ o _ d

s _ c _ n _

s _ _ _ _ d

What are these things, and whose are they?

______________ ______________ ______________

There is an apostrophe ‹s› missing from each of these sentences. Write them in.

Bee went to Inky house on Saturday morning. Inky liked Bee new red boots.

Grammar 29 – Contractions

Aim: Develop the children's knowledge of what a contraction is, and of how to use an apostrophe to write one. A contraction is the shortened form of a word or words. We use an apostrophe to show where the missing letter or letters used to be.

Introduction: Revise how to use apostrophe ‹s› to indicate belonging. Revise how to use the auxiliary verbs 'shall' and 'will' to describe the future. 'Shall' is added before a verb root for the first person ('I' and 'we'), and 'will' is added before a verb root for the second and third persons. Write some sentences on the board which describe future time, and in which the apostrophe is missing. With the children, identify the future verbs and add in the apostrophes.

Examples: I shall read Uncles book.
She will stroke Davids kittens.

Main point: Explain that an apostrophe is also used to show that a letter or letters are missing. Sometimes we shorten a pair of words by joining them together and leaving out some of their letters. We use an apostrophe to show where the missing letter or letters used to be. This is called a **contraction**. Write the word pair 'is not' on the board, and read it with the children. Now say the word pair in its shortened form, as the contraction 'isn't'. Ask which letter or letters have been left out. Erase the ‹o› from 'not', and replace it with an apostrophe. Explain that a contraction is always written as one word, not two. Repeat this exercise with other word pairs, such as 'does not' ('doesn't'), 'did not' ('didn't') and 'I shall'. In its shortened form, 'I shall' becomes 'I'll', and the apostrophe replaces the three missing letters ‹sha›.

Grammar sheet 29: In the first exercise, the children write out each contraction in full, as two words and with no letters missing. In the second exercise, they write each word pair as a contraction, missing out the appropriate letters and replacing them with an apostrophe.

Extension activity: Write more word pairs on the board for the children to write as contractions, and more contractions for the children to write out in full. The Writing Master on page 176 may be photocopied onto the back of the grammar sheets for the children to write on.

Rounding off: Go over the sheet with the class.

Contractions

We sometimes shorten pairs of words, by joining them together and leaving out some of the letters. We use an apostrophe to show where the missing letter or letters used to be. These shortened words are called contractions.

isn't

Write out each contraction in full, as two words and with no letters missing.

1. couldn't ________________
2. didn't ________________
3. haven't ________________
4. mustn't ________________

I shall **I'll**

Write each pair of words as a contraction, by joining them together and replacing some of the letters with an apostrophe.

I shall	I'll	we shall	____________
you will	you'll	you will	____________
he will	____________	they will	____________
she will	____________		
it will	____________		

We use contractions when we speak. They should not be used in writing except when writing speech, or in a friendly note.

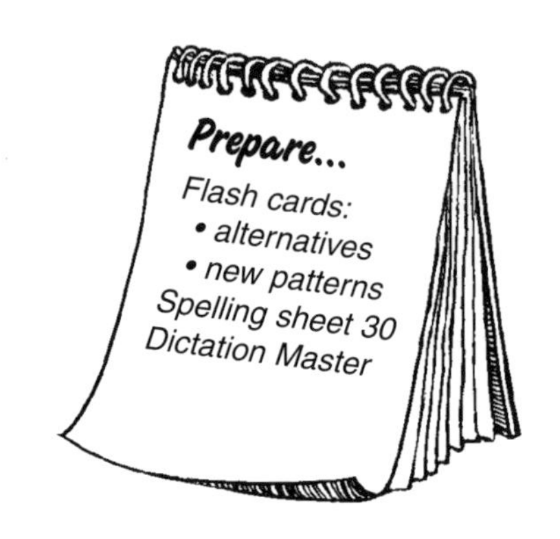

Spelling 30 – ‹**sion**›

Revision: Revise some of the spelling patterns and tricky words covered so far this year.

Main point: Introduce the ‹**sion**› spelling. At the end of a multi-syllabic word, this sounds something like /shun/. The /sh/ has a 'buzz' to it, as made by ‹s› in 'treasure', for example. The /u/ sound in the middle is a swallowed sound, known as a 'schwa', as is also found in words with the ‹tion› spelling. Although this sounds complicated, the children should have no problem with the ‹sion› spelling in context. They should listen to the sounds at the end of a word like 'invasion', and use analogy to spell these sounds in other words. With the children, make a list of words which use the ‹sion› spelling. To help them remember the words, the children could try making up silly sentences using as many of the words as possible, e.g. 'On this occasion we asked permission to watch the explosion on television.'

Spelling sheet 30: As a class, read the spelling list and the sentences, without filling in the gaps. Revise contractions. The children complete the words in the spelling list by writing in the missing letter pattern. Then they work through the exercises on the sheet.

Dictation: Read the words and sentences for the children to write down. The Dictation Master on page 175 may be photocopied onto the back of the spelling sheets for the children to write on.

Spelling list: Read the spelling words with the children. Point out that the ‹c› in 'occasion' is doubled with a ‹c›, not a ‹k›. Explain that the /ai/ sound in 'invasion' is spelt ‹a› and the /oa/ sound in 'explosion' is spelt ‹o›. Go over the measurement words '**fraction**' and '**estimate**'. Point out that the /shun/ sound at the end of 'fraction' is spelt ‹tion›. It helps the children remember the spelling of 'estimate' if they emphasise the /a_e/ sound in the last syllable, pronouncing it to rhyme with 'plate'.

Dictation

1. vision
2. tension
3. pension
4. division
5. extension
6. permission

1. He honestly needs his pension.
2. There was a huge explosion.
3. They watched television for hours.

Spelling List 30

1. fist
2. best
3. occasion
4. division
5. revision
6. invasion
7. explosion
8. television
9. **fraction**
10. **estimate**

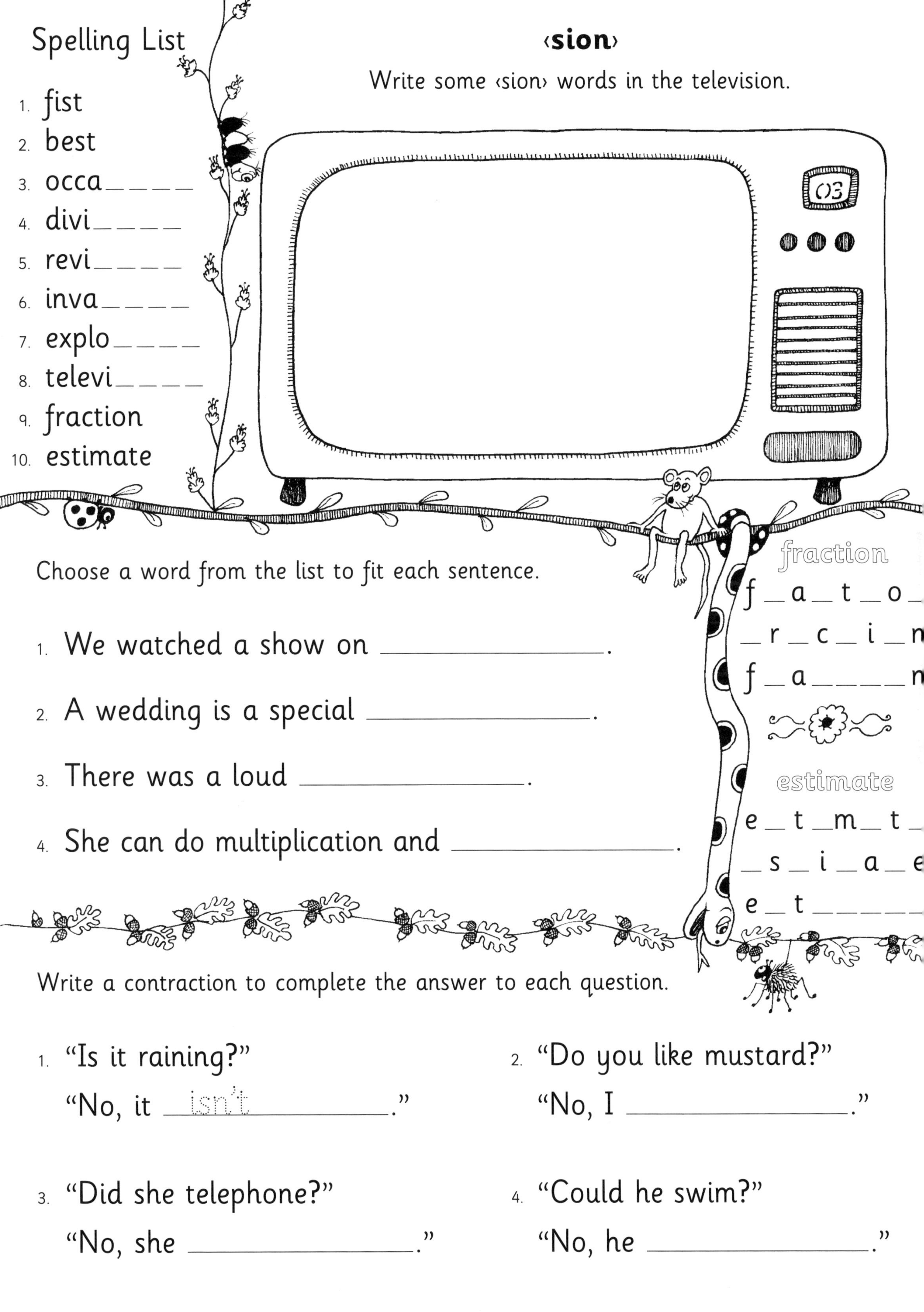

Spelling List

1. fist
2. best
3. occa_ _ _ _
4. divi_ _ _ _
5. revi_ _ _ _
6. inva_ _ _ _
7. explo_ _ _ _
8. televi_ _ _ _
9. fraction
10. estimate

‹sion›

Write some ‹sion› words in the television.

Choose a word from the list to fit each sentence.

1. We watched a show on ____________.
2. A wedding is a special ____________.
3. There was a loud ____________.
4. She can do multiplication and ____________.

fraction

f _ a _ t _ o _

_ r _ c _ i _ n

f _ a _ _ _ _ n

estimate

e _ t _ m _ t _

_ s _ i _ a _ e

e _ t _ _ _ _ _

Write a contraction to complete the answer to each question.

1. "Is it raining?"
"No, it isn't."

2. "Do you like mustard?"
"No, I ____________."

3. "Did she telephone?"
"No, she ____________."

4. "Could he swim?"
"No, he ____________."

Grammar 30 – Prepositions

Aim: Develop the children's understanding of prepositions. A preposition is a word that relates one noun or pronoun to another, often by describing where it is, or where it is moving towards.

Introduction: Revise the parts of speech covered so far: proper and common nouns, pronouns, adjectives, possessive adjectives, verbs, adverbs and conjunctions. Write some sentences on the board which feature prepositions. With the children, identify the parts of speech that have already been covered.

Examples: Bee^{N} flies^{V} over^{Pre} the wood^{N}.
Snake^{N} slithered^{V} slowly^{Adv} into^{Pre} a dark^{Adj} hole^{N}.
I^{P} dropped^{V} my^{Adj} pencil^{N} and^{C} it^{P} rolled^{V} under^{Pre} a chair^{N}.

Key: Noun^{N} Verb^{V} Pronoun^{P} Adjective^{Adj} Adverb^{Adv} Conjunction^{C} Preposition^{Pre}

Main point: Introduce **prepositions**. A preposition is a word that relates a noun or pronoun to another word in the sentence, often by describing where it is, or where it is moving towards. In the first example above, for instance, the preposition 'over' describes where Bee is moving in relation to the wood. Explain that 'pre' means 'before' and 'position' means 'place'. Together, 'preposition' means 'placed before', because a preposition is usually placed before a noun. A preposition is also placed before any describing words which may already come before the noun, such as adjectives, possessive adjectives or the articles 'a', 'an' or 'the'. In the second example above, for instance, the preposition 'into' comes before the article 'a' and the adjective 'dark'. With the children, identify the preposition in each of the example sentences, and underline it in green. Ask where else Bee might fly. With the children, make a list and identify the prepositions. The Prepositions Poem on page 218 may be enlarged, using a photocopier. Read it with the children.

Action: The action for prepositions is to point from one noun to another.

Colour: The colour for prepositions is green.

Grammar sheet 30: As a class, read the prepositions listed on either side of the sheet. The children write inside the outlined word, Prepositions, using a green pencil. Then they choose a preposition to complete each stage of Inky's journey. The children's answers are right as long as the prepositions chosen make sense in the sentence.

Extension activity: The children draw a picture map of Inky's journey, showing where she went and how she did so.

Rounding off: Ask some of the children to read out their work.

Green

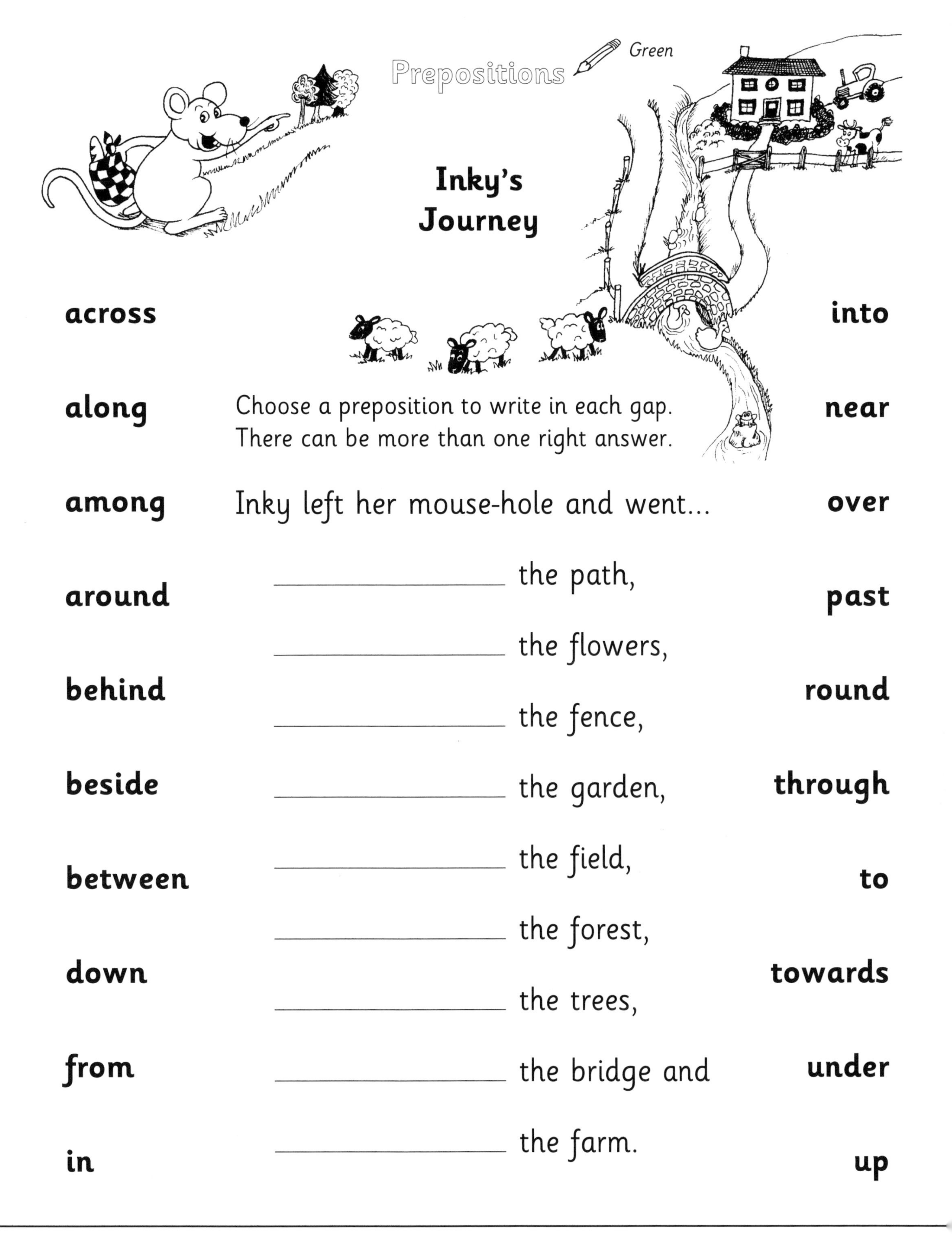

Inky's Journey

Choose a preposition to write in each gap.
There can be more than one right answer.

Inky left her mouse-hole and went...

________________ the path,

________________ the flowers,

________________ the fence,

________________ the garden,

________________ the field,

________________ the forest,

________________ the trees,

________________ the bridge and

________________ the farm.

across
along
among
around
behind
beside
between
down
from
in

into
near
over
past
round
through
to
towards
under
up

Action: Point from one noun to another.

Colour: Green

Prepare...
Flash cards:
• alternatives
• new patterns
Spelling sheet 31
Green pencils
Dictation Master

Spelling 31 – ‹**ei**› and ‹**eigh**›

Revision: Revise some of the spelling patterns and tricky words covered so far this year.

Main point: Most words with an /ai/ sound take the ‹ai›, ‹a_e› or ‹ay› spellings, but there are a number of exceptions which take ‹**ei**› or ‹**eigh**›. These need to be learnt. With the children, make a list of words which use ‹ei› or ‹eigh›. To help them remember the words, the children could try making up silly sentences using as many of the words as possible, e.g. 'Eight veiled neighbours weighed down the reindeer's sleigh.'

Spelling sheet 31: As a class, read the spelling list and the sentences, without filling in the gaps. Revise prepositions. The children complete the words in the spelling list by writing in the missing letter patterns. Then they work through the exercises on the sheet.

Dictation: Read the words and sentences for the children to write down. It may be necessary to explain the meaning of some of the harder words, such as 'vein' (a blood vessel). The Dictation Master on page 175 may be photocopied onto the back of the spelling sheets for the children to write on.

Spelling list: Read the spelling words with the children. Explain that 'eighty' has a 'toughy ‹y›' at the end. It helps the children remember the spelling of 'neighbour' if they emphasise the /ou/ sound in the second syllable, pronouncing it to rhyme with 'flour'. Go over '**child**' and its tricky plural, '**children**'.

Dictation

1. veil
2. vein
3. reins
4. sleigh
5. neigh
6. weight

1. That dictionary weighs a lot.
2. The horse neighed at my friend.
3. There are eight blackbirds in the pear tree.

Spelling List 31

1. grub
2. slug
3. eight
4. eighteen
5. eighty
6. weigh
7. reindeer
8. neighbour
9. **child**
10. **children**

Spelling List

1. grub
2. slug
3. _ _ _ _ _ t
4. _ _ _ _ _ teen
5. _ _ _ _ _ ty
6. w _ _ _ _ _
7. r _ _ ndeer
8. n _ _ _ _ _ bour
9. child
10. children

‹ei› / ‹eigh›

Write some ‹ei› and ‹eigh› words in the reindeer.

Choose a word from the list to fit each sentence.

1. Four plus four equals ________________.
2. Eight tens are ________________.
3. She is our next-door ________________.
4. A ________________ has antlers.

child

c __ i __ d

__ h __ l __

__ __ i __ __

children

c _ i _ d _ e _

_ h _ l _ r _ n

__ __ l __ __ n

Complete each sentence with a preposition. *Green*

to   from   in   beside   up

1. I want to sit ________________ my best friend.
2. Kayla climbed ________________ the ladder.
3. We read ________________ left ________________ right.
4. Grandpa keeps his keys ________________ his pocket.

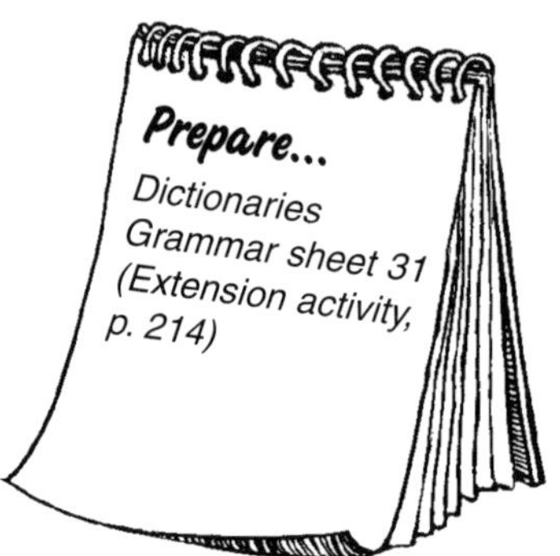

Grammar 31 – Finding the Meaning

Aim: Develop the children's ability to find words in the dictionary, and their familiarity with using it to find the meaning. Develop their understanding of homophones, and their ability to choose between homophones in their writing.

Introduction: Revise the alphabet in the four dictionary groups. Call out a letter. See how quickly the children can find the section of the dictionary for that letter. Repeat with other letters. Remind the children how to look up a word in the dictionary. Call out a word and see if the children can find it in the dictionary. Repeat with other words. Make sure all the words chosen are included in the dictionaries being used.

Main point: Remind the children that a dictionary can help by showing what a word means as well as how it is spelt. If they come across an unfamiliar word in their reading, the children can look up its meaning in a dictionary. Call out an unusual word and see how quickly the children can find its meaning in the dictionary. The first child to find the meaning reads it to the class. Repeat with other words. Make sure all the words chosen are included in the dictionaries being used. It may help to write the words on the board, so the children can focus on meaning without worrying about spelling.

Examples: cygnet, quintuplet, horizon

Remind the children that homophones are words that sound similar to one another despite having different meanings and spellings. The children can use a dictionary to check the meaning of a word, to avoid getting confused and using the wrong one in their writing. Otherwise their writing will not make sense.

Grammar sheet 31: As a class, read the pairs of homophones. Then the children use a dictionary to look up each word, and copy its meaning beside it.

Extension activity: The children complete sentences by choosing between two homophones, using the extension activity on page 214.

Rounding off: Go over the sheet with the class. Ask some children to read one of the meanings they found. Go over the extension activity, with the class checking their answers.

Finding the Meaning

Homophones sound the same but have different spellings and meanings.
Use a dictionary to find out which spelling has which meaning.
Write the meaning of each word on the line beside it.

beech ____________________

beach ____________________

flour ____________________

flower ____________________

right ____________________

write ____________________

wait ____________________

weight ____________________

whole ____________________

hole ____________________

meet ____________________

meat ____________________

sea ____________________

see ____________________

hear ____________________

here ____________________

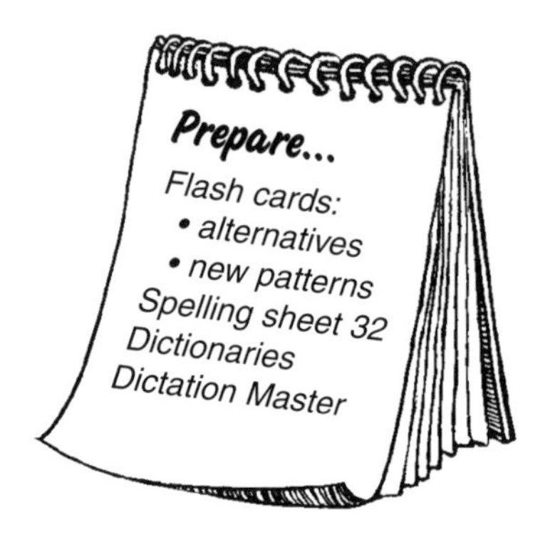

Spelling 32 – ‹**o**› for the **/u/** sound

Revision: Revise some of the spelling patterns and tricky words covered so far this year.

Main point: Most words with an /u/ sound take the ‹u› spelling, but there are a number of exceptions which take ‹**o**›. These need to be learnt. With the children, make a list of words which use the ‹o› spelling of the /u/ sound. To help them remember the words, the children could try making up silly sentences using as many of the words as possible, e.g. 'Somebody's mother's brother's son won dozens of gloves on Monday.'

Spelling sheet 32: As a class, read the spelling list and the sentences, without filling in the gaps. Revise homophones and explain when to use the homophones 'to', 'too' and 'two'. The children complete the words in the spelling list by writing in the missing letter pattern. Then they work through the exercises on the sheet.

Dictation: Read the words and sentences for the children to write down. The Dictation Master on page 175 may be photocopied onto the back of the spelling sheets for the children to write on.

Spelling list: Read the spelling words with the children. Remind them that the /ee/ sound in 'monkey' is spelt ‹ey›. For 'somebody', point out that the ‹d› is not doubled, and that there is a 'toughy ‹y›' at the end. Go over '**woman**' and its tricky plural, '**women**'. It helps the children remember the spelling of both words if they emphasise the 'long ‹o›' sound in the first syllable, pronouncing it to rhyme with 'home'.

Dictation

1. won
2. come
3. Monday
4. money
5. month
6. comforting

1. We won eight jars of honey.
2. My brother saw the explosion.
3. A wonderful smell was coming from the oven.

Spelling List 32

1. ark
2. clever
3. gloves
4. son
5. front
6. dozen
7. monkey
8. somebody
9. **woman**
10. **women**

Spelling List

1. ark
2. clever
3. gl _ ves
4. s _ n
5. fr _ nt
6. d _ zen
7. m _ nkey
8. s _ mebody
9. woman
10. women

‹o› for the /u/ sound

Write some ‹o› words in the glove.

Choose a word from the list to fit each sentence.

1. There are twelve eggs in a ________________.
2. I put on my hat, scarf and ________________.
3. The ________________ was swinging by his tail.
4. He has two daughters and a ________________.

woman

w _ m _ n

_ o _ a _

_ _ m a n

women

w _ m _ n

_ o _ e _

w o _ _ _

‘to’, ‘too’ or ‘two’?

1. I have ________ cats called Micky and Minnie.
2. We went ________ the mountains for our holidays.
3. There were ________ many of us ________ squeeze into the car.
4. I must go at ________ o’clock. Do you want to come ________?

Grammar 32 – Suffix: ‹-ing›

Aim: Develop the children's understanding of suffixes. A suffix is one or more syllables added at the end of a word to change its meaning.

Introduction: Revise prefixes. A prefix is one or more syllables added at the beginning of a word to change its meaning. Revise the four prefixes covered so far: ‹un-›, ‹dis-›, ‹mis-› and ‹im-›. With the children, think of examples of base words that can be changed with these prefixes. Think of some more prefixes and examples of base words that use them.

Examples:	*Prefix:*	*Meaning:*	*Examples of use with base word:*
	‹centi-›	hundred/hundredth	centipede, centimetre, centigrade
	‹pre-›	before/earlier	prefix, preposition, prehistoric

Main point: Explain that a **suffix** is similar to a prefix. A suffix is one or more syllables added at the end of a word to change its meaning, such as ‹-less› in 'hopeless', 'fearless' and 'harmless'. Ask if the children can think of any other suffixes. They already know the plural suffixes ‹-s›, ‹-es› and ‹-ies›, and they have learnt that the simple past tense of a regular verb is made by adding the suffix ‹-ed› to its root. Another suffix commonly used with verbs is ‹-ing›. Like ‹-ed›, the ‹-ing› suffix may be added in one of three different ways, depending on how the verb root is spelt:

a) If the verb root ends with a consonant which is not immediately after a short, stressed vowel sound, simply add ‹-ing›, e.g. 'jump' becomes 'jumping'.
b) If the verb root ends with the letter ‹e›, remove it before adding ‹-ing›, e.g. 'smile' becomes 'smiling'.
c) If the verb root ends with a consonant immediately after a short, stressed vowel sound, double the final consonant before adding ‹-ing›, e.g. 'pat' becomes 'patting'. Remind the children that the two consonants are needed to make a wall, to prevent 'magic' from the ‹i› jumping over to change the short vowel sound. (See page 23.)

Write some verb roots on the board. As a class, decide how to add ‹-ing› in each case.

Examples:							
	a)	knock	wish	try	look	boil	fight
	b)	save	complete	hide	joke	amuse	tease
	c)	wag	get	spin	drop	hug	plan

Grammar sheet 32: The children write inside the outlined word, Verbs, using a red pencil. Then they read the verb root in each fish body. They decide which way to add the ‹-ing› suffix in the fish tail, and write the new form of the verb on the line below.

Extension activity: The children add three more suffixes to base words, using the extension activities on page 201-3. The suffixes are ‹-ness›, ‹-ful› and ‹-er›.

Rounding off: Go over the sheet, with the children checking that they added each ‹-ing› suffix correctly. Then go over the extension activities.

Suffix – ‹-ing›

One of the most useful suffixes is ‹-ing›. Make new words by adding ‹-ing› to the verb roots, and write them on the lines below.

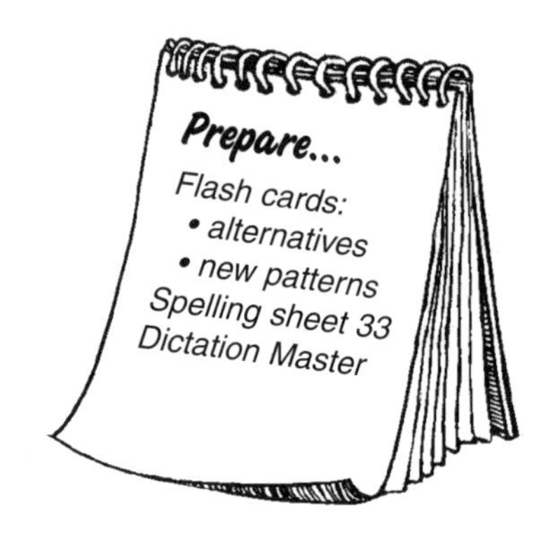

Spelling 33 – ‹**ture**›

Revision: Revise some of the spelling patterns and tricky words covered so far this year.

Main point: Introduce the ‹**ture**› spelling. At the end of a multi-syllabic word, this sounds something like /cher/. The /er/ is a swallowed sound known as a 'schwa', as is also found in words with the ‹tion› and ‹sion› spellings. Although this sounds complicated, the children should have no problem with the ‹ture› spelling in context. They should listen to the sounds at the end of a word like 'mixture', and use analogy to spell these sounds in other words. With the children, make a list of words which use the ‹ture› spelling. To help them remember the words, the children could try making up silly sentences using as many of the words as possible, e.g. 'My future picture will show the creature's nature adventure.'

Spelling sheet 33: As a class, read the spelling list and the sentences, without filling in the gaps. Revise how to add the ‹-ing› suffix. The children complete the words in the spelling list by writing in the missing letter pattern. Then they work through the exercises on the sheet.

Dictation: Read the words and sentences for the children to write down. The Dictation Master on page 175 may be photocopied onto the back of the spelling sheets for the children to write on.

Spelling list: Read the spelling words with the children. Explain that the /ue/ sound in 'future' is spelt ‹u›, the /ai/ sound in 'nature' is spelt ‹a› and the /ee/ sound in 'creature' is spelt ‹ea›. Go over '**mouse**' and its tricky plural, '**mice**'. Point out that the /s/ sound in 'mice' is spelt with a 'soft ‹c›'.

Dictation

1. texture
2. capture
3. fixture
4. vulture
5. structure
6. furniture

1. Your spare wheel has a puncture.
2. Come and photograph this creature.
3. Is the mixture ready to go in the oven?

Spelling List 33

1. shook
2. often
3. picture
4. future
5. nature
6. creature
7. fracture
8. adventure
9. **mouse**
10. **mice**

Spelling List

1. shook
2. often
3. pic_ _ _ _
4. fu_ _ _ _
5. na_ _ _ _
6. crea_ _ _ _
7. frac_ _ _ _
8. adven_ _ _ _
9. mouse
10. mice

‹ture›

Write some ‹ture› words in the picture.

Choose a word from the list to fit each sentence.

1. She painted a beautiful ______________.
2. A dragon is a fantastic ______________.
3. They had an exciting ______________.
4. Tomorrow is in the ______________.

mouse

m __ u __ e

__ o __ s __

m o __ __ __

mice

m __ c __

__ i __ e

m __ __ __

Add the suffix ‹-ing› to each verb root, and write the new word on the line.

make	______________	cook	______________
stop	______________	raise	______________
jump	______________	try	______________
swing	______________	whine	______________

Grammar 33 – Suffixes: ‹-er› and ‹-est›
Comparatives and Superlatives

Aim: Develop the children's understanding of suffixes, and their ability to use suffixes to make comparative and superlative adjectives.

Introduction: Revise suffixes. A suffix is one or more syllables added at the end of a word to change its meaning, such as ‹-ness› in 'goodness', 'lateness' and 'kindness'. Revise the rules for adding a suffix which starts with a vowel. The children have already learnt that a suffix which starts with a vowel may be added in one of three different ways (see Grammar 32). Now tell them to be careful when adding a suffix to a base word which ends with the letter ‹y›. If the letter before the ‹y› is a vowel, they simply add the suffix, e.g. 'grey' becomes 'greyness'. However, if the letter before the ‹y› is a consonant, they replace the ‹y› with ‹i› before adding the suffix, e.g. 'happy' becomes 'happiness'. As with ‹-ies› plurals, because the 'shy ‹i›' is not at the very end of the new word, it no longer needs to be replaced by 'toughy ‹y›'.

Main point: Introduce two new suffixes, **‹-er›** and **‹-est›**. The suffix ‹-er› is added to an adjective to make its **comparative**, and means 'more', e.g. 'small' becomes 'smaller'. The suffix ‹-est› is added to an adjective to make its **superlative**, and means 'most', e.g. 'small' becomes 'smallest'. Explain that short adjectives usually form their comparatives and superlatives with these suffixes, whereas longer ones often use the words 'more' and 'most', so we say 'prettier' and 'prettiest', but 'more beautiful' and 'most beautiful'. Comparatives and superlatives are special sorts of adjectives. They describe a noun by comparing it with one or more other items. A comparative is used for comparing a noun with one other item, and a superla-tive for comparing it with two items or more. Ask for examples of adjectives. With the children, practise saying each adjective followed by its comparative and superlative, e.g. 'high, higher, highest'. Ask the children which spelling they would use in each case.

Examples:							
	a)	short	tall	high	sweet	dark	soft
	b)	safe	blue	nice	close	rude	large
	c)	sad	red	big	hot	flat	thin
	d)	happy	heavy	silly	floppy	dusty	lazy

Grammar sheet 33: The children write inside the outlined words, using a blue pencil. Then they read the adjectives in 'Est-er' elephant and her friends. The children decide which way to spell the comparative and superlative for each adjective, and write them into the appropriate elephants.

Extension activity: The children add the ‹-er› and ‹-est› suffixes to make more comparative and superlative adjectives, using the extension activity on page 204.

Rounding off: Go over the sheet, with the class checking their answers. Then go over the extension activities.

Suffixes – ‹-er› and ‹-est›

Comparative and Superlative Adjectives

Blue

Two of the most useful suffixes are ‹-er› and ‹-est›.
Make comparatives and superlatives by adding ‹-er› and ‹-est› to the adjectives in Est-er Elephant and her friends.

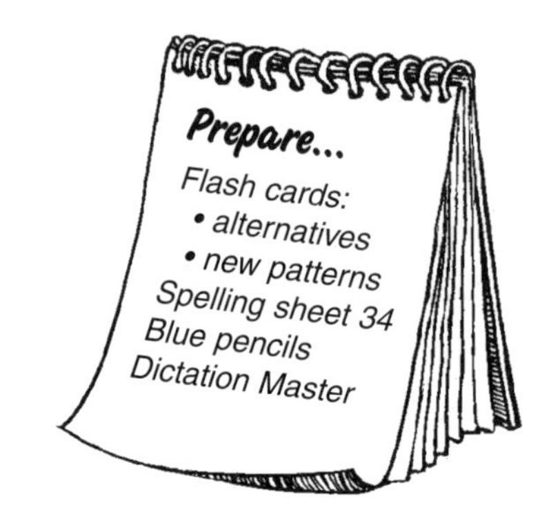

Spelling 34 – ‹**ie**› for the **/ee/** sound

Revision: Revise some of the spelling patterns and tricky words covered so far this year.

Main point: Although ‹ie› normally makes an /ie/ sound, as in 'pie', in some words it makes an /ee/ sound instead. Most words with an /ee/ sound take the ‹ee›, ‹ea›, ‹ey› or ‹y› spellings, but there are a number of exceptions which take ‹**ie**›. These need to be learnt. To help them remember the words, the children could try making up silly sentences using as many of the words as possible, e.g. 'It's my belief that the chief thief hid a piece of the shield in a field.'

Spelling sheet 34: As a class, read the spelling list and the sentences, without filling in the gaps. Revise how to add the ‹-er› and ‹-est› suffixes to adjectives, to make comparatives and superlatives. Remind the children that a comparative describes a noun by comparing it with one other item, and a superlative describes a noun by comparing it with two items or more. The children complete the words in the spelling list by writing in the missing letter pattern. Then they work through the exercises on the sheet.

Dictation: Read the words and sentences for the children to write down. The Dictation Master on page 175 may be photocopied onto the back of the spelling sheets for the children to write on.

Spelling list: Read the spelling words with the children. Point out that the /s/ sound in 'piece' is spelt with a 'soft ‹c›', followed by a 'silent ‹e›'. Go over the useful words '**library**' and '**computer**'. The children could use the 'Say it as it sounds' method for both words, pronouncing each syllable carefully to help them remember the spelling, i.e. 'lib-ra-ry' and 'com-put-er'.

Dictation

1. yield
2. wield
3. relief
4. fiend
5. series
6. handkerchief

1. A thief stole the royal crown.
2. "May I have a piece of pie?" I asked.
3. John took a picture of the cows and ewes in the field.

Spelling List 34

1. quit
2. sweet
3. field
4. piece
5. chief
6. thief
7. shield
8. belief
9. **library**
10. **computer**

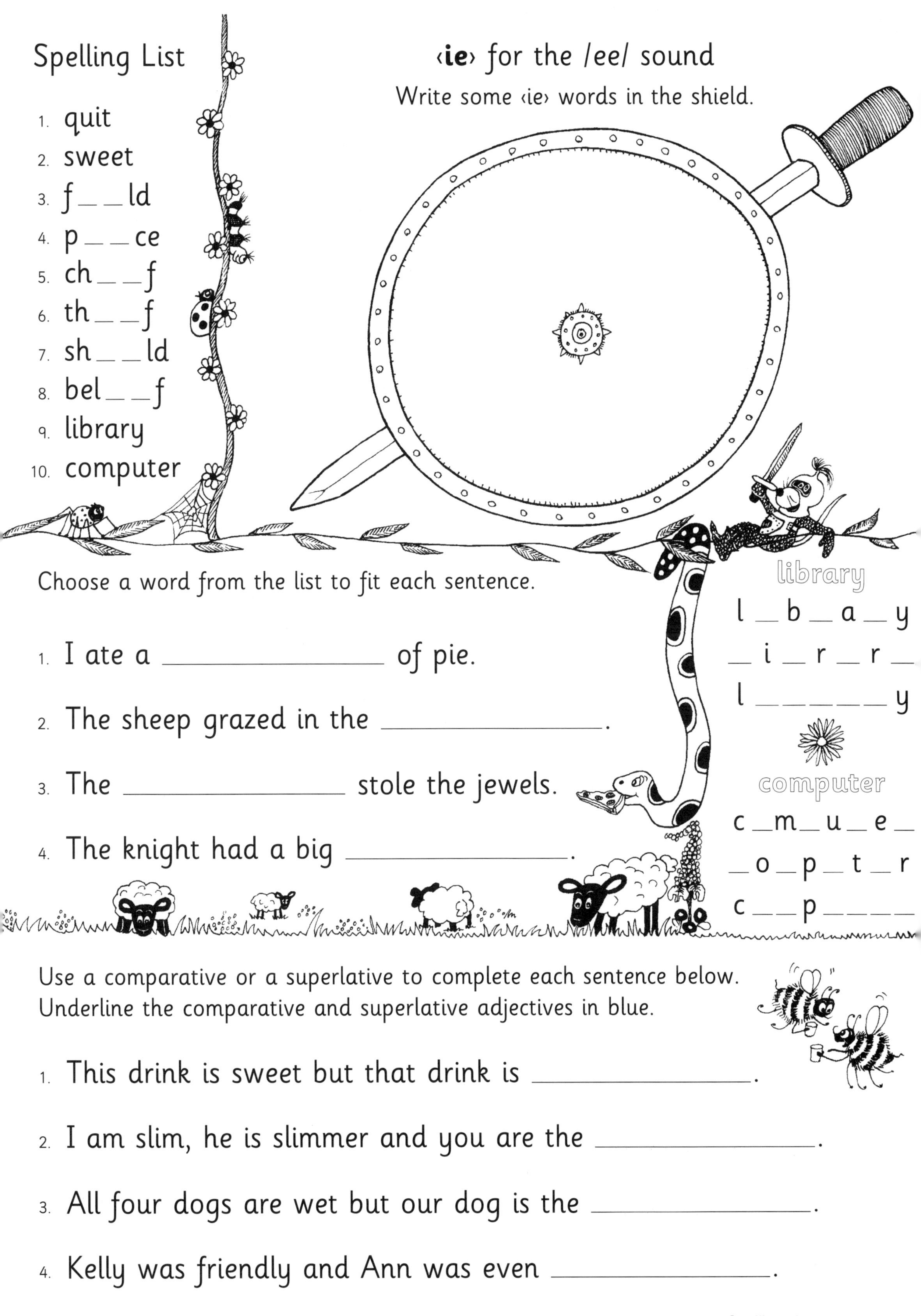

Spelling List

1. quit
2. sweet
3. f _ _ ld
4. p _ _ ce
5. ch _ _ f
6. th _ _ f
7. sh _ _ ld
8. bel _ _ f
9. library
10. computer

‹**ie**› for the /ee/ sound

Write some ‹ie› words in the shield.

Choose a word from the list to fit each sentence.

1. I ate a ______________ of pie.
2. The sheep grazed in the ______________.
3. The ______________ stole the jewels.
4. The knight had a big ______________.

library

l _ b _ a _ y

_ i _ r _ r _

l _ _ _ _ _ y

computer

c _ m _ u _ e _

_ o _ p _ t _ r

c _ _ p _ _ _ _

Use a comparative or a superlative to complete each sentence below.
Underline the comparative and superlative adjectives in blue.

1. This drink is sweet but that drink is ______________.
2. I am slim, he is slimmer and you are the ______________.
3. All four dogs are wet but our dog is the ______________.
4. Kelly was friendly and Ann was even ______________.

Grammar 34 – Interesting Words

Aim: Develop the children's ability to choose interesting words in their writing.

Introduction: Write two sentences on the board which feature commonly-overused words.

Examples: I went home.
Their house has a big garden.

With the children, read each sentence in turn. Ask which words could be replaced to make the sentences more interesting, while leaving the basic meaning unchanged.

Word:	*Some possible alternatives:*
went	walked, ran, strolled, hurried, cycled, drove
big	large, huge, vast, enormous, long, wide

Remind the children that a thesaurus lists words with similar meanings. Explain that to find a verb they should look up its root, so for 'went', which is a tricky past, they would look up 'go'.

Main point: Explain that writing becomes more vivid to the reader if the words are interesting and not overused. However, the children need to think carefully about which word to use in place of an overused one. It effects the meaning of a sentence when an overused word is replaced with a more interesting one. The new word should express what the children want to say as accurately as possible. Ask the children what effect each of their new words had, on the meanings of the example sentences.

Grammar sheet 34: As a class, read the sentences on the sheet. For each underlined word, the children think of an alternative to make the sentence more interesting, and write it on the line. They can use thesauruses to help them. Remind them that to find 'ran' and 'said', which are tricky pasts, the children should look up the verb roots 'run' and 'say'.

Word:	*Some possible alternatives:*		
ran	a) scuttled, scurried	b) rushed, hurried	c) chased, raced
nice	a) hot, sunny	b) delicious, tasty	c) kind, sweet
good	a) brilliant, fantastic	b) exciting, fun	c) wonderful, great
said	a) whispered, warned	b) ordered, insisted	c) called, invited
get	a) buy, choose	b) bring, fetch	c) grow, become

The children's answers are right as long as the words they choose make their sentences more interesting, while leaving the basic meaning unchanged.

Extension activity: The children expand sentences from the sheet by adding adjectives and adverbs. The Writing Master on page 176 may be photocopied onto the back of the grammar sheets for the children to write on.

Rounding off: Go over the sheet with the class. Ask some of the children to read out one of their sentences.

Interesting Words

We use some words too often. Think of a more interesting word to replace each of the underlined ones, and write it on the line provided. Use a different word in each sentence.

The spider ran across the floor. ____________

Tracy ran all the way home. ____________

Their dog ran after our cat. ____________

It was a nice day. ____________

We had a nice lunch. ____________

Everyone was very nice to me. ____________

The adventure park was good. ____________

The rides were good. ____________

I had a good time. ____________

“Sh! The baby is asleep,” said Dad. ____________

“Stop!” said the policewoman. ____________

“Come over here,” said the boys. ____________

I want to get new shoes. ____________

Please get me a glass of water. ____________

They will get angry. ____________

Prepare...
Flash cards:
• alternatives
• new patterns
Spelling sheet 35
(Thesauruses)
Dictation Master

Spelling 35 – ‹**ore**›

Revision: Revise some of the spelling patterns and tricky words covered so far this year.

Main point: Most words with an /or/ sound take the ‹or›, ‹al›, ‹au› or ‹aw› spellings, but there are a number of exceptions which take ‹**ore**›. These need to be learnt. To help them remember the words, the children could try making up silly sentences using as many of the words as possible, e.g. 'The store man swore more as he snored on the seashore.'

Spelling sheet 35: As a class, read the spelling list and the sentences, without filling in the gaps. Revise how to replace overused words with more interesting ones. The children complete the words in the spelling list by writing in the missing letter pattern. Then they work through the exercises on the sheet.

Dictation: Read the words and sentences for the children to write down. The Dictation Master on page 175 may be photocopied onto the back of the spelling sheets for the children to write on.

Spelling list: Read the spelling words with the children. Point out that the /ee/ sound in 'seashore' is spelt ‹ea›. Go over the useful words '**English**' and '**language**'. It helps the children remember the spelling of 'English' if they emphasise the short /e/ sound in the first syllable, pronouncing it like the ‹eng› in 'length'. They should practise saying the letter names for 'language'.

Dictation

1. core
2. tore
3. bore
4. sore
5. score
6. ashore

1. I wore gloves for the nature trail.
2. He washed his hands before supper.
3. Our neighbours used to live by the seashore.

Spelling List 35

1. swung
2. spring
3. more
4. wore
5. store
6. snore
7. before
8. seashore
9. **English**
10. **language**

Spelling List

1. swung
2. spring
3. m_ _ _
4. w_ _ _
5. st_ _ _
6. sn_ _ _
7. bef_ _ _
8. seash_ _ _
9. English
10. language

‹ore›

Write some ‹ore› words on the seashore.

Choose a word from the list to fit each sentence.

1. She ______________ a blue coat yesterday.
2. Please may we have some ______________?
3. I found a jellyfish on the ______________.
4. Did he arrive ______________ or after you?

English

E _ g _ i _ h

_ n _ l _ s _

_ _ _ l _ s h

language

l _ n _ u _ g _

_ a _ g _ a _ e

l _ n _ _ _ _ _

Think of a more interesting word to replace each of the underlined ones, and write it one the line.

1. She wore a <u>red</u> dress. ______________
2. The dinosaur gave a <u>loud</u> roar. ______________
3. It was a <u>cold</u> morning. ______________
4. He caught a <u>small</u> fish. ______________

Grammar 35 – Commas in Speech

Aim: Develop the children's understanding of commas, and of how to use commas in speech.

Introduction: Revise commas. Sometimes in the middle of a sentence, where it would be wrong to use a full stop, it is necessary to indicate a short pause. This helps the reader separate one idea from another. For this sort of pause we use a comma. Revise how to use commas to separate items in a list. On the board, write some sentences without any punctuation. With the children, read the text as it stands, and then punctuate it. There should be two capital letters, a pair of speech marks, two commas, a question mark and a full stop.

Example: when shall we bring the sandwiches cakes milk and lemonade for the party asked jenny

Main point: Explain that commas are not only used in lists. They are also used in sentences which include direct speech, to indicate a pause between the words spoken and the rest of the sentence. If the speech comes before the rest of the sentence, the comma belongs after the last word spoken but inside the speech marks. Point out that this is the same position that the question mark occupies in the corrected sentence on the board. A comma is not needed if there is already a question or exclamation mark in this position.

Example: "We would love to go on holiday," replied Mr Green.

If the speech comes after the rest of the sentence, the comma belongs after the last word that is not spoken but before the speech marks.

Example: Mr Green replied, "We would love to go on holiday."

Tell the children to start a new line for each new speaker. This makes it clear to the reader that someone else has started to speak.

Grammar sheet 35: As a class, read the first sentence. Ask the children to identify the speaker and which words are actually spoken. Help them decide where the missing punctuation should go. Then read the story, as a class. Help the children decide where the missing punctuation should go, and where to start each new line. The children punctuate the sentences. Next they copy out the story, adding punctuation and remembering to start a new line each time someone new starts to speak. The Writing Master on page 176 may be photocopied onto the back of the grammar sheets for the children to write on.

Extension activity: The children continue the story.

Rounding off: Go over the sentences with the class, checking where the commas and speech marks belong. Ask some children who continued the story to share their work with the class.

Commas in Speech

A comma is needed between the words actually spoken and the rest of the words in the sentence.

Add the missing commas and speech marks to these sentences.

1. My favourite colour is blue said the little girl .
2. The policewoman put her hand up and said Stop !
3. Hello said Uncle John How are you today ?
4. I know the names of all the dinosaurs said Toby and I've got a book about them at home .

A new line is needed each time someone different starts to speak.

Rewrite this conversation correctly.

Hello Bee called Inky. Hello Inky replied Bee, waving her antenna and flying over to her friend. Did you have a good time at the adventure park yesterday? asked Inky. Oh yes sighed Bee it was brilliant. I went on all the rides and we stayed all day. Did everyone from the hive go? wondered Inky. Yes said Bee and then she paused. Everyone who wanted to she corrected herself. Which rides did you think were the best? enquired Inky.

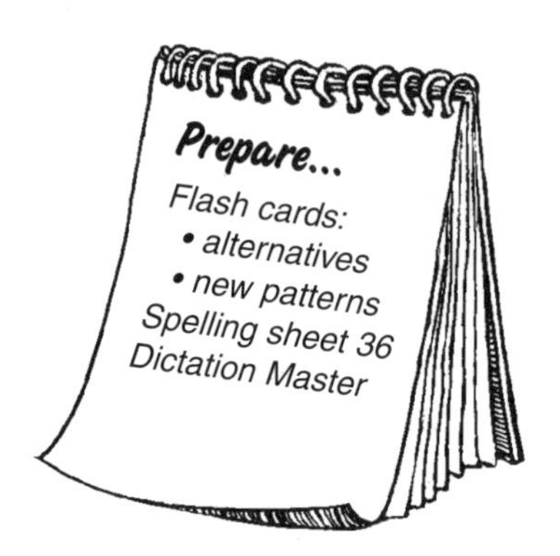

Prepare...
Flash cards:
• alternatives
• new patterns
Spelling sheet 36
Dictation Master

Spelling 36 – ‹le›

Revision: Revise some of the spelling patterns and tricky words covered so far this year.

Main point: Introduce the ‹**le**› spelling. At the end of a multi-syllabic word, this sounds something like /ool/. The little /oo/ sound in the middle is a swallowed sound, known as a 'schwa', as is also found in words with the ‹tion›, ‹sion› and ‹ture› spellings. The 'schwa' is a vowel sound, so the consonant doubling rule applies before it in words like 'paddle', 'kettle', 'nibble', 'topple' and 'snuggle'. No doubling is necessary in words like 'handle', 'twinkle' and 'jungle' because they already have two consonants between the short vowel and the ‹le›. (See the explanation and pictures on page 24.) With the children, make a list of words which use the ‹le› spelling. To help them remember the words, the children could try making up silly sentences using as many of the words as possible, e.g. 'The handle tumbled off the little bottle in the middle of the table.'

Spelling sheet 36: As a class, read the spelling list and the sentences, without filling in the gaps. Revise how to use commas in speech, and the other punctuation covered so far: full stops, question marks, exclamation marks, speech marks, commas in lists and apostrophes. The children complete the words in the spelling list by writing in the missing letter pattern. Then they work through the exercises on the sheet.

Dictation: Read the words and sentences for the children to write down. The Dictation Master on page 175 may be photocopied onto the back of the spelling sheets for the children to write on.

Spelling list: Read the spelling words with the children. Point out that the /i/ sound in 'syllable' is spelt with a ‹y›, although it is not at the end of the word. Go over the useful words '**continent**' and '**world**'. Tell the children to pronounce each syllable in 'continent' carefully to help them remember the spelling, i.e. 'con-ti-nent'. Point out that the /er/ sound in 'world' is spelt ‹or›.

Dictation

1. able
2. ankle
3. simple
4. uncle
5. tickle
6. bubble

1. The stable is in front of the field.
2. Somebody made the furniture wobble.
3. I put candles in the middle of the table.

Spelling List 36

1. damp
2. stand
3. apple
4. table
5. little
6. middle
7. bottle
8. syllable
9. **continent**
10. **world**

Spelling List

1. damp
2. stand
3. app _ _
4. tab _ _
5. litt _ _
6. midd _ _
7. bott _ _
8. syllab _ _
9. continent
10. world

‹le›

Write some ‹le› words in the apple.

Choose a word from the list to fit each sentence.

1. He asked for a ________________ of lemonade.
2. My ________________ sister is only two.
3. She laid the ________________ for dinner.
4. I baked an ________________ pie.

continent

c _ n _ i _ e _ t

_ o _ t _ n _ n _

c _ _ t _ _ _ _ _

world

w _ _ r _ _ d

_ _ o _ _ l _ _

w _ _ _ _ _ d

. , " ! ? " " Fill in the missing punctuation marks. " " ? ! " , .

□Do you want to come and play at my house□□ asked Josh□

Tammy replied□ □ I□ll have to ask my dad first□□

□Look□□ exclaimed Josh□ □There is your dad now□ Why don□t you ask him□□

□I will□□ Tammy agreed□

Grammar 36 – Parsing

Aim: Revise the parts of speech learnt so far.

Introduction: Revise the parts of speech covered so far: proper and common nouns, pronouns, adjectives, possessive adjectives, verbs, adverbs, conjunctions and prepositions. Call out a noun and ask the children to think of adjectives to describe it, e.g. 'green' or 'long' for 'grass'. Call out a verb and ask the children to think of adverbs to describe it, e.g. 'angrily' or 'happily' for 'to shout'. Call out a personal pronoun and ask the children for its possessive adjective, e.g. 'their' for 'they'. Call out two sentences and ask the children for a conjunction to join them, e.g. 'but' for 'We looked for her,' and 'We did not find her.' Ask the children to describe a journey, using prepositions, e.g. 'I walked across the bridge, down the hill, past the station and into the park.'

Main Point: This is a revision session, allowing the children to apply some of what they have learnt to a piece of writing. Choose a page from a big book, or the passage on Grammar sheet 36. Read it, with the children identifying the parts of speech they have learnt. A plastic sheet could be placed over the page, for the words to be underlined in the appropriate colours.

Grammar sheet 36: Read the story with the children. First the children write inside the outlined word, Nouns, in black, and underline all the proper and common nouns they can find. Then they repeat for the verbs, using red, and so on, using the appropriate colour for each part of speech. It is easier if the children concentrate on one part of speech at a time, rather than attempting to parse each word in order. It does not matter if they do not find all the parts of speech, as long as they can identify some of them. They may need more than one lesson to complete the sheet.

Extension activity: The children note and highlight each punctuation mark used in the passage.

Rounding off: Go over the sheet with the children. (See answers below.)

Key: Noun[N] Verb[V] Pronoun[P] Adjective[Adj] Adverb[Adv] Conjunction[C] Preposition[Pre]
(The asterisks indicate words that the children have not yet learnt to parse.)

'It[P] is[V] a sunny[Adj] morning[N]. Inky[N] and[C] Bee[N] are[V] in[Pre] the garden[N]. Inky[N] proudly[Adv] shows[V] Bee[N] her[Adj] birthday[Adj] present[N], a silver[Adj] chain[N]. It[P] glitters[V] in[Pre] the sunlight[N]. Suddenly[Adv], a magpie[N] swoops[V] to[Pre] the ground[N] and grabs[V] the chain[N].

"Stop[V]!" shout[V] Inky[N] and[C] Bee[N], but[C] the naughty[Adj] magpie[N] escapes[V] with[Pre] it[P]. Bee[N] flies[V] after[Pre] the magpie[N]. Inky[N] runs[V] quickly[Adv] along[Pre] the road[N] below[Pre] her[Adj] friend[N]. She[P] follows[V] the magpie[N] and[C] Bee[N] into[Pre] the forest[N]. She[P] sees[V] Bee[N] at[Pre] the bottom[N] of[Pre] a tall[Adj] tree[N].

"The nest[N] is[V] at[Pre] the top[N] of[Pre] the tree[N]," pants[V] Bee[N]. "I[P] can't[V] get[V] the chain[N] because[C] the magpies[N] are[V] bigger[Adj] than[C]* me[P]*." At[Pre]* this[Adj] moment[N] an empty[Adj] nutshell[N] lands[V] beside[Pre] Inky[N].

"I[P] am[V] sorry[Adj]!" calls[V] a squirrel[N] from[Pre] the tree[N].

"It[P] doesn't[V] matter[V]," Inky[N] replies[V]. "Could[V] you[P] help[V] us[P]* please[V]*?" She[P] explains[V] that[C]* the magpie[N] took[V] her[Adj] chain[N]. The squirrel[N] scampers[V] nimbly[Adv] up[Pre] the tree[N] and[C] fetches[V] it[P] from[Pre] the magpie's[N] nest[N].'

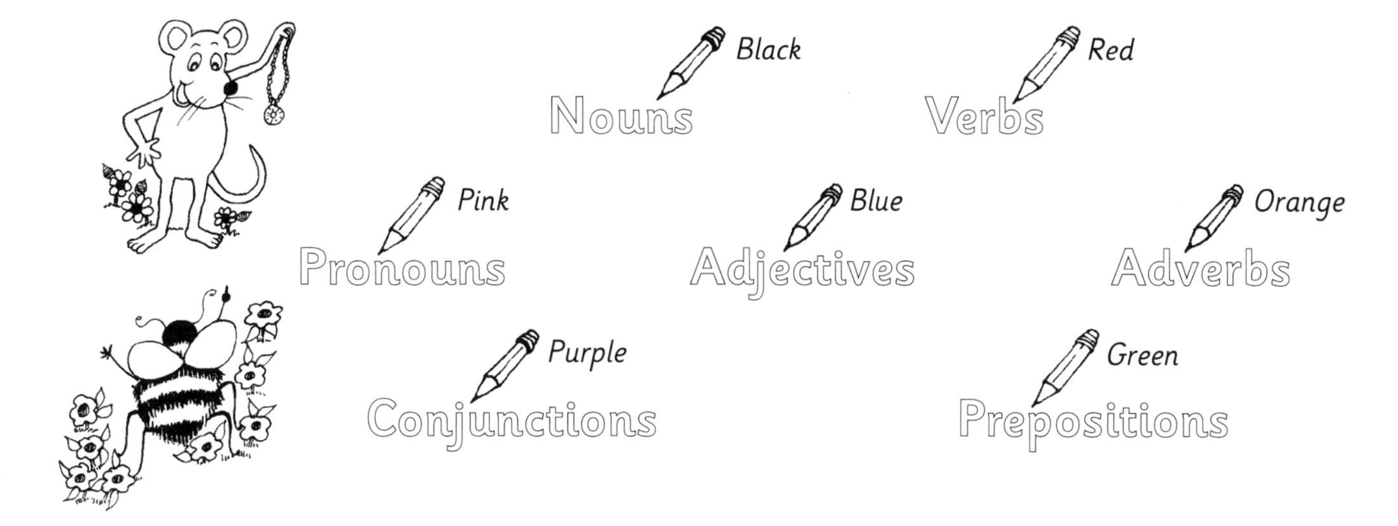

Underline as many of the different parts of speech as you can.

It is a sunny morning. Inky and Bee are in the garden. Inky proudly shows Bee her birthday present, a silver chain. It glitters in the sunlight. Suddenly, a magpie swoops to the ground and grabs the chain.

"Stop!" shout Inky and Bee, but the naughty magpie escapes with it. Bee flies after the magpie. Inky runs quickly along the road below her friend. She follows the magpie and Bee into the forest. She sees Bee at the bottom of a tall tree.

"The nest is at the top of the tree," pants Bee. "I can't get the chain because the magpies are bigger than me." At this moment an empty nutshell lands beside Inky.

"I am sorry!" calls a squirrel from the tree.

"It doesn't matter," Inky replies. "Could you help us please?" She explains that the magpie took her chain. The squirrel scampers nimbly up the tree and fetches it from the magpie's nest.

Photocopy Section 2

Master and Flash Card Sheets

Master Sheets (pages 175-76)

The Dictation Master on page 175 may be photocopied onto the back of the Spelling Sheets. It provides lines for the children to write the dictation words and sentences. The Writing Master on page 176 may be photocopied onto the back of the Grammar Sheets, when required. It provides extra lines which the children may need for their writing.

Flash Card Sheets (pages 177-83)

The seven Flash Card Sheets may be photocopied, cut up, and stuck onto card to make flash cards. Pages 177-80 feature digraphs (two letters which make a single sound) and the alternative ways of spelling vowel sounds. The children should already be familiar with both of these, but will benefit from regular practice.

In addition, pages 181-83 feature the new spelling patterns introduced in *The Grammar Handbook 2*. Many of these, such as ‹ph›, can only be pronounced one way, which makes flash card practice straightforward. Those which have more than one pronunciation, such as ‹c›, are marked with a plus sign (+) as a reminder to the children. Although some of these spellings, such as ‹ch›, are listed for their usual pronunciation among the earlier flash cards, they are still marked with the plus sign.

For practising the 'silent' letters, flash cards are provided with some common spelling patterns in which they occur, such as ‹rh› for 'silent ‹h›'. For those such as ‹sc› which can also be pronounced as a consonant blend, a plus sign is used as a reminder to the children.

Go through the flash cards as often as possible. A short burst of revision at the start of each spelling lesson is ideal.

Name: ______________________

Dictation

1. ______________ 2. ______________

3. ______________ 4. ______________

5. ______________ 6. ______________

Sentences

1. ______________________________

____

2. ______________________________

____

3. ______________________________

____

Name: ______________________

sh

ch

th

ng

qu

ar

ff

ll

ss

zz

ck

ay

a_e

ea +

igh

y +

i_e

ow

o_e

ew

u_e

oi

oy

or

al

au

aw

er

ir

ur

nk

wh

mb

wr

kn

ph

c

g

wa

ou

air

ey

rh

gh

sc +

are +

ear +

tion

sion

ei

eigh

o +

ture

ie +

ore

le +

Photocopy Section 3

Spelling and Tricky Word Sheets

Spelling List Sheets (pages 185-91)

Each week the children have a list of ten spelling words to take home and learn. The six sheets on pages 186-91 provide all the spelling lists ready to be photocopied, cut up, and stuck into the children's spelling homework books. To encourage parents to help their child, a parents' advice sheet has been provided. This can be copied, cut and stuck at the front of the spelling homework books. When the spelling tests have been marked, the results can be written into each book, to indicate to the parents how well their child has done.

Two words from the tricky word families are included in the weekly spelling list. However, it is useful to go over the tricky word families separately as well. Two types of sheet are provided for extra practice.

Silent 'b'
1. shin
2. bench
3. lamb
4. comb
5. thumb
6. crumbs
7. plumber
8. climbing
9. mother
10. father
10/10
1. chat
2. cash
3. write
4. wrist
5. wreck
6. wrong
7. answer
8. swordfish
9. sister
10. brother
GLUE

Tricky Word Family Spelling List Sheet (page 192)

The Tricky Word Family Spelling Lists group together the twelve tricky words from each six weeks. They may be photocopied, cut up, and given out as an extra spelling homework, either in the holidays, or if there are any weeks to spare.

'Look, Copy, Cover, Write, Check' (page 193)

The 'Look, Copy, Cover, Write, Check' method is an effective way for the children to learn to spell the tricky word families. Write the words in the left-hand column of the template for the children to practise one word family at a time, either at school or at home.

Parents' Advice Sheet

Dear Parent,

Each week your child will be given ten spellings. Please help him/her to learn them.

The first two spelling words are regular. These can be spelt by listening for the sounds and writing the letter(s) for them. The next six words use the spelling pattern of the week.

The last two words are usually irregular or tricky, and have to be learnt by heart. Your child can learn these harder words by saying the names of the letters as he/she writes them, e.g. for the word 'half', your child should say, 'aitch ai ell eff,' several times each day, until the word is known.

Dear Parent,

Each week your child will be given ten spellings. Please help him/her to learn them.

The first two spelling words are regular. These can be spelt by listening for the sounds and writing the letter(s) for them. The next six words use the spelling pattern of the week.

The last two words are usually irregular or tricky, and have to be learnt by heart. Your child can learn these harder words by saying the names of the letters as he/she writes them, e.g. for the word 'half', your child should say, 'aitch ai ell eff,' several times each day, until the word is known.

Dear Parent,

Each week your child will be given ten spellings. Please help him/her to learn them.

The first two spelling words are regular. These can be spelt by listening for the sounds and writing the letter(s) for them. The next six words use the spelling pattern of the week.

The last two words are usually irregular or tricky, and have to be learnt by heart. Your child can learn these harder words by saying the names of the letters as he/she writes them, e.g. for the word 'half', your child should say, 'aitch ai ell eff,' several times each day, until the word is known.

Dear Parent,

Each week your child will be given ten spellings. Please help him/her to learn them.

The first two spelling words are regular. These can be spelt by listening for the sounds and writing the letter(s) for them. The next six words use the spelling pattern of the week.

The last two words are usually irregular or tricky, and have to be learnt by heart. Your child can learn these harder words by saying the names of the letters as he/she writes them, e.g. for the word 'half', your child should say, 'aitch ai ell eff,' several times each day, until the word is known.

Dear Parent,

Each week your child will be given ten spellings. Please help him/her to learn them.

The first two spelling words are regular. These can be spelt by listening for the sounds and writing the letter(s) for them. The next six words use the spelling pattern of the week.

The last two words are usually irregular or tricky, and have to be learnt by heart. Your child can learn these harder words by saying the names of the letters as he/she writes them, e.g. for the word 'half', your child should say, 'aitch ai ell eff,' several times each day, until the word is known.

Dear Parent,

Each week your child will be given ten spellings. Please help him/her to learn them.

The first two spelling words are regular. These can be spelt by listening for the sounds and writing the letter(s) for them. The next six words use the spelling pattern of the week.

The last two words are usually irregular or tricky, and have to be learnt by heart. Your child can learn these harder words by saying the names of the letters as he/she writes them, e.g. for the word 'half', your child should say, 'aitch ai ell eff,' several times each day, until the word is known.

Spelling Lists 1-6

1.

Silent b

1. shin
2. bench
3. lamb
4. comb
5. thumb
6. crumbs
7. plumber
8. climbing
9. mother
10. father

2.

Silent w

1. chat
2. cash
3. write
4. wrist
5. wreck
6. wrong
7. answer
8. swordfish
9. sister
10. brother

3.

Silent k

1. song
2. trunk
3. knee
4. knit
5. know
6. knock
7. knight
8. penknife
9. grandma
10. grandpa

4.

wh

1. this
2. that
3. while
4. wheat
5. whip
6. whistle
7. whiskers
8. whatever
9. aunt
10. uncle

5.

ph

1. club
2. flag
3. phone
4. photo
5. dolphin
6. elephant
7. sphere
8. alphabet
9. nephew
10. niece

6.

ea

1. glad
2. plum
3. read
4. head
5. bread
6. weather
7. treasure
8. breakfast
9. cousin
10. friend

Spelling Lists 7-12

7.

Soft c

1. mill
2. tell
3. ice
4. dance
5. city
6. circle
7. police
8. cylinder
9. January
10. February

8.

Soft g

1. miss
2. cross
3. giant
4. magic
5. large
6. danger
7. orange
8. vegetable
9. March
10. April

9.

wa

1. luck
2. click
3. was
4. wash
5. wasp
6. swan
7. watch
8. swallow
9. May
10. June

10.

ou

1. thin
2. thick
3. touch
4. young
5. double
6. trouble
7. country
8. nourish
9. July
10. August

11.

air

1. cliff
2. off
3. air
4. hair
5. pair
6. stair
7. chair
8. hairbrush
9. September
10. October

12.

ch

1. buzz
2. fizz
3. echo
4. choir
5. chemist
6. stomach
7. Christmas
8. character
9. November
10. December

Spelling Lists 13-18

13.

/ai/

1. next
2. quit
3. make
4. pay
5. main
6. clay
7. waist
8. rainstorm
9. half
10. quarter

14.

/ee/

1. arm
2. shark
3. seen
4. three
5. seat
6. cream
7. please
8. teenager
9. eleven
10. twelve

15.

/ie/

1. club
2. flex
3. flying
4. sight
5. side
6. die
7. bright
8. sunshine
9. thirteen
10. fourteen

16.

/oa/

1. such
2. luck
3. home
4. froze
5. foal
6. stone
7. toast
8. snowball
9. fifteen
10. sixteen

17.

/ue/

1. sunk
2. book
3. huge
4. fuse
5. rescue
6. queue
7. ewe
8. useful
9. seventeen
10. eighteen

18.

/k/

1. hook
2. fork
3. back
4. brick
5. deck
6. flock
7. struck
8. rucksack
9. nineteen
10. twenty

Spelling Lists 19-24

19.

/er/

1. drip
2. plug
3. third
4. winter
5. bird
6. over
7. hurt
8. butterfly
9. thirty
10. forty

20.

/oi/

1. drag
2. trip
3. join
4. spoil
5. point
6. joy
7. royal
8. ointment
9. fifty
10. sixty

21.

/ou/

1. snap
2. swam
3. loud
4. cloud
5. found
6. now
7. crowd
8. sunflower
9. seventy
10. eighty

22.

or

1. twig
2. from
3. pork
4. walk
5. jaw
6. north
7. straw
8. saucepan
9. ninety
10. hundred

23.

ey

1. film
2. kept
3. key
4. honey
5. money
6. donkey
7. chimney
8. journey
9. thousand
10. million

24.

y

1. grip
2. milk
3. baby
4. lady
5. holly
6. fairy
7. happy
8. family
9. zero
10. equals

Spelling Lists 25-30

25.

Silent h

1. belt
2. farm
3. hour
4. ghost
5. rhyme
6. rhythm
7. honest
8. rhinoceros
9. centimetre
10. metre

26.

Silent c

1. land
2. quiz
3. scene
4. scent
5. muscle
6. science
7. scissors
8. crescent
9. gram
10. kilogram

27.

are

1. film
2. kept
3. hare
4. care
5. share
6. scare
7. square
8. nightmare
9. millilitre
10. litre

28.

ear

1. grip
2. milk
3. bear
4. tear
5. pear
6. wear
7. swear
8. underwear
9. weight
10. volume

29.

tion

1. must
2. stuck
3. nation
4. station
5. relation
6. action
7. fiction
8. dictionary
9. minute
10. second

30.

sion

1. fist
2. best
3. occasion
4. division
5. revision
6. invasion
7. explosion
8. television
9. fraction
10. estimate

Spelling Lists 31-36

31.

ei

1. grub
2. slug
3. eight
4. eighteen
5. eighty
6. weigh
7. reindeer
8. neighbour
9. child
10. children

32.

o

1. ark
2. clever
3. gloves
4. son
5. front
6. dozen
7. monkey
8. somebody
9. woman
10. women

33.

ture

1. shook
2. often
3. picture
4. future
5. nature
6. creature
7. fracture
8. adventure
9. mouse
10. mice

34.

ie

1. quit
2. sweet
3. field
4. piece
5. chief
6. thief
7. shield
8. belief
9. library
10. computer

35.

ore

1. swung
2. spring
3. more
4. wore
5. store
6. snore
7. before
8. seashore
9. English
10. language

36.

le

1. damp
2. stand
3. apple
4. table
5. little
6. middle
7. bottle
8. syllable
9. continent
10. world

Tricky Word Family Spelling Lists

1. mother
2. father
3. sister
4. brother
5. grandma
6. grandpa
7. aunt
8. uncle
9. nephew
10. niece
11. cousin
12. friend

13. January
14. February
15. March
16. April
17. May
18. June
19. July
20. August
21. September
22. October
23. November
24. December

25. half
26. quarter
27. eleven
28. twelve
29. thirteen
30. fourteen
31. fifteen
32. sixteen
33. seventeen
34. eighteen
35. nineteen
36. twenty

37. thirty
38. forty
39. fifty
40. sixty
41. seventy
42. eighty
43. ninety
44. hundred
45. thousand
46. million
47. zero
48. equals

49. centimetre
50. metre
51. gram
52. kilogram
53. millilitre
54. litre
55. weight
56. volume
57. minute
58. second
59. fraction
60. estimate

61. child
62. children
63. woman
64. women
65. mouse
66. mice
67. library
68. computer
69. English
70. language
71. continent
72. world

Look Say the letter names.	**Copy** Try writing the word. **Cover**	**Write** **Check** Is it right?	Have another go!

Photocopy Section 4

Extension Activity and Poem Sheets

Extension Activity Sheets (pages 195-214)

A number of Extension Activity Sheets are provided for further practice. To save on preparation time, most of these are ready for photocopying. However, in some cases a blank template is provided as well, so words can be chosen to suit. The templates can be used again and again, with a different set of words each time. The extension activities are intended to supplement the following lessons:

Grammar work

Alphabetical order, dictionary and thesaurus work

Poem Sheets (pages 215-18)

The Poem Sheets may be enlarged, using a photocopier, for whole-class teaching. The poems are intended to supplement the following lessons:

Add the past tense ending to each verb root.

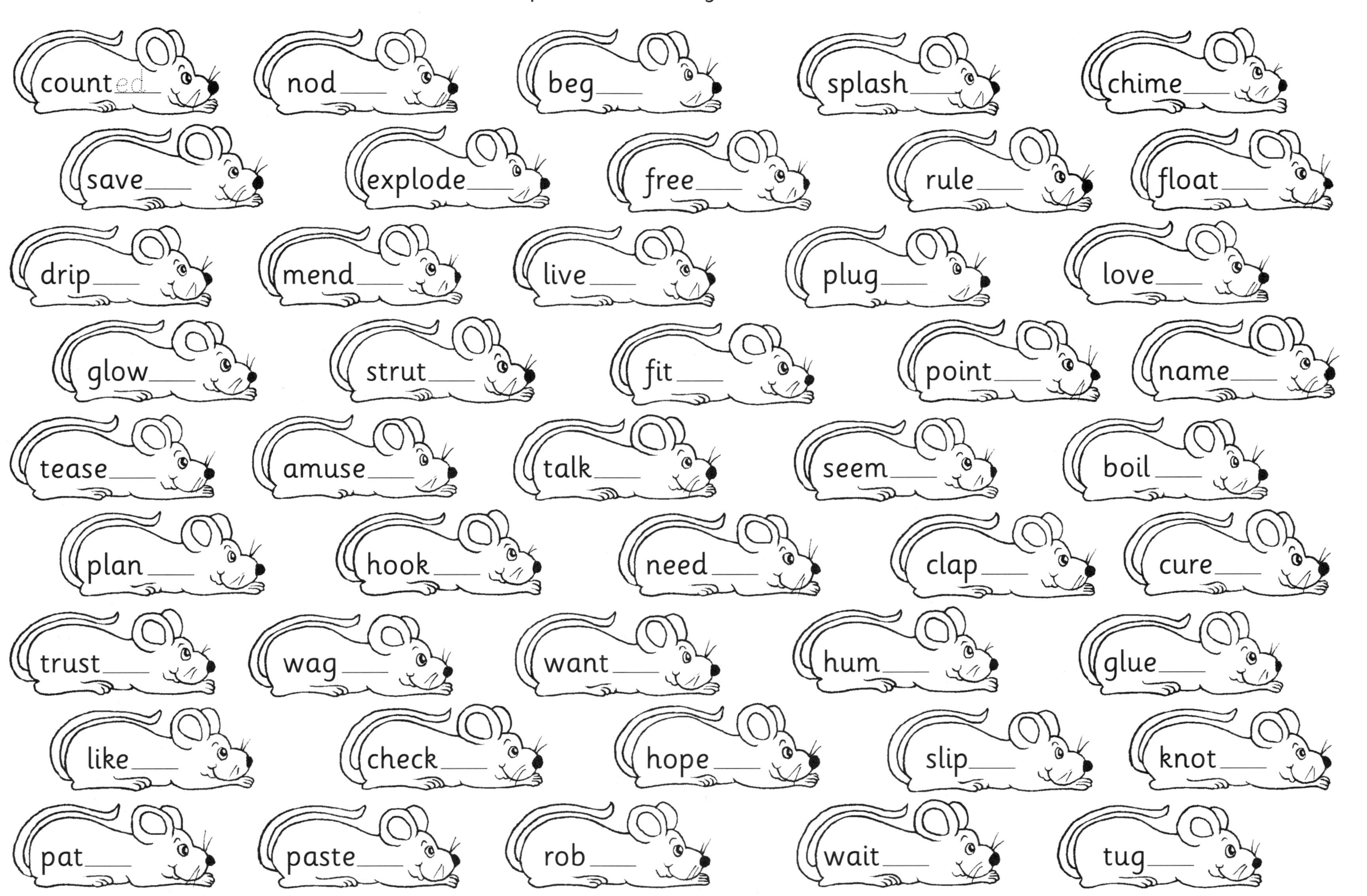

Add the past tense ending to each verb root.

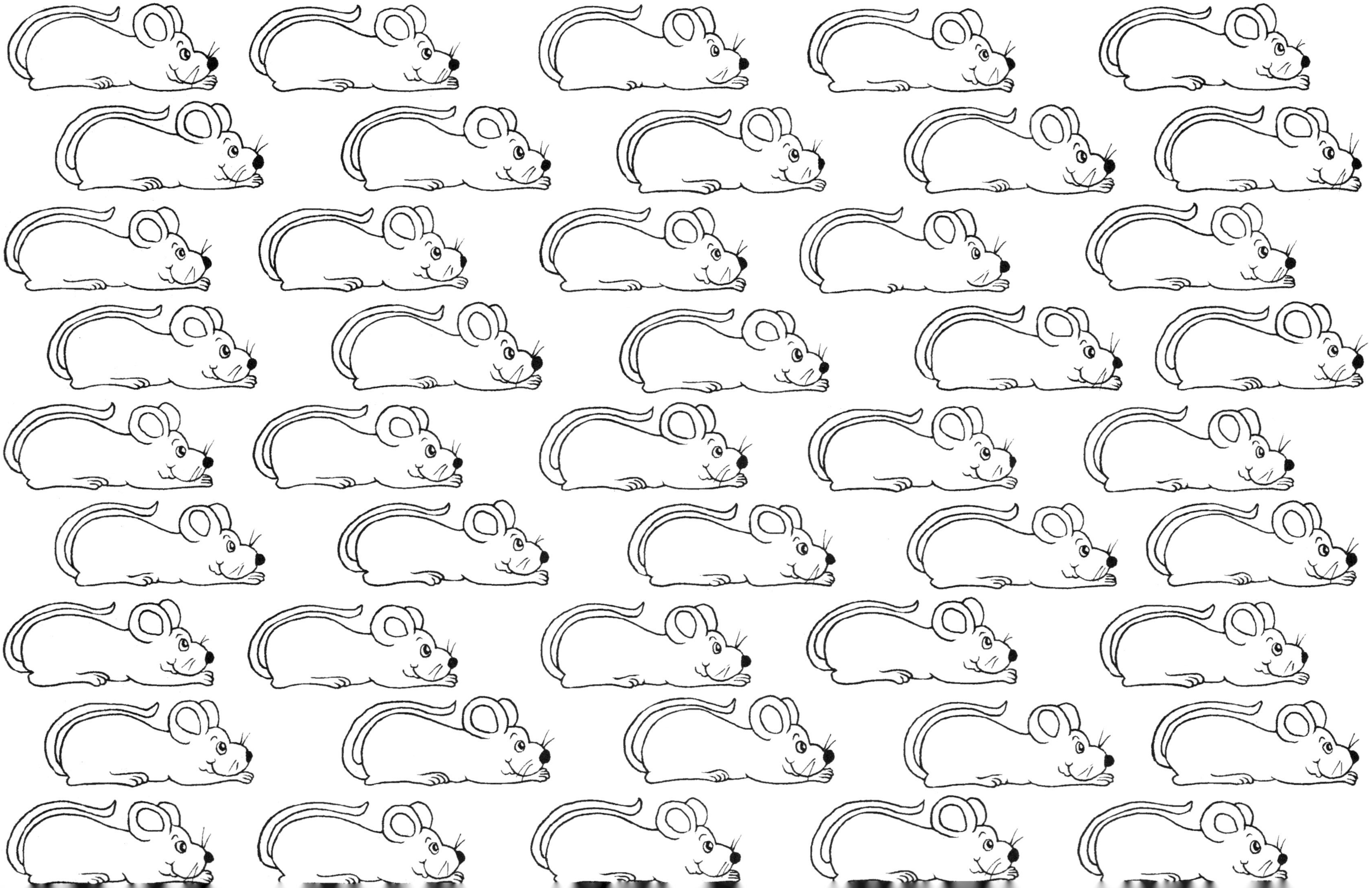

Each of these verb roots has a tricky past. Write each past tense in the honeycomb.

Each of these verb roots has a tricky past. Write each past tense in the honeycomb.

Complete each sentence with a conjunction. 

and but because or so while

1. Grandpa was angry ______________ I was rude.
2. Nina likes peanuts, ______________ she hates almonds.
3. Can you swim, ______________ do you need help?
4. We baked a cake ______________ it was his birthday.
5. The children hid ______________ Dad counted to fifty.
6. I brushed my teeth ______________ went to bed.
7. Judy loves drawing, ______________ we gave her some coloured pencils.
8. I lost my ring, ______________ my mother found it.
9. Please wait ______________ I get my coat.
10. Have you forgiven me, ______________ are you still angry?
11. My feet were cold, ______________ I put on my socks.
12. Ted wrote this story himself, ______________ he drew all the pictures too.

Prefixes

There are many prefixes. These are five useful ones.

undo middle not half again

Choose a prefix to go in front of each of the base words in the fish bodies, and write it on the line in the fish's head.

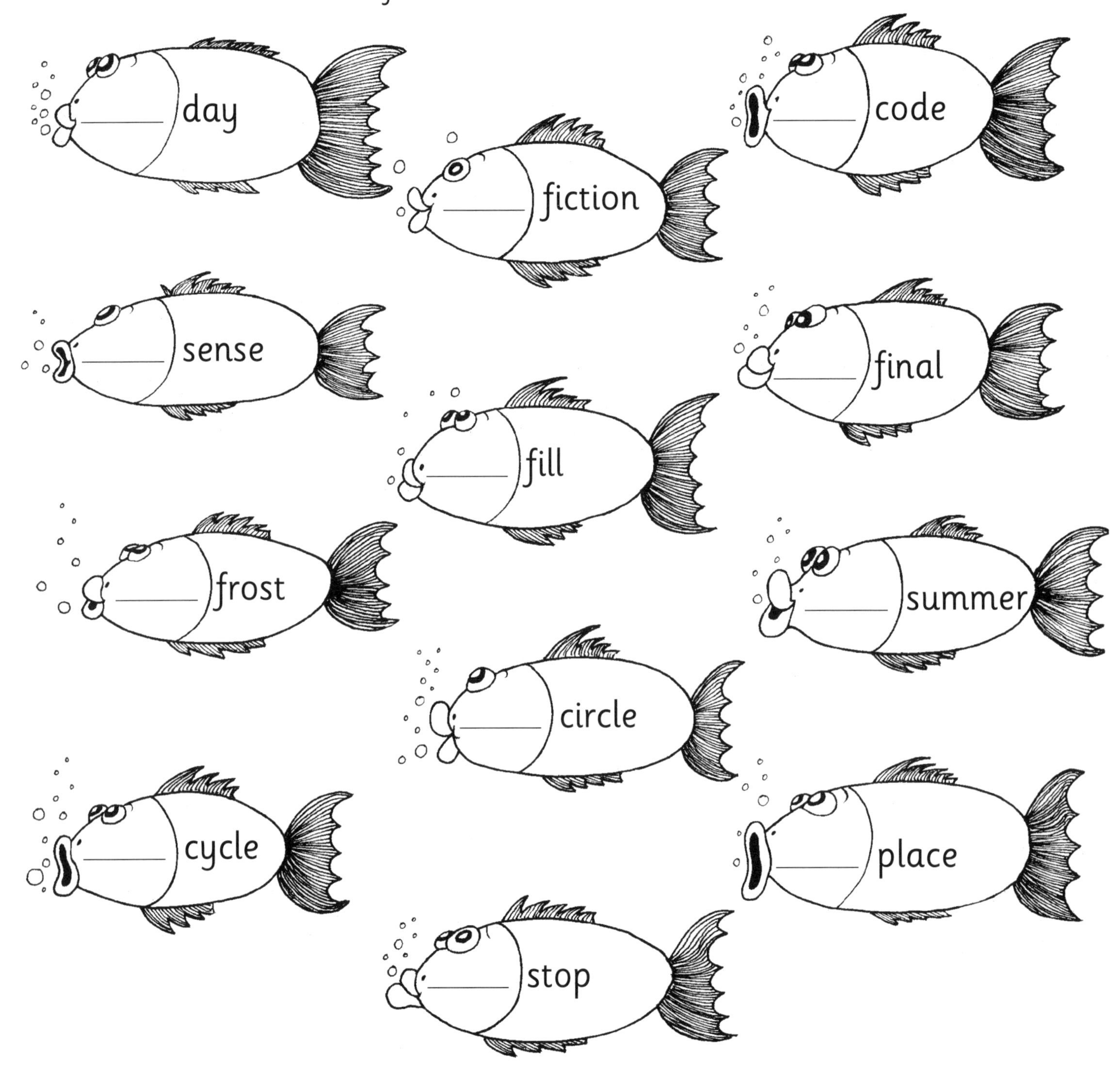

You can use a dictionary to check whether you have chosen the right prefixes.

Suffix – ‹-ness›

Make nouns by adding ‹-ness› to the adjectives, and write them on the lines below.

ness

Suffix – ‹-ful›

Make adjectives by adding ‹-ful› to the nouns, and write them on the lines below.

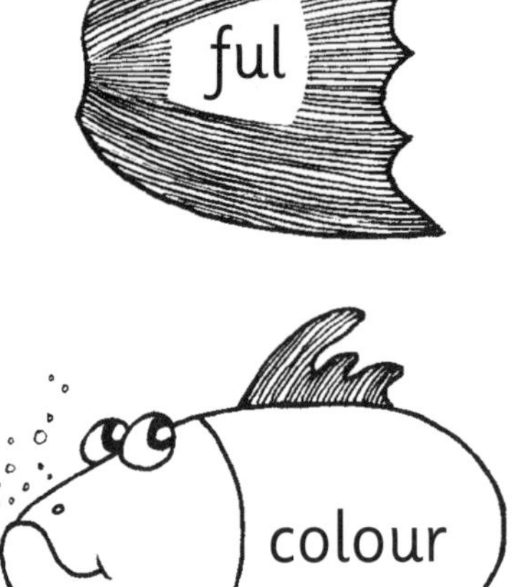

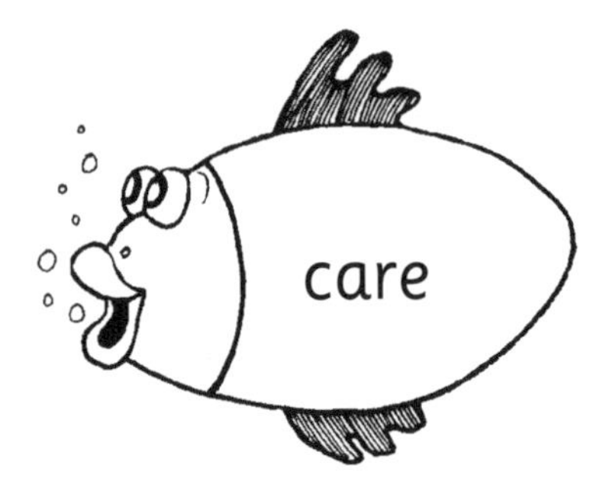

Suffix – ‹-er›

Make nouns by adding ‹-er› to the verbs, and write them on the lines below.

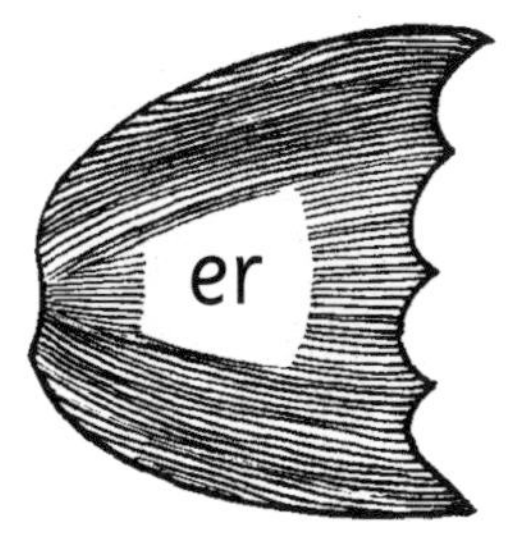

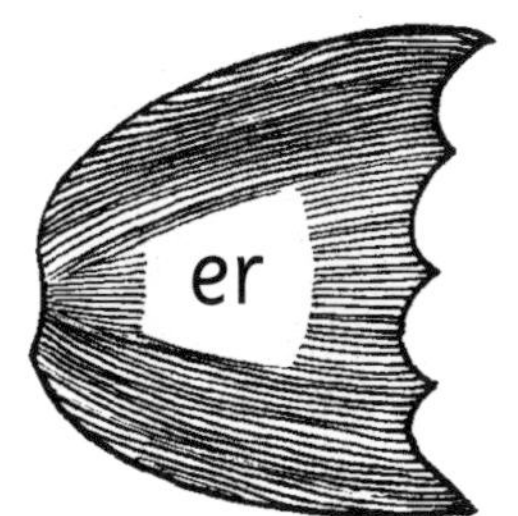

Suffixes – ‹-er› and ‹-est›

Comparative and Superlative Adjectives

Blue

Two of the most useful suffixes are ‹-er› and ‹-est›.
Make comparatives and superlatives by adding ‹-er› and ‹-est› to the adjectives in Est-er Elephant and her friends.

Suffixes – ‹-er› and ‹-est›

Blue

Comparative and Superlative Adjectives

Two of the most useful suffixes are ‹-er› and ‹-est›.
Make comparatives and superlatives by adding ‹-er› and ‹-est› to the adjectives in Est-er Elephant and her friends.

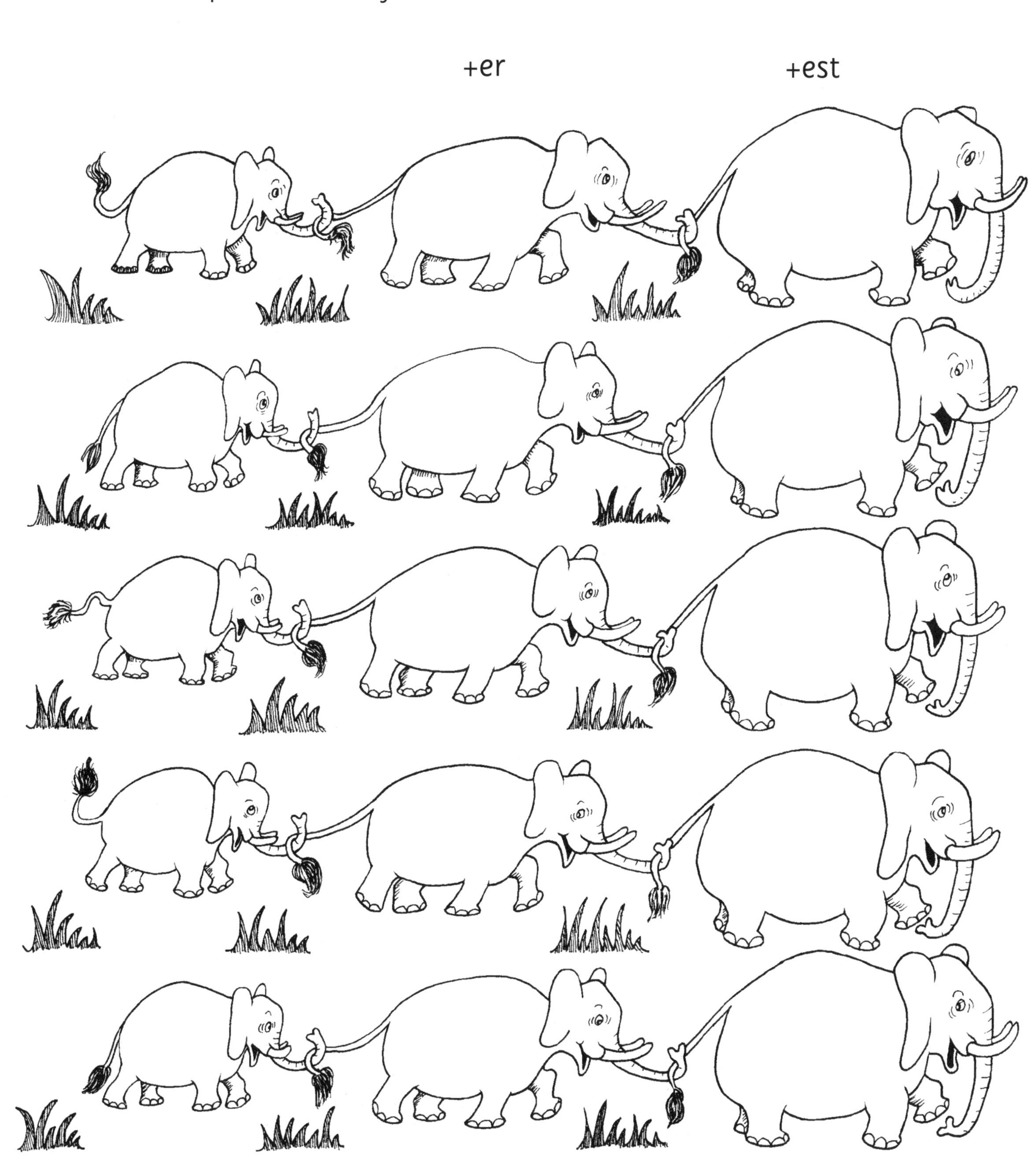

Draw a ring around the word that would come first in the dictionary.

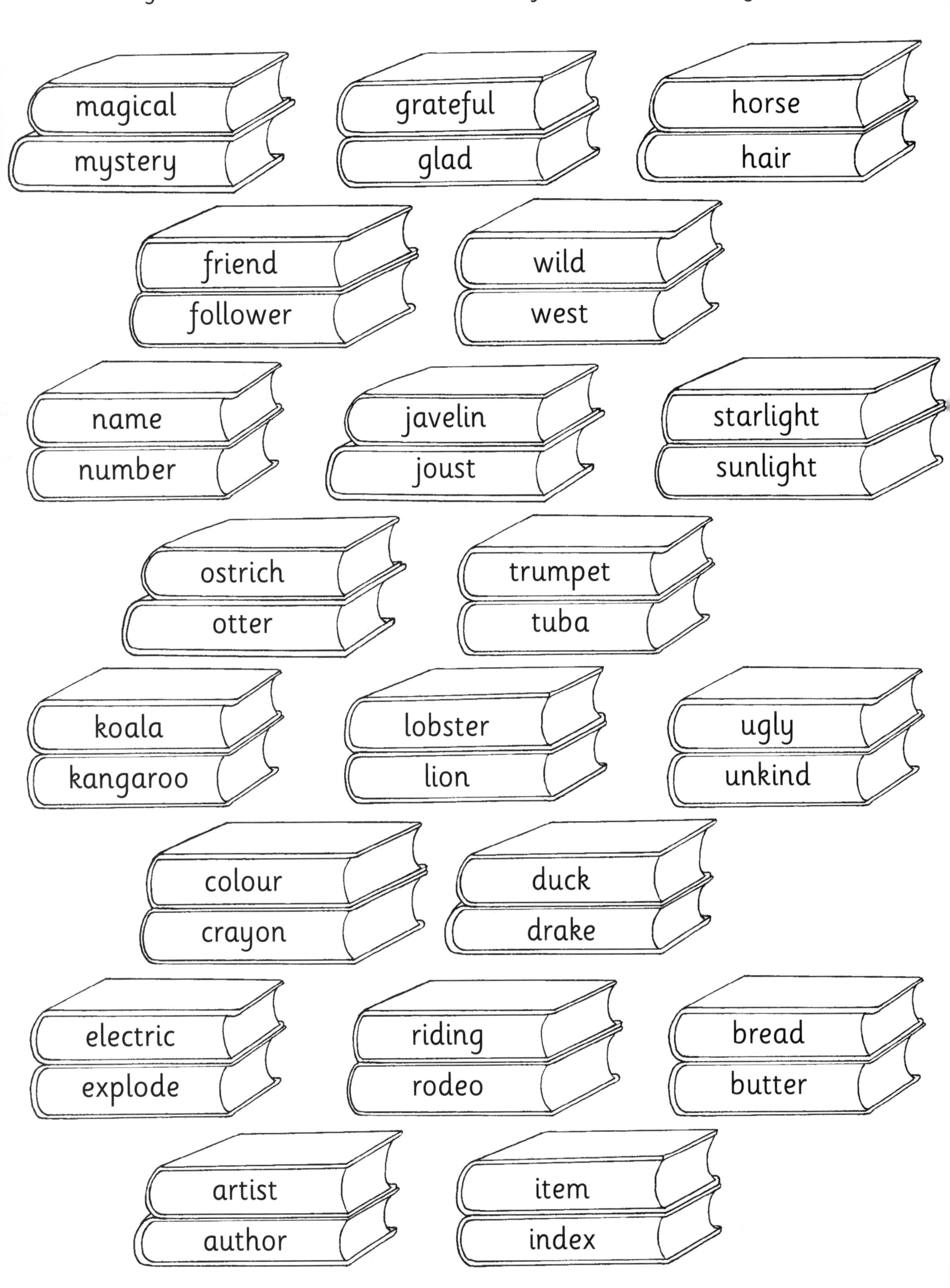

Draw a ring around the word that would come first in the dictionary.

In each group of three, decide which word comes first (1st), which word comes second (2nd) and which word comes third (3rd). The words start with the same two letters, so remember to look at the third letter of each word.

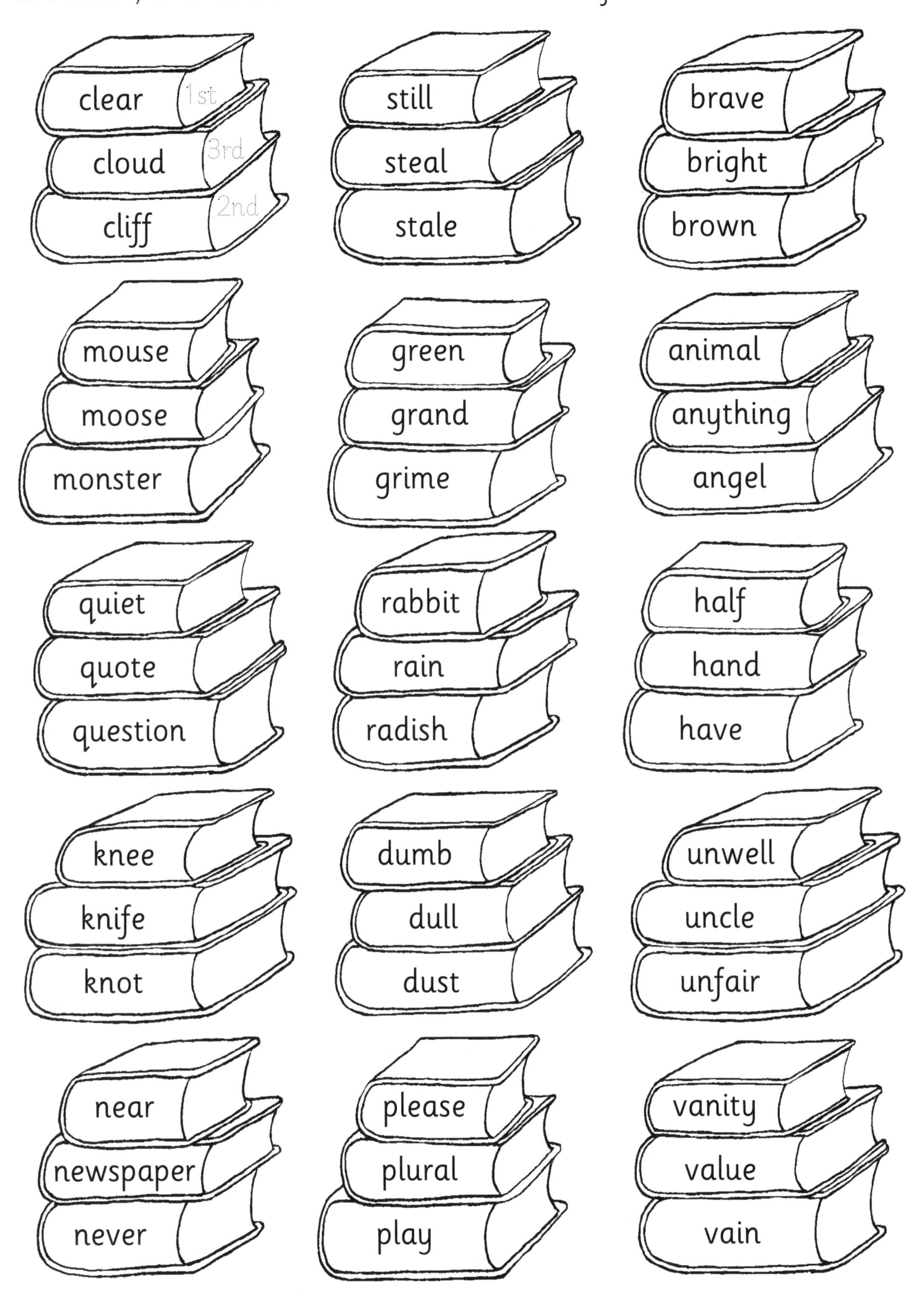

In each group of three, decide which word comes first (1st), which word comes second (2nd) and which word comes third (3rd). The words start with the same two letters, so remember to look at the third letter of each word.

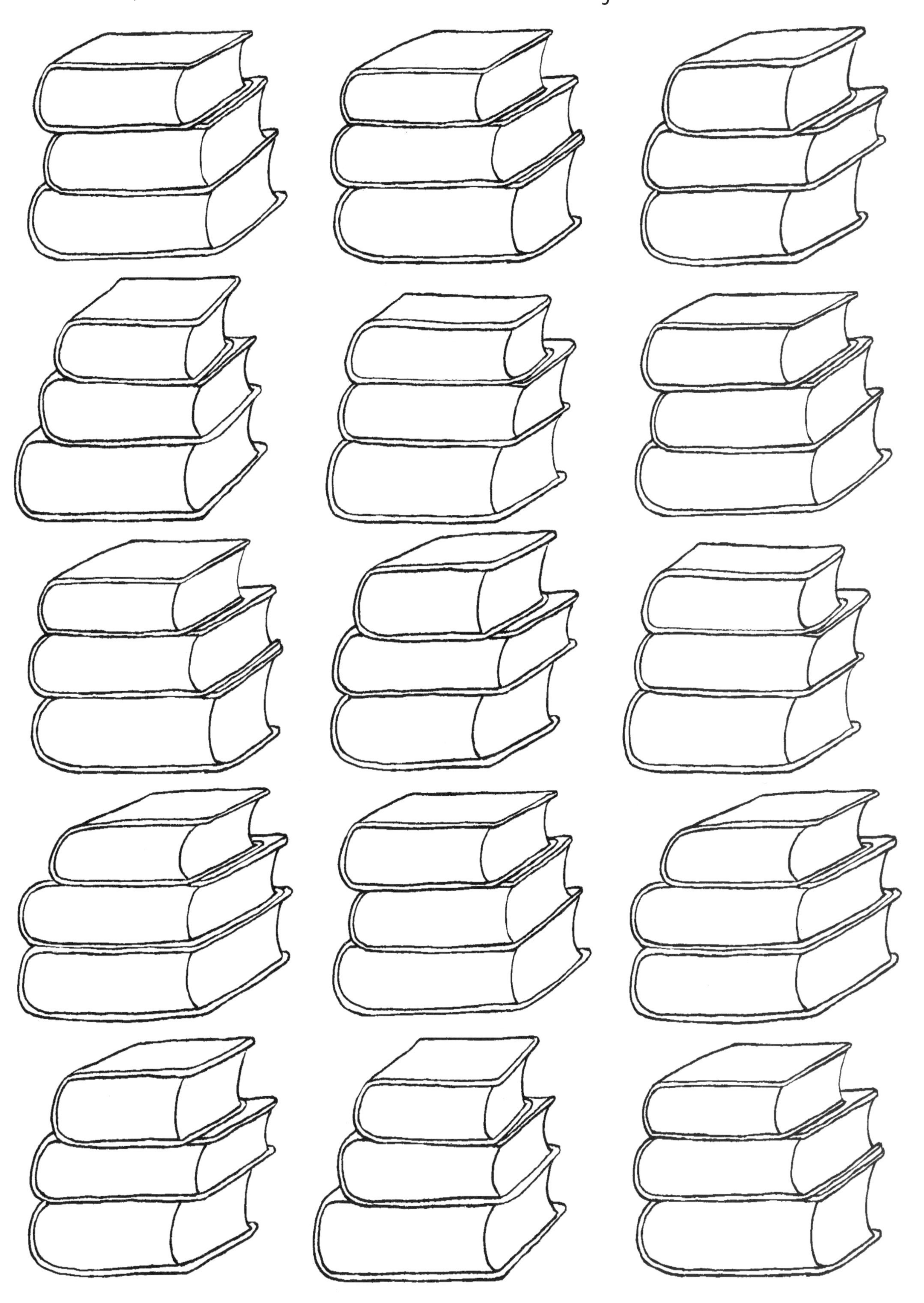

Look up each word in the dictionary. Read the meaning and draw a picture for it.

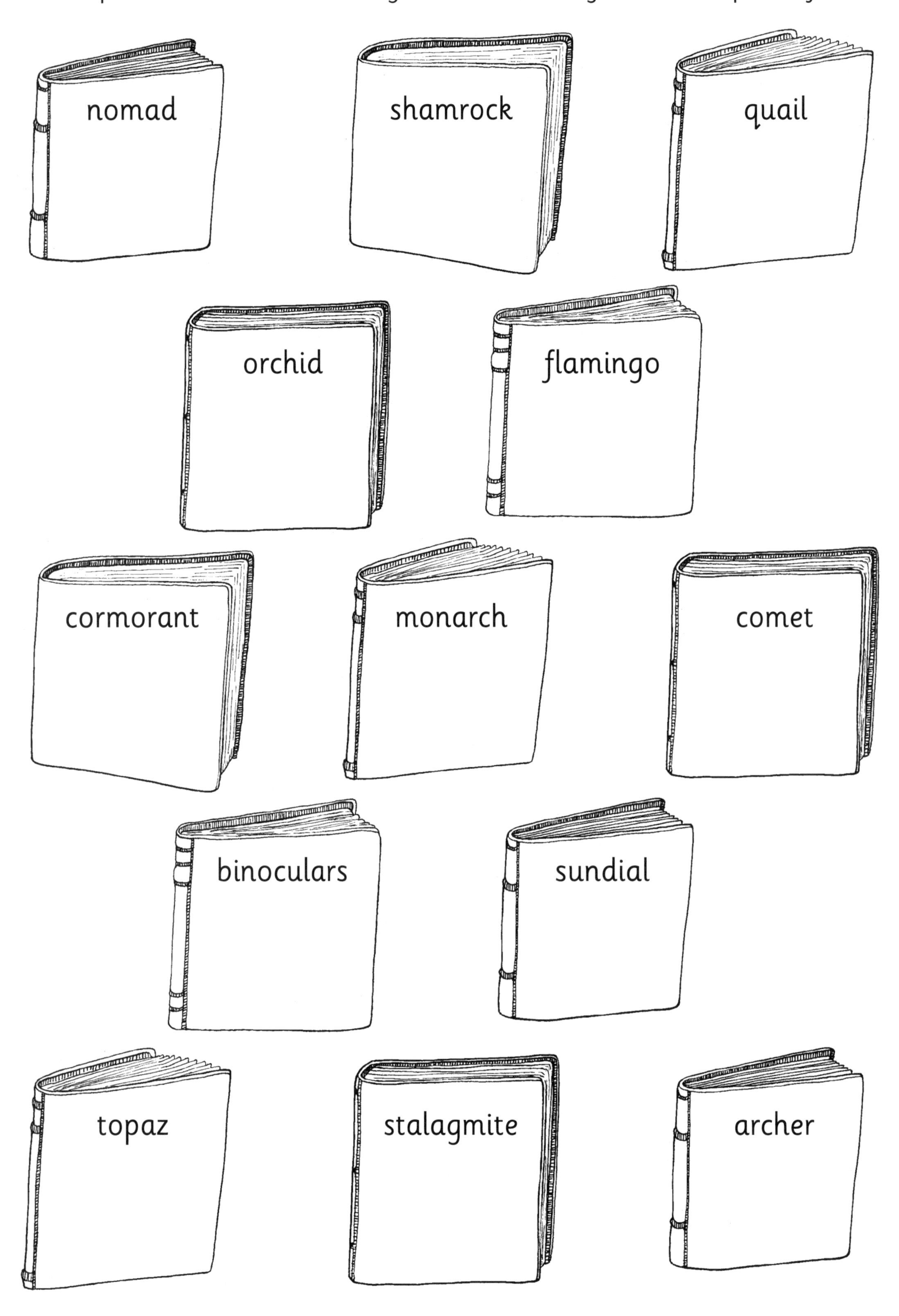

Look up each word in the dictionary. Read the meaning and draw a picture for it.

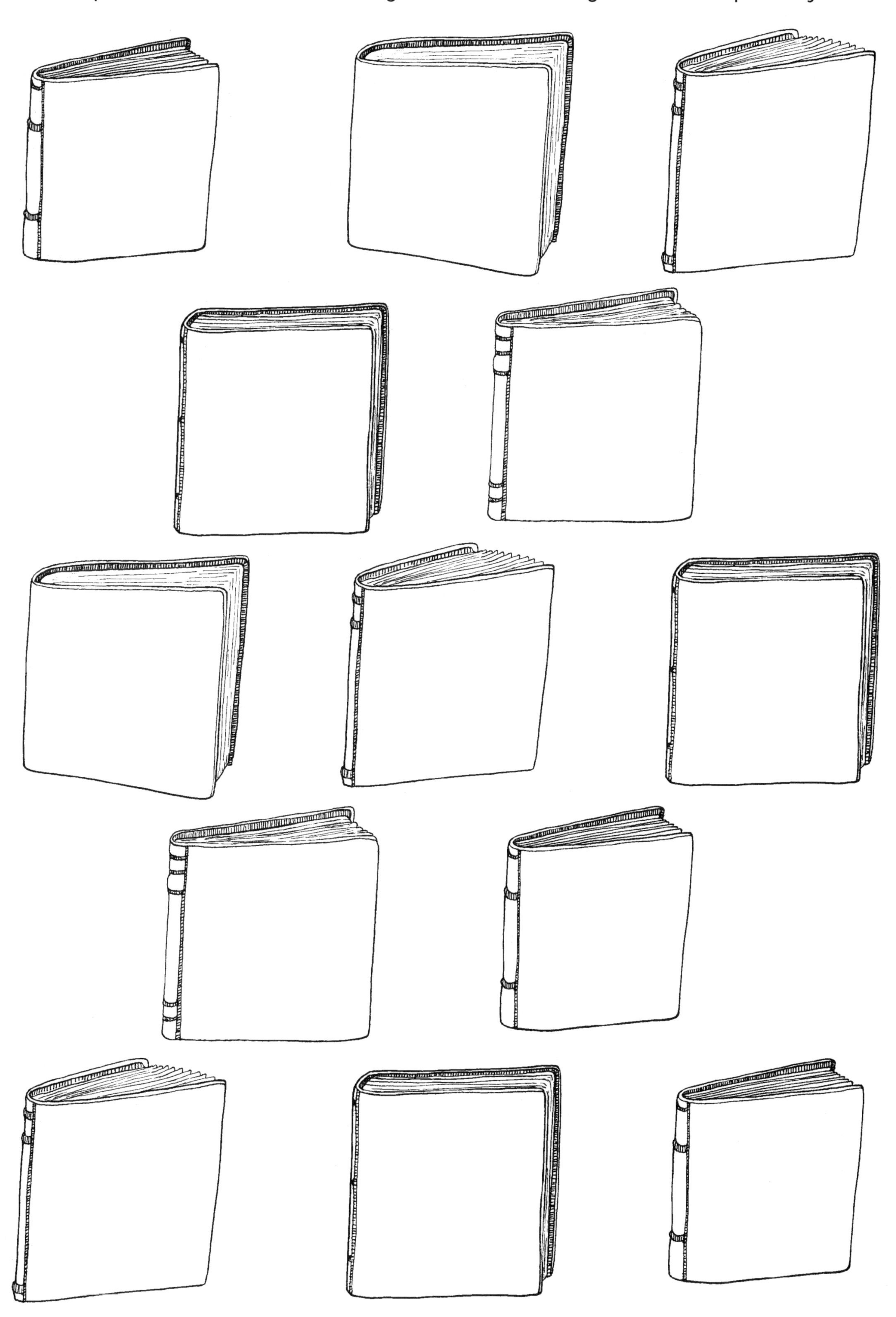

Word Webs

In the spaces of each word web, write words which could be used instead of the word in the middle.

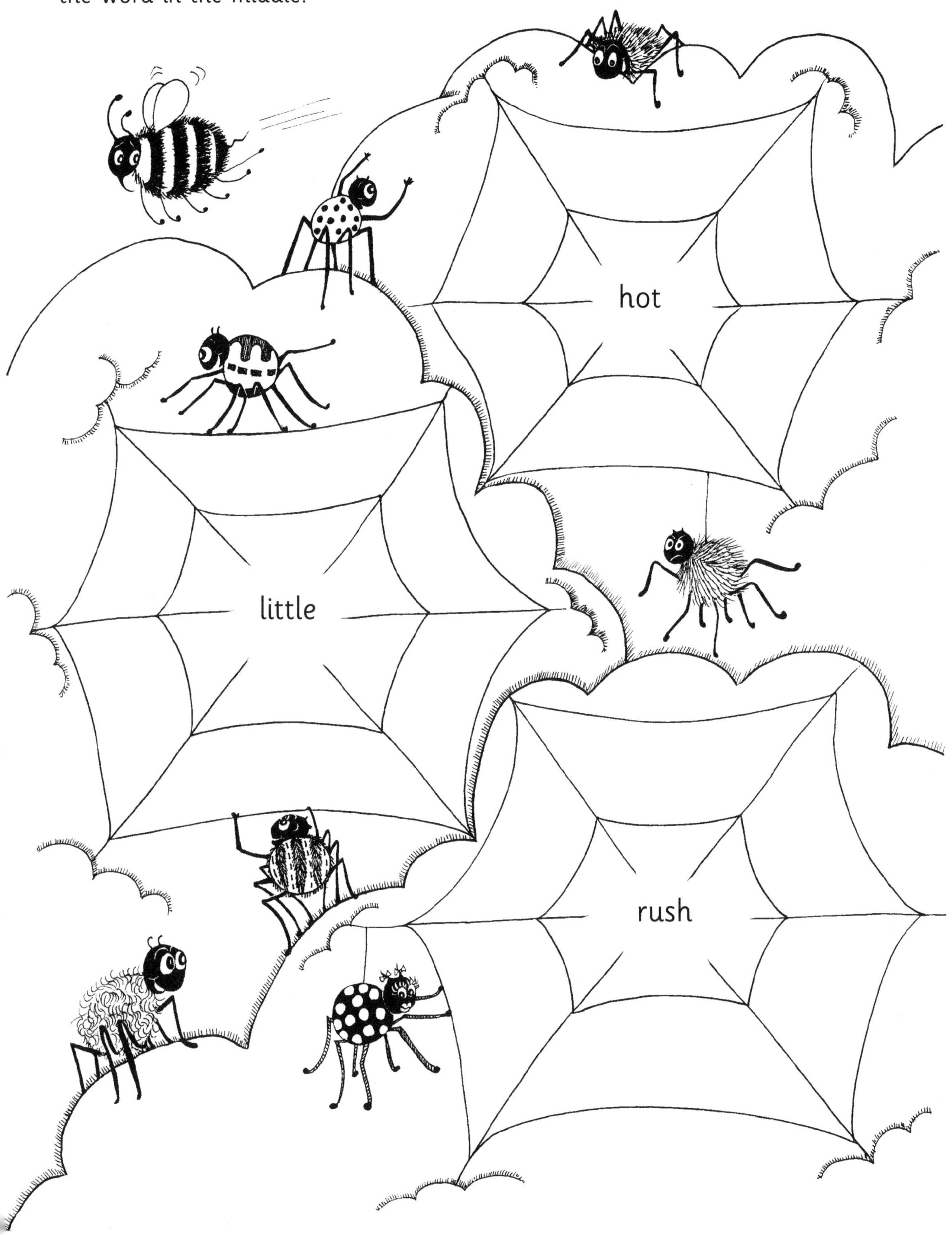

Word Webs

In the spaces of each word web, write words which could be used instead of the word in the middle.

Choose the right word to complete each sentence.

pair or **pear ?**

1. I have a new ________________ of shoes.
2. Dylan has a ________________ in his lunch box.

wear or **where ?**

1. "________________ are we going?" asked Kelly.
2. I want to ________________ my favourite sweater.

witch or **which ?**

1. "________________ of these is your bike?" asked Josh.
2. The ________________ has a broomstick and a black cat.

right or **write ?**

1. We must ________________ a thank-you letter to Grandma.
2. Tick the answer if you got it ________________.

for or **four ?**

1. I painted this picture ________________ you.
2. Two plus two equals ________________.

Possessive Adjectives – a rhyming poem

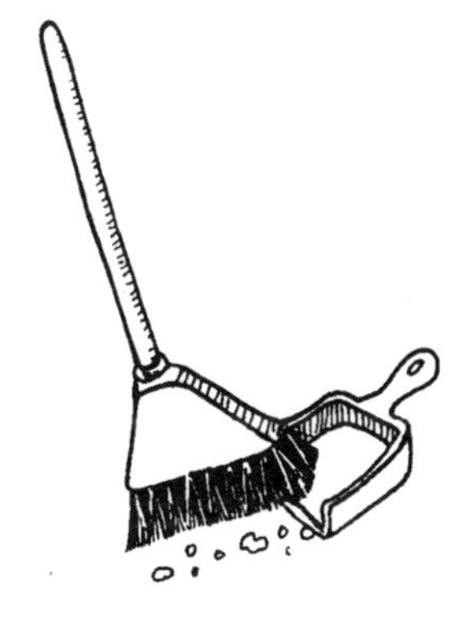

My broom,
Your room,
His flag,
Her bag,
Its bone,
Our phone,
Your mothers and
Their brothers.

Adverbs – My Day

I wake suddenly,
I get out of bed reluctantly,
I eat my breakfast messily,
I go to school happily,

I work neatly,
I listen attentively,
I play noisily,
I speak clearly,

I go home quickly,
I watch television quietly,
I wash carefully,
I go to bed slowly,

I sleep soundly and
I dream sweetly.

Apostrophe ‹s› – an alliterative poem

Anna's apple,
Ben's book,
Claire's cat,
Debbie's dress,
Ethan's elephant,
Fred's fish,
Graham's goat,
Hannah's hat,
Iman's iguana,
Joanne's jeans,
Kim's kite,
Liam's letter,
Molly's mouse,
Natasha's notebook,
Oscar's octopus,
Paul's picture,
Quentin's quilt,
Rashid's rabbit,
Sita's sari,
Tom's tortoise,
Una's umbrella,
Vera's violin,
Wong's watch,
Xander's xylophone,
Yolanda's yogurt and
Zoe's zither.

Prepositions – Inky's Journey

Inky left her mouse-hole and went...

along the path,
among the flowers,
past the fence,
down the garden,
across the field,
through the forest,
between the trees,
under the bridge and
towards the farm.